Rewriting Success in Rhetoric and Composition Careers

LAUER SERIES IN RHETORIC AND COMPOSITION
Series Editors: Catherine Hobbs, Patricia Sullivan, Thomas Rickert, and Jennifer Bay

The Lauer Series in Rhetoric and Composition honors the contributions Janice Lauer has made to the emergence of Rhetoric and Composition as a disciplinary study. It publishes scholarship that carries on Professor Lauer's varied work in the history of written rhetoric, disciplinarity in composition studies, contemporary pedagogical theory, and written literacy theory and research.

OTHER BOOKS IN THE SERIES

Writing a Progressive Past: Women Teaching and Writing in the Progressive Era by Lisa Mastrangelo

Greek Rhetoric Before Aristotle, 2e, Revised and Expanded Edition by Richard Leo Enos

Rhetoric's Earthly Realm: Heidegger, Sophistry, and the Gorgian Kairos by Bernard Alan Miller (2011) *Winner of the Olson Award for Best Book in Rhetorical Theory 2011

Techne, from Neoclassicism to Postmodernism: Understanding Writing as a Useful, Teachable Art by Kelly Pender (2011)

Walking and Talking Feminist Rhetorics: Landmark Essays and Controversies, edited by Lindal Buchanan and Kathleen J. Ryan (2010)

Transforming English Studies: New Voices in an Emerging Genre, edited by Lori Ostergaard, Jeff Ludwig, and Jim Nugent (2009)

Ancient Non-Greek Rhetorics, edited by Carol S. Lipson and Roberta A. Binkley (2009)

Roman Rhetoric: Revolution and the Greek Influence, Revised and Expanded Edition, by Richard Leo Enos (2008)

Stories of Mentoring: Theory and Praxis, edited by Michelle F. Eble and Lynée Lewis Gaillet (2008)

Writers Without Borders: Writing and Teaching in Troubled Times by Lynn Z. Bloom (2008)

1977: A Cultural Moment in Composition, by Brent Henze, Jack Selzer, and Wendy Sharer (2008)

The Promise and Perils of Writing Program Administration, edited by Theresa Enos and Shane Borrowman (2008)

Untenured Faculty as Writing Program Administrators: Institutional Practices and Politics, edited by Debra Frank Dew and Alice Horning (2007)

Networked Process: Dissolving Boundaries of Process and Post-Process by Helen Foster (2007)

Composing a Community: A History of Writing Across the Curriculum, edited by Susan H. McLeod and Margot Iris Soven (2006)

Historical Studies of Writing Program Administration: Individuals, Communities, and the Formation of a Discipline, edited by Barbara L'Eplattenier and Lisa Mastrangelo (2004). Winner of the WPA Best Book Award for 2004–2005.

Rhetorics, Poetics, and Cultures: Refiguring College English Studies (Expanded Edition) by James A. Berlin (2003)

REWRITING SUCCESS IN RHETORIC AND COMPOSITION CAREERS

Edited by
Amy Goodburn, Donna LeCourt,
and Carrie Leverenz

Parlor Press
Anderson, South Carolina
www.parlorpress.com

Parlor Press LLC, Anderson, South Carolina, USA

© 2013 by Parlor Press
All rights reserved.
Printed in the United States of America

S A N: 2 5 4 - 8 8 7 9

Library of Congress Cataloging-in-Publication Data

Rewriting success in rhetoric and composition careers / edited by Amy Goodburn, Donna LeCourt, and Carrie Leverenz.
   p. cm. -- (Lauer Series in Rhetoric and Composition)
   Includes bibliographical references and index.
   ISBN 978-1-60235-292-6 (pbk. : alk. paper) -- ISBN 978-1-60235-293-3 (alk. paper) -- ISBN 978-1-60235-294-0 (adobe ebook) -- ISBN 978-1-60235-295-7 (epub)
   1. English language--Rhetoric--Study and teaching--United States. 2. Report writing--Study and teaching (Higher)--United States. 3. English language--Rhetoric--Study and teaching--Authorship. 4. English language--Rhetoric--Study and teaching--Research. 5. Interdisciplinary approach in education. 6. Writing centers. I. Goodburn, Amy M. II. LeCourt, Donna, 1963- III. Leverenz, Carrie, 1959-
   PE1405.U6R49 2012
   808'.042071173--dc23
                              2012005610

Cover image © 2008 by Geoffrey Holman. Used by permission.
Cover design by David Blakesley.
Printed on acid-free paper.

Parlor Press, LLC is an independent publisher of scholarly and trade titles in print and multimedia formats. This book is available in paper, cloth and Adobe eBook formats from Parlor Press on the World Wide Web at http://www.parlorpress.com or through online and brick-and-mortar bookstores. For submission information or to find out about Parlor Press publications, write to Parlor Press, 3015 Brackenberry Drive, Anderson, South Carolina, 29621, or email editor@parlorpress.com.

Contents

Introduction   *vii*
   Donna LeCourt, Carrie Leverenz and Amy Goodburn

Section 1: Redefining Work in Academic Institutions

1 Field Notes from a Composition Adjunct at the Biomedical Engineering Outpost   *3*
   Mya Poe

2 Moving Up in the World: Making a Career at a Two-year College   *18*
   Malkiel Choseed

3 Nontraditional Professionals: A Successful Career with a PhD in Rhetoric and Composition?   *32*
   Ildikó Melis

4 Opportunity and Respect: Keys to Contingent Faculty Success   *51*
   Sue Doe

5 Disclaimer: "Professional Academic on a Closed Course: Do Not Attempt this at Home."   *69*
   Heather Graves

Section 2: Redefining Valuable Knowledge Beyond Academe

6 Coming to Terms: Authority in Action and Advocacy   *83*
   Moira K. Amado-McCoy

v

7 Ten Ways English Studies Contributes to User
Experience Research, or: How to Retrofit
an English Studies Degree   *104*
    Dave Yeats

8 Establishing a Writing Curriculum at a Law Firm   *117*
    Benjamin Opipari

9 My Unexpected Success as a Technical Editor   *132*
    Shannon Wisdom

10 Conversing with the Same Field: Same
Questions, Different Road   *145*
    Nick Carbone

Section 3: Working for Change

11 Mentoring for Change   *158*
    Cindy Moore

12 Composing a Life: Negotiating Personal, Professional,
and Activist Commitments within the Academy   *175*
    Jennifer Ahern-Dodson

13 Researching to Professionalize, not Professionalizing
to Research: Modular Professionalization
and the WIDE Effect   *191*
    Stacey Pigg, Kendall Leon, and Martine Courant Rife

14 Bridging Town and Gown through
Academic Internships   *209*
    Lara Smith-Sitton and Lynée Lewis Gaillet

Index   *227*

Contributors   *237*

Introduction

Donna LeCourt, Carrie Leverenz and Amy Goodburn

> *Professionalization means making your field a research discipline, with lots of journals. Making your field a research discipline means giving it a limited focus—ideally, in the humanities, one with a historical side, and one also with an empirically verifiable subject.*
>
> —J. Hillis Miller

> *When I started teaching basic writing, I had believed I had found a new and important context for the kind of intellectual and political work I had always wanted to do. I felt that my work teaching was part of a larger struggle for a literate and participatory democracy. Today, for better and for worse, I feel I am part of a profession that has arrived.*
>
> —John Trimbur

This collection began with a 2008 panel proposed for the Conference on College Composition and Communication in response to a 2007 featured session introducing the book *Women's Ways of Making It in Rhetoric and Composition* by Michelle Ballif, Diane Davis, and Roxanne Mountford. *Women's Ways of Making It in Rhetoric and Composition* reports the results of a national survey as well as in-depth interviews with eight women leaders to illuminate the working lives of female academics in rhetoric and composition. Unfortunately, the book offers a definition of "making it" based primarily on the experiences of full-time, tenured professors and their scholarly success. (See *Composition Studies* 39.1, 2011, for additional critiques of this definition of "making it.") In contrast, our panel sought to critique the assumptions that success lies primarily with scholarship and that what makes scholarship successful is its status in the field rather than its value to the researcher herself, to those who might make use of it, or to the larger public. We felt compelled to critique this limited view of success because although each of us holds tenure at a PhD-granting institution, we have also made career choices that seem to violate both spoken and unspoken guidelines for being successful. We have held administrative positions prior to tenure, have sought alternative means of scholarship, and have often rejected the advice to put our need to publish ahead of doing things that we thought were important to do. We have also allowed family responsibilities to affect our work. What we sought to demonstrate in our panel, by sharing our stories and all the messiness therein, is a deceptively simple insight: if we continue to value our academic lives primarily in terms of what we publish and its authorized effects, then what we spend most of our time doing—teaching, administering, mentoring—becomes implicitly devalued.

This panel, and the responses we received, prompted us to ask what it means to have a successful career in rhetoric and composition beyond our own stories, which are, admittedly, still located within universities and are thus perhaps overly influenced by the very model we sought to question. Although each of us must inevitably define success for herself, our answers will be influenced by the dominant discourses of the profession, by those people and texts authorized to define the field and to mete out its rewards. Ironically, many choose an academic career because of the seeming freedom to shape one's work life, and yet the process of academic training, of securing a position, of meeting expectations, can seem anything but liberating. While this process of acculturating members into a profession's values is inevitable, we believe it is time to reexamine those values and to question the consequences of our current definition of success.

In questioning how we should define success, we recognize that we are not the only ones making different choices and that the invisibility of alternative paths to success may, in fact, limit who joins the profession and the kinds of work rhetoric and composition professionals do. As we listened to the stories evoked in the proposals we received for this collection, it struck us how clearly composition's identity as a discipline, so hard fought for the past forty years, is actually disciplining us in an almost too typical Foucauldian matrix. The more rhetoric and composition becomes institutionalized through graduate degrees, undergraduate concentrations, and writing programs, the more it takes on a disciplinary status that seeks to delimit both its knowledge and its speaking subjects. In the last few decades, rhetoric and composition has become an increasingly important part of academic institutions. As such, our field has taken on the power/knowledge relations embedded in those institutions such that it is difficult for the individual scholar to look at her knowledge production outside of the explicit (and implicit) value systems of that institution. As authorized subjects of a particular strand of academic discourse, those of us who have "succeeded" in the terms of our institutional and disciplinary locations have a limited vision. We may seek institutional change, but our positions within the institution limit our ability to see alternatives.

In spite of critiques arguing that over-specialization and a disproportionate emphasis on research fail to prepare PhD students in English for the actual teaching and service work they are likely to do, most institutions and the graduate programs operating within them inevitably act to replicate the status quo. And those seeking power, like programs in rhetoric and composition, feel compelled to adopt the values held by those in power. What we have learned in putting this collection together is how differently success is being defined by those who have resisted these dominant values and who are thus not typically authorized as speaking subjects in our scholarly conversations— those working in community colleges, in non-tenure track positions, and outside the academy—whose very locations on the margins can provide them with a clearer perspective from which to gaze upon the discipline critically. Even in our well-intentioned attempts to address adverse labor conditions for those who work part-time or off the tenure track, we typically do not see their contributions as "scholarly," nor do we often include their voices in our scholarship. Yet those for whom "publish or perish" does not apply have a unique perspective on the value of scholarship, on how disciplinary knowledge figures into both their teaching lives and their work with writing outside the academy. This group, we believe, has something important to tell us about the costs of our definitions of "success" within such tightly closed institutional parameters. They might also help us redefine "useful knowledge" in our discipline and provide alternative visions of the field.

This collection, then, is our attempt to represent those alternative narratives and, through those narratives, argue for expanding predominant definitions of professional success beyond the research-focused university career. While we believe this redefinition is necessary to widen career options for those entering the field of rhetoric and composition, we also seek to extend the ways the field creates and makes use of knowledge about writing and to critique the narrowing effects of disciplinarity. *Rewriting Success,* that is, concentrates attention on the interrelation of three points—career training, knowledge-making, and disciplinarity—to examine both how rhetoric and composition literally "disciplines" itself via its assumptions about what constitutes its work (materially and intellectually) and how such assumptions manifest themselves in our graduate training and career advice. Forging its critique from the ground up, this book offers a view of the discipline from sites of practice in diverse settings, and as such, argues that a discipline is defined not only by its scholarship but also by how a discipline commodifies its knowledge, illustrated most poignantly in how that knowledge "sells" in the marketplace where jobs are acquired and careers made. Thus, our goal in this book is two-fold: we offer, we hope, both a new view of the discipline that can help us reimagine our work within multiple structures of value and a range of alternative career paths for those in rhetoric and composition.

The need to expand our definition of "success" in rhetoric and composition is linked both to concerns about our disciplinary identity and about the larger social and material conditions of our work: the declining labor market for our graduate students for tenure-track positions and the personal contingencies that can make even those available positions undesirable. Jack Schuster and Martin Finkelstein's 2006 meta-analysis of the American faculty reports that by the 1990s "[t]he pattern is striking and unequivocal: among new hires . . . the majority were being appointed to non-tenure-eligible positions" and "term-limited full-time positions have become the modal type of full-time appointment for new entrants to academic careers" (195). The American Federation of Teachers' 2009 report, *American Academic: The State of the Higher Education Workforce, 1997–2007,* confirms this trend, noting that "the number of full-time tenured and tenure-track faculty members declined from approximately one-third of the instructional staff in 1997 to just over one-quarter in 2007" (5). In rhetoric and composition the numbers are quite pronounced, with perhaps as much as 50% of the instruction in composition done off the tenure-track, according to the Coalition on the Academic Workforce report in 1999 (Tables 2 and 2A). Given current economic trends, one can only speculate that these numbers have increased in the last ten years. Indeed, the 2009 *MLA Report on Doctorate Recipients from U.S. Universities* found that even though the number of doctorates in English has declined by 34.3% from a high of 752 in 1995 to 494 in 2009, job prospects have also continued to decline. As MLA reports, in 2009, of the 1,233 doctorate recipients in the Survey of Earned Doctorates' category of "letters," "53% reported having definite employment at the time of graduation, 8.7% had definite postdoctoral study, and 34.6% were seeking positions" (4).

Although tenure-track positions in rhetoric and composition continue to be advertised at a higher rate proportionate to the number of qualified job seekers than do positions in literature, the institutional trend away from tenure-track positions is clear. Coupled with the ongoing reduction in tenure-track jobs is a dramatic decline in the number of jobs advertised, thanks to the current economic crisis. According to MLA's analysis of the *Job Information List* (*JIL*) midway through the 2008–2009 job search, the *JIL* advertised 21.9% fewer jobs than the previous year, "the biggest one-year drop in the thirty-four year history of the JIL" (MLA Office of Research). In light of such data, we can no longer assume that our students will be heading off into positions just like ours. Nor should we assume that they want to, given that landing one of the few available tenure-track jobs often requires being willing to relocate and accepting job responsibilities that may not be a good fit.

Such labor realities remind us that our assumptions about success have the potential to negatively impact new members of our profession. As long as we continue to view success as defined by a tenure-track position in a research institution and by the currency of one's scholarship in the field, we send the implicit message that not securing this type of position or not wanting to define one's work by one's research means that the discipline deems that person less valuable or less able to contribute knowledge to the field (see Choseed and Melis in this collection). While we may advise our graduate students that "it's okay to look at the community college," or "you can always take a term appointment until something else opens up," such advice continues to send the message that "okay" is somehow not good enough. Such messages can come at great cost to students as evidenced by Mysti Rudd's post to the *KairosWiki* in an unsolicited response to our CCCC session:

> After the session ended, I was prompted to pose the question to myself, freewriting in my journal about what it means, to me, to feel successful—as a student and a teacher, as a writer and a reader, as a parent and a partner—coming face to face (nose to penny?) with the places where I have been punishing myself by wearing the girdle of some left-over rubric that was not created for me, or by me, nor would aid me in becoming a better teacher/thinker/writer. I had read enough articles in *The Chronicle of Higher Education* about women academics disproportionately denied tenure to realize that success in the academy was in dire need of revision—that I was not alone in my struggle to see myself as successful.

As Rudd implies here and throughout her review of our session, it had never occurred to her that questioning the "publish or perish" model of success was possible or that the triumvirate of "teaching, research, and administration" as currently defined may not be the best standard by which to judge one's ability to contribute to the field. Nor may an academic position be the only venue in which the knowledge produced by our field can be useful.

It is not surprising that Rudd found herself unable to imagine alternatives, as these alternatives are rarely made visible in the typical process of disciplinary acculturation. The impulses that steer rhetoric and composition away from the narrowness and elitism typical of other disciplines are directly countered by impulses to meet standards and achieve recognition. Virginia Anderson and Susan Romano make a similar observation in their introduction to *Culture Shock and the Practice of Profession: Training the Next Wave in Rhetoric and Composition*:

> Rhet/comp graduates struggle with the field's desire to be the "same"—to exploit the goods and assets available to a credentialed academic discipline, and to be simultaneously "other"—to resist the culture and the structures that have made these assets possible. Graduates meet head-on the tensions generated by their calling's desire to be "in" while making openings through which outsiders—nonacademic practices or nonsanctioned populations—enter. (6)

One way to address this struggle is to revise graduate programs so that rhetoric and composition PhDs will be better prepared to respond to the "culture shock" they will experience in the institutions where they must make their home. As Anderson and Romano put it, "The majority of junior faculty contributors tell us that they must be prepared to reinvent themselves on the job. They must be prepared to find that the views their new colleagues hold about their expertise and function do not match those they were trained to expect" (6). Anderson and Romano recognize as a problem that the discipline of rhetoric and composition lacks consensus regarding "the degree to which its path from novice to professional will track that of traditional English departments or will evolve in more flexible, innovative directions that may diverge from accepted standards in academe" (8). Rhetoric and composition may wish to create a different kind of discipline, but as long as we reside within institutions with established practices for earning tenure and promotion through peer review, how free are we to be different? Ultimately, what contributors to *Culture Shock and the Practice of Profession* recommend is "a more honest sense of how they can fit the model of a rhet/comp professional into the spaces where it must ultimately survive" (8).

Addressing this problem of "fit" in perhaps a more positive way, Lori Ostergaard, Jeff Ludwig, and Jim Nugent's collection, *Transforming English Studies: New Voices in an Emerging Genre,* explores how the "difference" represented by rhetoric and composition might have a transforming influence on English Studies. But the authors included here do not underestimate the difficulty of doing so. Matthew Abraham, in his contribution, "Transforming Fragmentation into Possibility: Theory in the Corporate University" reminds readers that we cannot forget "the often fundamental purpose of the university: to preserve dominant culture and to transmit dominant values" (123) even as he argues for the potential of theory to imagine a different model. Other essays in *Transforming English Studies* explore how curriculum, program definition, and institutional practices such as hiring can be transformed with the active engagement of those committed to such transformation. Ultimately, Ostergaard, Ludwig, and Nugent argue that for responses to disciplinary crisis to be transformative, they must be characterized by "a prolonged interrogation of the discipline's seemingly mundane assumptions, a respect for how local contexts shape reform, and an acknowledgment of the diversity of our (inter) discipline" (15).

Like these authors, we recognize the challenge of bringing the qualities that make rhetoric and composition different—a commitment to inclusivity, concern for the marginalized, an interest in teaching nonspecialists, attention to service and administration as intellectual work—into traditional academic positions that depend primarily on research productivity to measure success. And while we believe that as a discipline we need to continue to try to make change from within traditional institutional structures, the contributors to *Rewriting Success in Rhetoric and Composition Careers* highlight the ways in which professionals in rhetoric and composition might also enact these values—sometimes with less struggle—in alternative locations both inside and outside the university. Despite its beginnings in the first-year composition classroom, rhetoric and composition as a field has much to contribute to the larger mission of higher education and produces knowledge that can also find a home outside academic institutions. Given the state of the academic job market, such alternatives to tenure-track positions should, rightly, form more a part of our vision of success than they do.

In seeking essays for this collection, we contacted eighteen well-established PhD programs in rhetoric and composition and asked for help locating graduates who had chosen nonacademic jobs. Several directors had names and email addresses at their fingertips, and a number of those contacts are represented here. But just as interesting were the responses from directors who revealed their difficulty in imagining how a PhD in rhetoric and composition might lead to anything but a tenure-track job. One admitted being puzzled by our question, since PhDs in rhetoric and composition, unlike an MA in professional writing or even a PhD in technical writing, are intended to lead to an academic career. Another noted that all of the PhD students in his program had gotten academic jobs, since that was his program's focus. A third confessed that he couldn't think of a single PhD student who had taken a non-academic job but suggested that was a good reason for publishing this book.

While it is clear that we need to expand the options our graduate students might imagine for their future careers, we would also argue that defining success through a singular model has had a negative impact on how we envision our field. The limitations we put upon who can produce knowledge and what counts as knowledge are intimately caught up in our assumptions about value. By designating scholarship the primary site of value, we also, in Bruce Horner's terms, commodify the product of our labor such that scholarship does not seem to be a product of labor at all. As Horner explains:

> Labor is commodified when the value of the product of that labor is identified as an objective property of the product itself. In the academy, intellectual labor, in the form of "scholarship," is deemed to be one's own work, treated as divorced from material and social conditions, a product of the autonomous scholar. It is thereby commodified simultaneously with commodification of the scholar herself. (2)

Divorcing scholarship from its material conditions results in the assumption that intellectual labor is not labor at all but work, and "non-material work" at that (Horner 13). Work is personal, fed by individual desire; labor is imposed, an economic relation where one is separated from the product produced, in classic Marxist terms, alienated from the product of her labor. By designating scholarship "work" in this way, we operate under the illusion that it is not invested in processes of capital, that it is not commodified. Yet by not recognizing the materiality of our scholarly work, by presuming it is not part of an exchange relation, we, as rhetoric and composition professionals, come to be as much a commodity as the scholarship we produce. Thus, our "success" becomes determined by how well our commodity "sells" in the academic marketplace. But the influence also goes much further, impacting our sense of personal worth.

Those not producing scholarship or those making "use of" writing knowledge outside of academic circulation routes (as those working outside the academy do) presumably see little exchange value in their labor as it resists commodification from a disciplinary perspective. Or more specifically, those of us invested in the current system see little value—to the profession—in their work. The cost within academic institutions is high: those not directly involved with scholarship signify as having less value, and (if we extend the logic of the argument) are accorded with different labor conditions, thus justifying the use of adjunct labor and contributing to the "corporatization" of the university. Teaching becomes a site of labor rather than "work" where use and exchange function more dialectically. In Horner's view, "the value of the product of teaching is more clearly tied to material social conditions" such that these "ties make the work of teaching resistant to such commodification" (2). This devaluing of teaching is one disciplinary argument that rhetoric and composition has taken on directly, but the result is such that teaching knowledge, then, enters the commodification process through scholarship. Outside of this production cycle, it remains labor and thus of less value. Practitioner knowledge comes to be seen as "lore" (North), something that circulates within much different networks that have more use than exchange value, that are not easily commodified and thus not easily seen to accrue academic capital.

The stories we offer in this collection attempt to resist this production cycle of academic capital by examining how one's institutional location—academic or otherwise—allows one to produce different kinds of knowledge, frequently unavailable to those of us in tenured positions at research institutions. The relationship between the use and exchange value of such knowledge is deeply impacted by its local context where hierarchies of scholarship/teaching need not apply. Even more importantly, the authors in this collection highlight how our most prominent positions (the valued tenured spot at a research institution) may actually limit the knowledge we produce and the kind of cultural capital that knowledge can accrue in other venues. In offering their different stories of success, that is, the authors in this collection speak directly to problems of institutionalized disciplinarity wherein the commodification of our labor limits both how our knowledge might be constructed and how it might circulate. In taking us to the more silenced parts of the academy (tribal colleges, community colleges), speaking from positions not often seen as authorized to create knowledge (nontenured positions, writing across the curriculum programs), and even going beyond the academy (to law firms and community centers), the authors in this collection invite all of us to broaden our definitions of both work and success. As we consider the value of our work differently, we also hope that we can offer more alternatives in graduate training, more career options to those beginning in the field, and perhaps a return to the valued sites that once defined our discipline: teaching, literacy, and public rhetoric.

We also hope this collection serves as a call to action by suggesting how institutions can do a better job of supporting and encouraging alternative career paths, by welcoming adjuncts and term instructors as full members of the profession, and by actively mentoring in ways that honor all kinds of career options. These are grand hopes, more than one short collection can provide, but they are worthy goals which begin with listening to our "other" colleagues whose voices are too often drowned out by assumptions about their locations and choices.

OVERVIEW OF THE COLLECTION

Rewriting Success in Rhetoric and Composition Careers redefines success in rhetoric and composition in three ways: 1) by highlighting the unique knowledge and perspectives gained by teacher/scholars in presumably marginal positions, thus offering an expanded view of the "work" of composition and the new collaborations not always possible within restrictively defined tenure-track positions; 2) by making visible how graduate training in rhetoric and composition can support careers outside academe, thus extending the reach and value of the field's knowledge-making; and 3) by considering how institutions in the process of training, professionalizing, and evaluating its members can better support alternative career paths.

Section 1, "Redefining Work in Academic Institutions," encourages us to see the value of knowledge produced in a variety of institutional locations. For example, Malkiel Choseed and Mya Poe both demonstrate the unique potential that can be found in marginalized institutional positions. As a community college teacher, Choseed argues that such sites are perhaps the most fruitful for understanding relations between theory and practice that are at the heart of our research endeavors, yet he locates the "use value" of such relations within the classroom itself. Directly challenging the idea that teaching at a two-year college is "moving down," Choseed illustrates how valuable his scholarly background has been to his teaching and administrative work in a two-year college. Taking a different tack, Poe examines the kinds of knowledge we professionally create about writing in the disciplines and the limitations our institutional locations force upon that work. As Director of Technical Communication at MIT (a non-tenure track position), she was afforded the opportunity not only to engage with writing in the disciplines (WID) in a longterm relationship but also as a co-teacher in disciplinary courses. Such practitioner knowledge, she argues, leads to much different research questions, producing scholarship that takes into account the "fault lines of disciplinary discourse or its silencing tendencies" that are more difficult to see from an outsider's perspective.

Choseed and Poe highlight the new opportunities for knowledge-making in their institutional locations, but Ildiko Melis takes this critique one step further, arguing that our scholarship is actually impacted by our labor practices, that the "corporatization" of our universities has resulted in scholarship that seems to be removed from the realities of the undergraduate writing classroom. As a writing teacher in a tribal college, Melis examines how "the lack of publicly visible demonstrations of 'success'—or rather, a range of possible successes—within rhetoric and composition sends a mixed message about the value of writing, and the expertise involved in it, to our students." She argues for a new, ecological model of success that would "include more of the experiences of nontraditional professionals who work in our field and whose success is shaped by a variety of complex local conditions." This focus on local conditions—both institutionally and personally—is picked up in Sue Doe's chapter and her study of non-tenure track professionals' definitions of success. Through this study, Doe not only expands our concept of success but also offers these redefinitions as a new way of viewing adjunct labor as a potentially productive rather than presumptively oppressive situation: "in the liminal space between the gold standard of tenure and the willful use of an untenurable underclass lie well supported non-tenure track faculty positions that, for the foreseeable future, offer a productive faculty space." But, she cautions, this productivity does "require particular kinds of support to make them viable," support structures that she outlines in her conclusion.

While the chapters above argue forcibly for the value of teaching as a site of knowledge-construction and refiguring our sense of temporary and permanent teaching positions, the final chapter in this section takes a much different tack by examining the problems with the "gold standard" tenure-track job itself. Adding a counter-voice to this conversation, Heather Graves examines how the triumvirate of "teaching, research, and service" actually makes research not only difficult but almost impossible. As someone who identifies first as a researcher, Graves emphasizes the value of research/writing both within and without traditional academic institutional structures which, ironically, tend to value research the most yet accord it the least time or priority in terms of our work lives. In this way, the materiality of labor conditions is transposed to the traditional model of success as Graves reports on why she left her tenured position to pursue a writing career. As such, Graves's chapter sets up our second section focused on narratives from those who, like Graves, have chosen career paths that took them out of the university.

The alternative perspectives and implicit critique of the field's value system continues in Section 2, "Redefining Valuable Knowledge in Rhetoric and Composition," where the authors underscore how one's location highlights the differing value systems that might be accorded to "writing studies" in all its manifestations. In Section 2, authors trained in rhetoric and composition who have chosen to work outside of academe reflect on how they use their expertise in unanticipated ways and suggest how rhetoric and composition programs might better prepare graduates for these alternative kinds of work. Moira Amado-McCoy analyzes her experience transitioning from a tenure-track position to become executive director of a nonprofit group dedicated to LGBTQ support, arguing that training in rhetoric and composition—with its focus on public uses of language, on teaching, on writing for multiple audiences—is ideal preparation for advocacy work. She also notes the ways in which the political ends of rhetorical training might be pursued more effectively in the public sphere than in universities, especially departments of English, where the inherent interdisciplinarity of rhetoric is looked on suspiciously, and advocacy work and other real-world uses of language are discouraged. Like Amado-McCoy, Dave Yeats also notes the ways in which universities can constrain the kind of work one is able to do, ultimately deciding to leave his tenure-track position to become a user-experience researcher. Although Yeats finds he prefers the unpredictability and flattened hierarchy of his current work environment, he nevertheless credits his training in literature, creative writing, rhetoric, and technical communication for preparing him for his responsibilities conducting empirical research on how people interact with technologies in the interest of improving product design.

Not all such alternative careers came after leaving tenure-track positions. In their contributions to this collection, both Shannon Wisdom and Ben Opipari share how the writing and teaching expertise gained in graduate school led them to nonacademic positions and how those positions have challenged and extended their rhetoric and composition training when applied outside of the traditional classroom. As a technical editor for a communications technology firm, Wisdom makes frequent use of her ability to read critically from multiple points of view. Her graduate experience with peer responding and collaborative writing has also been vital as she negotiates and builds relationships with the subject matter experts who write the content she edits. Indeed, the skill of effective collaboration is one she recommends graduate programs focus on even more. Opipari also practices the fine art of collaboration in his role as a writing consultant in an international law firm. Once a university writing center director, Opipari has been able to draw on his past academic experience to understand the writing needs of lawyers, even as the highly specialized nature of legal writing and the hierarchical organization of law firms have made writing consultation in this context challenging. Though both Wisdom and Opipari intended to pursue academic careers, their stories demonstrate that nonacademic positions hold promise for intellectual engagement and career satisfaction.

For Nick Carbone, choosing a career track parallel to but different from that offered by a tenure-track university position has allowed him to develop more fully his interests in teaching and technology. Now a technology specialist in composition with Bedford/St. Martin's Press, Carbone believes his current position enables him to have a broader influence on the teaching of writing than his previous position on the tenure track, where writing for specialists via journal and book publication is valued over communicating in multiple forms with a wide range of writing teachers, which is now a regular part of his work. Taken together, the essays in this section make a clear case for the ways rhetoric and composition training can be put to use outside of the academy and an even clearer case for the importance of re-seeing success in the field as more than tenure and promotion.

Building upon the insights in the first two sections, Section 3, "Working for Change," features stories of individuals' and institutions' attempts to intervene in the dominant models of success by providing alternative forms of training and professionalization, models of scholarship, and faculty work profiles. The section begins with Cindy Moore's chapter on mentoring graduate students differently. Specifically, Moore proposes a "student-focused community mentoring model" to provide MA students with a comprehensive sense of career possibilities. Drawing upon her experiences at three MA-granting institutions as well as her work on mentoring in the profession more broadly, Moore argues that in maintaining the status quo in mentoring, "we risk not only being unresponsive to our students' needs but to the changing realities of American life." Moore provides extensive comments from students whom she has mentored to illuminate some of the questions that mentors and mentees should consider in relation to graduate study in rhetoric and composition.

Considering different options as part of one's graduate training also potentially opens up opportunities both within and outside of the university. Jennifer Ahern-Dodson's chapter illustrates how a non-tenure track postdoctoral writing fellow position at Duke University provided her opportunities to collaborate on the teaching of writing with academics in other disciplines and to engage in service learning partnerships. These experiences subsequently led her to pursue her current position as the Community Partnership Coordinator for Scholarship with a Civic Mission at Duke. While some view the development of postdoctoral positions as attempts to dismantle the tenure-track system, Ahern-Dodson complicates this argument, illustrating how the postdoctoral fellow position provided her institutional support to devote time to her teaching in a way that ultimately enabled her to pursue a fulfilling position that utilizes her expertise.

The final two chapters in this section pick up on Ahern-Dodson's insights by describing programs that offer graduate students explicit research and/or internship experiences to provide professional development for graduate students beyond teaching and administration. In this way, they seek to locate the new connections and possibilities Ahern-Dodson experienced within graduate programs. For example, Stacey Pigg, Kendall Leon, and Martine Rife chronicle the insights they gained as graduate students in a research center. These three authors describe how their experiences at the Writing in Digital Environments Research Center (WIDE) at Michigan State University have prepared them to consider broader types of work beyond academe. Based on their experiences with WIDE, they propose that "modular" models of participation and development are best suited for preparing composition and rhetoric graduate students to occupy multiple and diverse locations. Claiming that "much of the literature on graduate student training and professionalization" focuses on teacher training, writing, and writing program administration, they argue that "the reality is that graduate student opportunities in rhetoric and writing extend beyond those to which these activities are specifically linked" and, thus, that we need to prepare graduate students for "multiplicity" rather than linearity. In a similar vein, Lynée Gaillet and Lara

Smith describe an internship program at Georgia State University for the South Atlantic Modern Language Association that provides opportunities for undergraduate and graduate students in English to gain professional development in areas such as conference planning, journal and monograph publishing, and administration of programs. Concurring with Pigg, Leon, and Rife, Gaillet and Smith suggest that there is a wide range of work that occurs in academia that is not restricted to teaching or writing program administration. They describe this internship program as offering a different kind of pedagogical experience, one that teaches students to communicate within a specific organization and that offers insights into other forms of work outside of the traditional tenure-track teaching position.

While *Rewriting Success* ends with recommendations to alter our practices in graduate training and mentorship, such changes alone are not enough to change the landscape our graduates encounter. Instead, we hope that this collection will inspire all of us to challenge our local institutions and wider disciplinary structures to expand our models of success, make the productive potential within alternative positions easier to access for those working in such positions, and to revalue, in our best tradition, the wide range of work and knowledge-making by rhetoric and composition specialists both within the classroom and without.

Works Cited

Abraham, Matthew. "Transforming Fragmentation into Possibility: Theory in the Corporate University." *Transforming English Studies: New Voices in an Emerging Genre*. Ed. Lori Ostergaard, Jeff Ludwig, and Jim Nugent. West Lafayette, IN: Parlor Press, 2009. 122–40. Print.

American Federation of Teachers. *American Academic: The State of the Higher Education Workforce, 1997–2007*. February 2009. Web. 30 March 2010.

Anderson, Virginia, and Susan Romano, eds. *Culture Shock and the Practice of Profession: Training the Next Wave in Rhetoric and Composition*. Cresskill, NJ: Hampton, 2006. Print.

Ballif, Michelle, Diane Davis, and Roxanne Mountford. *Women's Ways of Making It in Rhetoric and Composition*. New York: Routledge, 2008. Print.

Coalition on the Academic Workforce. "Who Is Teaching in U.S. College Classrooms? A Collaborative Study of Undergraduate Faculty, Fall 1999." *American Historical Association*. AHA, 22 Nov. 2000. Web. 26 March 2009.

Deleuze, Gilles. *Foucault.* Trans. Sean Hand. Minneapolis: U of Minnesota P, 1988. Print.
Horner, Bruce. *Terms of Work for Composition: A Materialist Critique.* Albany: SUNY P, 2000. Print.
Miller, J. Hillis. Foreword. *Publishing in Rhetoric and Composition.* Ed. Gary A. Olson and Todd W. Taylor. Albany: SUNY P, 1997. xi-xiv. Print.
Modern Language Association. *MLA Report on Doctorate Recipients from U.S. Universities* 2009. Web. 2 June 2009.
MLA Office of Research. "Mid-Year Report on the 2008–09 MLA *Job Information List.*" *Modern Language Association.* 26 March 2009. Web. 2 June 2009.
North, Stephen M. *The Making of Knowledge in Composition: Portrait of an Emerging Field.* Upper Montclair: Boynton, 1987. Print.
Olson, Gary A., and Todd W. Taylor, eds. *Publishing in Rhetoric and Composition.* Albany: SUNY P, 1997. Print.
Ostergaard, Lori, Jeff Ludwig, and Jim Nugent, eds. *Transforming English Studies: New Voices in an Emerging Genre.* West Lafayette, IN: Parlor P, 2009. Print.
Rudd, Mysti. Rev. of "Writing beyond the Discipline: Alternative Strategies for 'Making It' in Rhetoric and Composition." *Kairos* 13.1. Fall 2008. Web. 22 March 2009.
Schuster, Jack H., and Martin J. Finkelstein. *The American Faculty: The Restructuring of Academic Work and Careers.* Baltimore, MD: Johns Hopkins UP, 2006. Print.
Trimbur, John. "Close Reading: Accounting for My Life Teaching Writing." *Living Rhetoric and Composition: Stories of the Discipline.* Ed. Duane H. Roen, Stuart C. Brown, and Theresa Enos. Mahwah, NJ: Erlbaum, 1999. 129–42. Print.

REWRITING SUCCESS IN RHETORIC AND
COMPOSITION CAREERS

1 Field Notes from a Composition Adjunct at the Biomedical Engineering Outpost

Mya Poe

To say that the status of adjunct labor in higher education is highly debated would be an understatement ("Contingent"; Street). The increasing use of contingent labor along with the poor conditions of employment for adjuncts (poor pay, low status, no unions, yearly contracts, isolation) are well documented (Wee; Schell and Stock), yet many institutions readily rely on adjuncts for much college-level teaching (ADE; Jaschik). Within composition and rhetoric, the place of adjunct labor has an uneasy presence. While adjuncts clearly have a presence in composition classrooms and disciplinary lore, the contributions of adjunct labor do not seem to figure in the advancement of composition and rhetoric research (Schell; CCCC). As a non-tenure-track lecturer for five years and a non-tenure-track director for the last three years, I am sympathetic to the struggles of non-tenure-track labor in composition and the importance of advocating for non-tenure-track labor rights. Until institutions make longterm commitments to non-tenure-track employees and professional organizations support their non-tenure-track members in the same way that they support tenured faculty, I have no illusion that the employment conditions of adjunct labor will dramatically improve. I also believe that we miss something important in our discipline when we do not value the contributions adjuncts bring to our classrooms and even to the profession itself. As Eileen Schell has pointed out, the expertise of part-time teachers has been important in shaping the history and practice of composition and rhetoric because adjuncts possess important "practitioner knowledge."

In writing across the curriculum (WAC) and writing center work, practitioner knowledge is not only important in delivering writing instruction but also in managing programs. Not acknowledging the contributions of adjuncts in WAC scholarship misses the expertise these individuals provide to the field. Moreover, because adjuncts can spend years teaching in disciplinary classes (i.e., they can move outside traditional departmental structures), they can provide important, longitudinal insights about how to best teach writing in the disciplines. It is such practitioner knowledge that is most important in delivering WAC pedagogy to our colleagues across the university; faculty are not so much interested in case studies of individual students or program descriptions but in practices for teaching writing and evidence that those practices work.

As director of technical communication at the Massachusetts Institute of Technology (MIT), my professional non-tenure-track identity is defined by my administrative duties and by my teaching responsibilities in the writing across the curriculum program.[1] Although my administrative duties take most of my time, my teaching collaborations with science and engineering faculty have been most engaging for me as teacher and researcher. My goals in working with scientists and engineers are to improve how writing is taught in their classes and to get students to think about disciplinary discourses critically. Thus, I am not interested in simply describing disciplinary discourses but in teaching students rules for participation in disciplinary communities and exposing students to the conflicts and tensions found in disciplinary ways of communicating.

My teaching goals resonate with Donna LeCourt's call in "WAC as Critical Pedagogy" for "a more open and critical approach to disciplinary discourses" (397). LeCourt identifies three directions to provide a critical approach to disciplinary discourses, including recognition that disciplinary discourses are sites of contestation, that social discourses impact disciplinary discourses, and that disciplinary discourses both silence as well as engender conversation. By opening disciplinary discourses to such scrutiny, we avoid reductionist, assimilationist approaches to the teaching of disciplinary writing and speaking (i.e., that which we have rejected in the teaching of first-year writing but still use in disciplinary writing classes). LeCourt writes: "An uncritical approach to disciplinary communities—the assumedly reified authority of already constituted practices—only serves to perpetuate and instantiate the worldview and ways of knowing already valued within the dominant professional ideology" (395). Working almost exclusively within disciplinary classes and departments for the last nine years has helped me better understand the ways that conflict, social forces, and silencing play out in disciplinary communication. I believe exposing alternative disciplinary discourses is an important project that WAC has long ignored, but I also believe that attention *solely* to these aspects of disciplinary communication isn't sufficient. Somehow we must balance making the norms of disciplinary communication explicit in our teaching while also challenging those norms.

In this chapter, I share how my ideas about teaching disciplinary writing have evolved to include both critical explorations of disciplinary writing alongside teaching disciplinary conventions explicitly. My ability to make such changes has been possible because I reside in an adjunct's outpost in biomedical engineering. In essence, I'm paid to stay away from the writing program home. In this chapter, I do not purport to have an ideal model for how to make changes to the ways we teach disciplinary writing, but I do propose some working ideas that might help advance the field's research on writing in the disciplines and highlight how adjuncts might help us do that. I begin with a review of WID research to contextualize some of the issues and problems in the literature. I then discuss a biomedical engineering course where my goal has been to get students to understand the social construction of knowledge in scientific data-driven arguments. Following this example, I discuss several other examples in classes where we have tried to address the impact of social influences on disciplinary communication and reconceptualize assimilationist approaches to the teaching of disciplinary writing.

Writing, Learning, and Teaching in the Disciplines

The writing across the curriculum and writing in the disciplines movements have been formative in shaping our understandings of writing practices in the disciplines and suggesting how writing can improve learning of technical content. As Bazerman et al. point out, the WID movement was based on "the awareness that prior assumptions we had about what constituted good writing and what writing should be taught were based on literary models" (10). To help students with writing in disciplinary classes, we needed to know about the writing that was done within the disciplines. This emphasis on *what* the disciplines are teaching rather than *why* those disciplinary norms are used has had a profound impact on WID research. In an effort to understand disciplinary norms for writing, WID researchers have tended to focus on identifying disciplinary discourses and looking at students' uptake of these discourses (and struggles of that uptake) as they adopt professional identities. Yet, because WID studies have tended to focus on programs and students, they have typically not taken a longitudinal approach to disciplinary discourses within classrooms to understand *why* disciplinary discourses have certain formations and *how* to facilitate critical uptake of those discourses.

In my opinion, one of the major shortcomings of WID research is that few studies are informed by longterm participation in disciplinary classes by writing teachers. Despite all of the research on writing in the disciplines, most composition and rhetoric faculty do not teach *in* disciplinary classes. Simply put, writing researchers aren't in the field long enough to see the fault lines of disciplinary discourses or their silencing tendencies. Instead, WID researchers have been positioned outside the classroom while studying students' struggles in learning disciplinary discourses. For example, in an early study, Berkenkotter, Huckin, and Ackerman report on the struggles of a graduate student in composition and rhetoric through interviews and analysis of his writing. Also, while Berkenkotter, Huckin, and Ackerman tell us about Nate's struggles to adopt the disciplinary discourse of composition and rhetoric, they do not critique the discourse of composition and rhetoric itself or question whether Nate's assimilation has a positive outcome. Dorothy Winsor's study of engineering students also provides insights related to the socialization of students into the profession through the written genres. In *Writing like an Engineer,* Winsor explores "how professional ideology teaches developing engineers to deny the rhetorical nature of their work at the same time as professional practice and experience teach those same developing engineers to write strategically" (vii). Winsor's research confirms that the engineering students she studied saw engineering communication as arhetorical, aimed only at other engineers, and situated solely within the workplace: "After five years of being socialized into the engineering community, the students seem to have concluded that [writing like an engineer] means to write to other engineers about data and facts and to leave persuasiveness to managers" (99).

Research studies such as that by Berkenkotter, Huckin, and Ackerman and Winsor are important because they show the socially constructed nature of disciplinary writing while also showing how the rhetorical nature of that writing is often muted in the teaching of disciplinary communication. Yet, while such studies are important in understanding the development of professional identities and the role of communication in that process, they do not necessarily translate into specific classroom practices for teaching writing.

Another line of research on writing in the disciplines has focused on faculty values and classroom activities. Some of these studies have exposed disconnects between professional practice and individual classroom pedagogy. For example, Herrington's research on chemical engineering classrooms shows that faculty come to writing activities often with very different goals and expectations. Herrington's findings question the use of singular notions of disciplinary discourses or the transparency of community values within the disciplines. More recently, Chris Thaiss and Terry Myers Zawicki interviewed faculty in fourteen different disciplines for *Engaged Writers, Dynamic Disciplines*. They describe faculty who work squarely within disciplinary conventions and those who struggle to find alternatives to conventional discourse usage "to meet exigencies important to them and the readers whom they most want to reach" (57). In describing these various faculty approaches, Thaiss and Zawicki show a wide array of purposes and approaches to teaching writing in the disciplines, many of which deviate from conventional disciplinary communication forms. Studies such as Herrington's and Thaiss and Zawicki's are important in showing the varied ways disciplinary faculty approach subject content and disciplinary practices. Again, however, such studies do not translate into practices for disciplinary faculty to use in their classrooms.

Finally, collections such as Monroe's *Writing and Revising the Disciplines,* and Segall and Smart's *Direct from the Disciplines: Writing Across the Curriculum* consist of essays from disciplinary faculty on teaching writing. For example, Segall and Smart's collection includes essays from a political scientist, a cognitive psychologist, a mathematician, an occupational therapist, and a biologist, among others. Such collections are important contributions to WID and WAC scholarship because they represent the perspectives of faculty in the disciplines, but they rarely offer a critical perspective on disciplinary discourses.

From a teaching perspective, the lack of involvement of composition and rhetoric faculty in disciplinary classes has led to a dearth of teaching materials for those of us (adjuncts, fellows, and graduate students) who do teach in disciplinary classes. Certainly there are seemingly innumerable technical writing textbooks and handbooks, but just as first-year writing teachers often find textbooks and handbooks stifling, so do disciplinary writing teachers. Instead of asking students to read pages from a textbook and complete an exercise at the end of the chapter, I want students to read the primary literature in their field and be able to identify the rhetorical moves that the authors use. I want students to question the data in the scientific papers they read, and I want them to participate in current disputes in the field. Finally, I want materials that help students think about the ways a field poses certain values over other values and not all participants in a disciplinary community come to the table equally. For example, what does it mean that many authorship disputes are reported by international collaborators (Scheetz; Wilcox)? What does it suggest when a field such as "tissue engineering" re-brands itself "regenerative medicine" after many of the start-up companies in the field failed? What about the numerous National Institutes of Health grants that claim a clinical goal of treating cancer patients, even when the proposed research in the grant is at least a decade away from clinical trials?

Quantitative Physiology: Early Notes from the Field

The lack of disciplinary-specific resources for advanced writing in the disciplines became obvious when I started teaching in biomedical engineering classes at MIT. In my first year, I was assigned to several workshop-style classes and given a number of "consulting" assignments in communication intensive courses.[2] It quickly became apparent that these types of interventions were only marginally integrated with the course content and that general advice about genres of scientific writing was not sufficient to help students. I began to work with disciplinary faculty to shelve the infamous writing lecture that MIT students heard repeatedly. Instead, I began working to tailor assignments to individual classes that reflected the values in those disciplines. In doing so, I drew upon rhetoric of science (Gross; Bazerman; Myers), the sociology of science (Cetina; Latour and Wolgar; Latour), and philosophy of science (Kuhn). Thus, my practitioner problem about the lack of complexity in WID research regarding disciplinary discourses became a site of inquiry.

The place where my thinking about teaching disciplinary writing crystallized was in a course called Quantitative Physiology. Quantitative Physiology is a large-lecture, upper-level course in biomedical engineering in the MIT department of Electrical Engineering and Computer Science (EECS). The course is designed around these central inquiries: (1) Which molecules are transported across cellular membranes, and what are the mechanisms of transport? How do cells maintain their compositions, volume, and membrane potential? (2) How are potentials generated across the membranes of cells? What do these potentials do? In the course, students complete two research projects—a "bench" project in which they use microfluidics devices to study changes in cells due to osmosis and diffusion, and a theoretical study of the Hodgkin Huxley (HH) model using computer simulation. The faculty who teach Quantitative Physiology strongly tie the purpose of the course to professional development, and one explicit goal of the course is to prepare students for careers in biomedical engineering. There is a strong assimilationist agenda to the course, but the faculty members are also aware that most MIT students won't become work-a-day biomedical engineers. (Many MIT graduates go to medical school, graduate school, or work in the financial sector).

Prior to my involvement, Professor Denny Freeman had worked with the WAC program for several years, trying various ways of integrating writing instruction into the course. Initially, he tried workshop sessions outside of class time, but only a few students showed up to the workshops. By 2000, the workshops outside of class time were eliminated, and Freeman began looking for other ways to integrate communication instruction into the course, such as adding revisions and peer review. We first set out to improve the grade sheet, clarifying expectations for the assignments, offering a writing clinic where we could talk with students about our comments, and adding end-of-semester course evaluations. We changed a report assignment into an oral presentation assignment, and we added project proposals. But all these improvements only marginally improved the students' writing.

In 2003, Freeman and I started giving lectures together on how to write technical papers, and through that collaboration the curriculum began to change substantially. Rather than instructing students on general technical writing issues about audience and genre, we began to focus on the issues that were central to quantitative physiology—namely, data. In our discussions about student communication, we had often noted that the source of student writing problems was in their data. Students didn't know how to present data and how to use data throughout the article to make a convincing case for their work. This led to a series of problems in the writing, including underdeveloped analyses of findings, poor logical progression from one finding to the next finding, and lack of coherence between the findings presented in the results section and the methods and discussion sections. Students also seemed more concerned with making the data fit the theory while ignoring "interesting" findings or presenting all of their findings without thinking through why they were presenting those findings.

Freeman suggested that we use the storyboarding method in which designers use graphic organizers to help them sequence the narrative of a film. Freeman had found the method useful to help him focus on telling an interesting "story" with his research findings. He used the approach with his graduate students and found equal success, observing that by sketching out slides by hand and laying them out, his graduate students were pushed to make conclusions about their findings. Students were asked to answer questions like these:

> So why are you showing me this slide? So why did you show me this set of four slides? So why did you show me this set of 24 slides? [When you answer these questions,] you're addressing the thing that's on the minds of the audience. They don't want to know how you spent your summer vacation; they don't care. They want to know why you find this interesting.

In translating the storyboarding approach to undergraduates, we identified three underlying concepts to storyboarding: 1) data drive scientific research; 2) each figure in a report tells its own "story," and different kinds of visual presentations lead readers to interpret data in particular ways; and 3) in sum, the figures in a report tell a narrative of the research. Overall, our goal was to help students see that data do not "speak for themselves" and are not "obvious" to readers. Researchers must choose what data are interesting to present and construct a plausible narrative to convey their understanding of that data to an audience. We also wanted students to understand that argument is not woven around data but through the process of collection and analysis. Every methodological choice in data collection and analysis is a decision, which allows researchers to "see" certain results and not others.

Certainly, our goals for student learning were driven by a desire to initiate students into disciplinary discourse—to get them thinking like scientists. Yet, we didn't want students to think blindly about scientific discourse as some transparent conveyer of facts. Scientific facts are constructed, and the primary means by which that construction occurs is through data-driven arguments (i.e., scientists use data to advance their own ideas and the knowledge of the field). And data-driven arguments aren't without their tensions. For example, it's not so difficult to manipulate data, and the ethics of publishing multiple articles from the same data set are murky. Students in quantitative physiology encounter this tension when they engage in the process of selecting some data for their manuscripts while leaving out other data. There are no right or wrong data to present; there is only the evidence researchers provide to the readers and their supporting narrative. Students often question whether the selection and formatting of data to prove a particular point is ethical, which leads us to discuss with them how scientists can tell certain stories with more veracity than others, such as through the replication of studies.

Another goal was that we wanted "to convey writing in a way that [didn't] alienate" (Villanueva 172). We wanted students to see themselves in disciplinary writing; the stories they chose to tell with data were stories of their own making. Scientific research can often be alienating because students don't see how scientific research can be driven by their own desires and interests. By allowing students to design their own experiments, they come to take ownership (if even in a small way) of science. Certainly, our approach doesn't address some of the challenges laid out by feminist critiques of science (e.g., Spanier), for example, but I do think that getting students to critically assess scientific arguments helps them demystify scientific knowledge and, hopefully, will encourage them to challenge scientific arguments that are assaults to their identities (such as data about the ability of women to do math).

Such changes to a course like Quantitative Physiology would have been difficult if I only had an outsider's perspective of biomedical engineering. It took years for me to understand what made for convincing arguments in the field, the typical learning trajectory of students in the major, how we might use data as a way to teach students about the social construction of scientific knowledge, and how writing about data might help students gain ownership of their scientific identities. It was only by adopting an anthropological perspective that I believe my understanding of biomedical epistemologies came about. Instead of listening to *what* faculty were saying about writing or biological engineering, I listened to *how* faculty were talking about the relationship between writing and disciplinary knowledge. I was only offered the time that I needed to develop such an understanding precisely because I was not a faculty member whose time was needed to teach courses in my tenure home. I could stay in the field because biomedical engineering was an adjunct's outpost.

In the last year, I've been able to take my insights from quantitative physiology and use them to complete a study of student learning. Along with two colleagues, I undertook a year-long study of seventeen students in seven disciplinary classes. Because we are not tenure-track faculty, we had no release time for research, but we did have some support from the dean for transcription of interview tapes. My research on quantitative physiology focused on gaining a better understanding of what students were learning about arguing with data and how that understanding was facilitated (or not) through storyboarding. Through surveys and case study analyses of five students, I found that because the storyboard focus repeatedly required students to engage with their research data and consider it rhetorically, students' language about their research changed markedly over the semester. Initially, students talked about what they were doing methodologically and how they were doing it. Later, students talked about why certain data were interesting and what limitations or possibilities accompanied that data. It was also clear, as Winsor shows in her research with engineers, that genres were places for making knowledge and that different genres led to different ways of making knowledge with data. In other words, genres were important in *how* (not *what*) students' learning was changing in making data-driven arguments. Using different genres forced students to work with data in different ways—different audiences, different formats, different purposes. Moreover, faculty feedback that modeled professional feedback (what I call "authentic feedback") guided students' understandings of using data in making scientific arguments. Students began to adopt rhetorical ways of describing data, using phrases such as a "believable trend" and a "convincing finding."

The importance of authentic feedback was another important *how* in student writing development.

In the end, the research on student learning in quantitative physiology has been useful for sharing with other teachers. However, one of the disappointments for me was that my co-researchers and I did not address other kinds of identities in our research. (We focused solely on the notion of student and professional identities). Of the seventeen students in the seven classes studied in this book, eleven were women and six were men. Seven students were white, seven were Asian, two were African-American, and one was Latino. Our students included both native-born students as well international students. Unfortunately, we didn't address *these* identities in our research. Once again, we had succumbed to the WID research tradition of looking at identity along the axis of novice/expert and silencing other features that are salient in the formation of professional identity.

OBSERVATIONS FROM FURTHER AFIELD

As a first foray into a broader vision of WAC pedagogy, quantitative physiology helped shape my ideas about how to initiate WAC collaborations that would advance more critical explorations of writing in the disciplines. While the "critical" aspect of quantitative physiology was limited to exposing the constructed nature of scientific arguments, my work outside of quantitative physiology has brought other possibilities. For example, in a graduate level biomedical engineering course, we talk about grant writing conventions along with such topics as NIH funding politics, the impact of public perception on scientific research, and the ways that grant scoring is influenced by reviewers' own interests. After all, highly contested discourses about disciplinary knowledge play out in grants because scientific funding is tied so closely to the genre. A WID pedagogy that does not acknowledge this aspect of grant writing now seems to me remarkably superficial.

Likewise, a recent collaboration with two Mexican universities has made me consider how WAC and WID pedagogies are often exported without consideration of their potential to silence other ways of teaching (Donahue). In our case, we are trying to avoid that possibility by using a transnational, collaborative approach where information and ideas flow both ways across our borders. Any introduction of WAC will include attention to Mexican educational and cultural norms that add to existing WAC approaches. We are also keen to keep in focus why our colleagues are interested in adopting WAC, their goals for student learning, and the institutional resources available to them that will reshape the implementation of WAC at their universities. In return, we hope to learn more about autonomous learning centers and other ways that Mexican universities have successfully negotiated these resource issues in language instruction.

In future research in the field, I want to explore the relationship between the diverse workplaces in which scientists work and the world Englishes at play in those spaces with the decidedly narrow range of written language that appears in scientific journals. Scientists' attitudes towards language and literacy practices in those multilingual lab spaces might provide important insights for faculty in other disciplines as well as for the teaching of writing.

In the end, my work in quantitative physiology and other classes has given me insight into the developmental trajectory of students in the sciences and ways to integrate more critical perspectives on disciplinary discourses in our teaching of scientific writing. The question for me is *when* to integrate these perspectives and *how* these changes will impact students learning in the disciplines. Should we start by teaching students how to make a convincing story with their data, how to cite strategically, or how reasonably to "stretch" interpretations drawn from findings? Or should we start by talking about how scientific discourse silences individual perspectives or even the deaths of animals used in testing?

Conclusion

As non-tenure-track positions go, my job is a good one. It's not without its problems—low prestige, little power, and an institution that doesn't quite know what to do with the legions of adjunct labor who far outnumber the tenure-track faculty. I knew these issues when I took my job, and yet, because of my position as non-tenure-track faculty, I've been afforded opportunities for collaboration and research that would not have been possible in a traditional tenure-track faculty position.

After teaching in science and engineering classes for nine years, I've come to a much deeper understanding of disciplinary discourses and to a fuller understanding of the potentials and problems found in the ways we teach disciplinary discourse. Through teaching collaborations with faculty, I've also reaffirmed my belief that teaching writing in the disciplines can be effective and that we actually know little about how to do it well. While we have more than twenty-five years of research on writing in the disciplines, we still need to know much more if we are to teach students about the rich world of disciplinary communication and the ways that disciplinary discourses silence certain perspectives while giving voice to others. We also need to better understand how to teach writing in the disciplines if we are to hope that students will participate in the contests that get played out in disciplinary discourses and be able to engage with the social discourses that impact what gets said and done in their chosen professions. It is by listening to *why* and *how* certain disciplinary norms get played out, rather than simply *what* norms are played out, that we might have a WID pedagogy that moves beyond assimilationist outcomes. The adjuncts who work with faculty and students in the disciplines on a daily basis are the ones who are best suited to take up this challenge. By drawing on their practitioner expertise, we could substantially contribute to composition and rhetoric research while rewriting how we think about the contributions of adjunct labor. My notes from the field suggest that the making of knowledge in composition and rhetoric needs those adjunct perspectives from the field.

Notes

1. At MIT, the WAC program employs about forty full- and part-time lecturers, three directors, and one associate director. Although our specific appointments vary, none of the directors are tenure-track faculty. I teach five courses per year and have a minor publishing requirement. MIT supports travel to conferences through a discretionary fund and grants from the dean of the School of Humanities and Social Sciences.

2. MIT has a communication intensive (CI) curriculum in which students are required to take four CI classes during their four undergraduate years at MIT. Two of these CI courses must be in a students' major.

Works Cited

2007 ADE Ad Hoc Committee on Staffing. "Education in the Balance: A Report on the Academic Workforce in English." Association of Departments of English, Dec. 2008. Web. 9 February 2009.

Bazerman, Charles. *Shaping Written Knowledge: The Genre and Activity of the Experimental Article in Science.* Madison: U of Wisconsin P, 1988. Print.

Bazerman, Charles, Joseph Little, Lisa Bethel, Teri Chavkin, Danielle Fouquette, and Janet Garufis. *Reference Guide to Writing Across the Curriculum.* West Lafayette, IN: Parlor P, 2005. Print.

Berkenkotter, Carol, Thomas Huckin, and John Ackerman. "Conventions, Conversations, and the Writer: An Apprenticeship Tale of a Doctoral Student." *Genre Knowledge in Disciplinary Communication* Ed. Carol Berkenkotter and Thomas Huckin. Hillsdale: Erlbaum, 1995. 117–44. Print.

CCCC Executive Committee. "Statement of Principles and Standards for the Postsecondary Teaching of Writing." *College Composition and Communication* 40.3 (1989): 329–36.

Cetina, Karin Knorr. *Epistemic Cultures: How the Sciences Make Knowledge.* Cambridge: Harvard UP, 1999. Print.

"Contingent Appointments and the Academic Profession." *American Association of University Professors.* AAUP, 2003. Web. 9 February 2009.

Donahue, Christiane. "'Internationalization' and Composition Studies: Reorienting the Discourse." *College Composition and Communication* 61.2 (2009): 212–43. Print.

Gross, Alan. *The Rhetoric of Science.* Cambridge: Harvard UP, 1990. Print.

Herrington, Anne. "Writing in Academic Settings: A Study of the Contexts for Writing in Two College Chemical Engineering Courses. *Research in the Teaching of English* 19.4 (1985): 331–61. Print.

Jaschik, Scott. "Breadth of Adjunct Use and Abuse." *Inside Higher Ed.* 3 Dec. 2008. Web. 9 February 2009.

Kuhn, Thomas. *The Structure of Scientific Revolutions.* 3rd ed. Chicago: U of Chicago P, 1970. Print.

Latour, Bruno, and Steve Woolgar. *Laboratory Life: The Construction of Scientific Facts.* Princeton: Princeton UP, 1986. Print.

Latour, Bruno. *Science in Action: How to Follow Scientists and Engineers through Society.* Cambridge: Harvard UP, 1987. Print.

LeCourt, Donna. "WAC as Critical Pedagogy." *JAC* 16.3 (1996): 389–405. Print.

Monroe, Jonathan. *Writing and Revising the Disciplines.* Ithaca: Cornell UP, 2002. Print.

Myers, Greg. *Writing Biology: Texts in the Social Construction of Scientific Knowledge.* Madison: U of Wisconsin P, 1990. Print.

Scheetz, M. "Office of Research Integrity: A Reflection of Disputes and Misunderstandings." *Croatian Medical Journal.* 40.3 (1999): 321–25. Print.

Schell, Eileen. E., and Patricia L. Stock, eds. *Moving a Mountain: Transforming the Role of Contingent Faculty in Composition Studies and Higher Education.* Urbana, IL: NCTE, 2001. Print.

Schell, Eileen E. *Gypsy Academics and Mother-Teachers: Gender, Contingent Labor, and Writing Instruction.* Portsmouth, NH: Boynton/Cook-Heinemann, 1998. Print.

—. "Toward a New Labor Movement in Higher Education: Contingent Faculty and Organizing for Change." *Workplace: A Journal for Academic Labor* 4.1. 2001. Web. 9 February 2009.

Segall, Mary T., and Robert A. Smart. *Direct from the Disciplines: Writing Across the Curriculum.* Portsmouth, NH: Boynton/Cook, 2005. Print.

Spanier, Bonnie B. "Encountering the Biological Sciences: Ideology, Language, and Learning." *Writing, Teaching, and Learning in the Disciplines.* Ed. Anne Herrington and Charles Moran. New York: MLA, 1992. 193–212. Print.

Street, Steve. "Avenues for Change Adjuncts can Believe In." *Inside Higher Ed.* 19 Jan. 2009. Web. 9 Feb. 2009.

Thaiss, Chris, and Terry Myers Zawacki. *Engaged Writers, Dynamic Disciplines: Research on the Academic Writing Life.* Portsmouth, NH: Boynton/Cook, 2006. Print.

Villanueva, Victor. "The Politics of Literacy Across the Curriculum." *WAC for the New Millennium.* Ed. Susan H. McLeod, Eric Moraglia, Margot Soven, and Christopher Thaiss. Urbana, IL: NCTE, 2001. 165–78. Print.

Wee, Eric L. "Professor of Desperation: Bad Pay, Zero Job Security, No Benefits, Endless Commutes. Is This Any Way to Treat PhDs Responsible for Teaching a Generation of College Students?" *Washington Post* 21 July 2002: W24. Print.

Wilcox, Linda J. "Authorship: The Coin of the Realm, the Source of Complaints." *Journal of the American Medical Association* 280.3 (1998): 135–36. Print.

Winsor, Dorothy. A. *Writing like an Engineer: A Rhetorical Education.* Mahwah, NJ: Erlbaum, 1997. Print.

2 Moving Up in the World: Making a Career at a Two-year College

Malkiel Choseed

At some point during the semester in my first-year composition classes, a student will ask me about my PhD dissertation. I like to use this question as an excuse to discuss different kinds of graduate education and how these might become part of students' professional or academic goals. Eventually, the questions will come back to my dissertation and my graduate work. I try my best to describe objectively the process and what it involved, both from a professional and a personal standpoint.

In my case, I started my MA program in the fall of 1997 and did not graduate with a PhD until the spring of 2007, two years after starting as an assistant professor at Onondaga Community College. After I explain the time and work involved in writing a dissertation, a student will invariably ask me, "Was it worth it?" At this, I always pause. This question can be answered in so many ways—financially, personally, professionally. Colleagues on both the university and two-year college level have asked me versions of the same question. To put it bluntly, was my doctoral training a waste of time when I could be doing the same job with an MA? The question can be asked in a more productive way, however, a way that opens up conversation and lines of inquiry as opposed to shutting them down. Has my research background and graduate training impacted my work teaching first-year writing students in positive ways? The answer to this question is "yes."

From undergrad to my MA program to the start of my PhD coursework, I saw myself on an upward path, but taking this job was the biggest "moving up" that I had ever done. Most people pursuing a traditional PhD probably do not imagine themselves following a teaching-centered career trajectory at a two-year college. While the state of the economy combined with the tight academic job market may eventually change this perception, many of my peers and faculty at Research I institutions, like the one I attended, would perceive my choice to work at a community college as "moving down."

Graduate school colleagues, if they thought of it at all, saw it as a stopgap measure, something to pay the bills while I finished my dissertation. Once I had the dissertation finished, I could then look for a "real" tenure-track job at a school where the production of scholarship is both privileged and primary. After all, why put myself through the ordeals of a PhD program if I was not going to use the skills and training on a regular basis? In academia now, to teach at a university or four-year college is to understand oneself primarily as a researcher—a producer of knowledge, someone whose "work" is done primarily outside of the classroom. To teach at a two-year college is to understand oneself primarily as teacher, someone whose work is done primarily in the classroom with undergraduates. This distinction is a false one, or should be, when applied to rhetoric and composition.

Advanced graduate training in the history, theory, and practice of composition and its related fields is especially valuable for those working in teaching-intensive colleges, and, I argue, especially two-year, open admissions colleges. This kind of background facilitates the teacher-scholar's ability to recognize the links and intersections between theory and practice, collapsing that somewhat useful but ultimately false binary. Whereas this kind of background and training is not essential to good teaching (some of the best and smartest teachers of composition I know have never taken a graduate seminar in composition theory), it can be, to say the least, extremely helpful. It puts the practitioner in a position to assume a leadership position in the department, to think programmatically and institutionally, and impacts classroom pedagogy by helping the teacher-scholar to ask and answer the most important questions about teaching and learning. It is potentially a place to put into practice and bring to life our years of study, as well as the most fertile ground for composition research. Those within composition ought to see teaching at the two-year college not as a step down, a second choice, or even as a transitional job between graduate school and that elusive research institution, but as an upward movement.

There is an inherent prestige in the culture of American academics associated with research-intensive universities. One need only look at the articles on tenure and the job search that crop up toward the end of the year in *The Chronicle of Higher Education* and *Inside Higher Ed* to see this. Why this has come to be a complex issue has a long history (disciplinary and institutional histories of the field, like those of James Berlin, Susan Miller, John Brereton, and Jean Ferguson Carr, Stephen Carr, and Lucille Schultz address this implicitly or explicitly). Like it or not, we are defined professionally by our scholarly or research output. This mindset, however, implicitly devalues the intellectual work of teaching.

Some of those in the field of rhetoric and composition, like the teacher-scholars represented in this collection, have begun the slow process of rewriting academic culture for the better. Through his work on the scholarship of teaching, Ernest J. Boyer brought the dichotomy between teaching and research to the collective attention of the American professoriate. This work has been prefigured and extended in the field of composition through a diverse array of approaches. From Stephen North's work on "lore" to Robin Varnum's history of composition at Amherst to Bruce Horner's materialist critique of composition to the advocacy of the Council of Writing Program Administrators for the recognition of teaching as scholarly work, composition studies is exploding with new ideas and paradigms for understanding and evaluating our work in and out of the classroom. By detailing my own experience putting theory into practice, I'd like to add my voice to this list and attempt to help break down the theory/practice binary that persists, despite this work, in many peoples' minds. In the hopes that our efforts to equally value practitioner-knowledge not be relegated to the past nor rest solely on theoretical critiques, I would like to see teaching valued differently and help those seeking to determine whether a teaching-focused job might best meet their needs as practitioners *and* scholars of rhetoric and composition.

Composition, Institutional Context, and the Binary between Theory and Practice

My new colleagues at my community college were gracious and welcoming, but I wondered if they thought they were taking a chance on hiring me. After all, because I was drawn to the school by a geographical convenience, there was not much holding me there. I now know that some of the department members worried that I would complete my PhD and immediately go on the market, essentially wasting their time and effort in the hiring process. In addition to this very reasonable concern, I sensed, from some corners of the department, a distrust of university training and a research or scholarly agenda. While it was not pervasive, it was palpable, especially at meetings to discuss preferred qualifications for future hires, curriculum development, and our programmatic approach or philosophy. The idea seemed to be that community college faculty were dedicated to a practical life of teaching and that "university types" were mostly focused on abstractions and avoiding the classroom as much as possible to pursue "scholarship." Or, if the skills and knowledge that a PhD program gave to someone were appreciated, they were thought not to be relevant to this particular job. My experience with both my two-year and four-year colleagues reinforced this growing sense that our academic culture is divided, a culture in which researchers disparage teaching and teachers disparage research.

There is a split between theory and practice, a binary which still needs to be deconstructed in our field in general and which lies at the heart of this essay. To be fair, however, there is also a very real set of differences between the worlds of the two-year college and the four-year university. One need only look at what is valued and rewarded at each institution. On the two-year college level, our extremely busy teaching schedules force us to focus on the everyday act of teaching at the expense of traditional scholarship. That being said, I am continually amazed by my colleagues who, while teaching a heavy load, make the time to write and publish scholarly, creative, popular and pedagogical work. While these efforts are appreciated by the institution, the focus for tenure and promotion is always on the classroom and service to the department and college. As graduate students, we all vied for the elusive non-teaching fellowship so that we, like our mentors, could focus on our "real" work. In fact, one of my former graduate colleagues was hired at a prestigious, public four-year university with the promise that, if he taught the requisite freshman writing courses his first year on the job, he would not have to teach them anymore.

What is appealing about a job like mine that includes undergraduate advising, committee work, and a five/five teaching load with a minimum of six classes per year at the first-year composition (FYC) or developmental level? First, what the job does not require: publish or perish does not exist. If you wish to pursue publication (and can find time for it), you can. If you choose not to, you do not have to. I can begin a writing project because I believe I have something to add to the conversation, not because a tenure-review clock is ticking like a time bomb. Second, the job allows a focus on teaching and working with students, a place that shares and supports the values of true, liberal arts education, and a place to meet some of the most diverse and interesting people you will ever encounter and make a positive impact in their lives. In one class, I had a former U.S. Marine sniper, a recent immigrant from Cuba, a retired truck driver, and other traditional and nontraditional students of every hue and creed. In that same class, one student told me that his life's goal was to be "middle class." He wanted a future that was, above all else, stable and saw our community college as the key to that future.

Focusing on teaching allows, even forces, a person to collapse the false binary between theory and practice. When you can focus on teaching, as the focus has to be at a community college, you get the chance to make real the theories and ideas that were for the most part abstractions in graduate school. Of course, there are challenges, disappointments, and even heartbreak, but the ability to impact real people for the better cannot be quantified.

The Reciprocal Relationship between Professional Knowledge and Teaching

Traditionally, the dissertation and the preparation for it represent an area of specialization which will be carried over into the professional life of the academic. The dissertation, that all-consuming ogre with its insatiable appetite for resources and, most importantly, time, is (usually) the first book-length manuscript an academic produces. The process of writing and defending it is as much about learning how to write a monograph (the pinnacle achievement for academics) as it is learning how to specialize in a field of knowledge or producing the final product itself.

Historically, the dissertation represents the contribution of new knowledge to a particular field. This is the essence of graduate, research training. If we return to the beginning of this essay, then, my students' questions take on a new resonance. I will never teach a graduate seminar. I will never direct graduate student committees or devise qualifying exams. If I choose to, I will never have to seek publication in peer-reviewed journals or at academic presses. In fact, I will never get to teach a dedicated senior seminar or even a junior-level class (we only have first-year and sophomore students). Most of our classes are designed to transfer and are therefore "service" courses (composition and technical writing) or sophomore level survey courses (American Literature I, World Literature II, Introduction to Drama, etc.).

Currently, we only offer four composition classes: developmental, two required first-year courses, and one intermediate composition course. What is the value, then, of my research background for these students? Using the teaching of Shakespeare as a case study, my dissertation argued that English studies as it took form in the developing American system of higher education in the late nineteenth and early twentieth centuries was shaped by classroom pedagogy as represented in collegiate level textbooks. When I walk into our developmental classroom or when I draft a syllabus for one of our FYC classes, what purpose does the dissertation serve, either for me or my students?

What is unique about a graduate-level specialization in composition, though, is that with very few exceptions, our work is always relevant to those students in the FYC classroom. In my case, I spent years reflecting on how classrooms actually work and how knowledge gets created in those classrooms instead of simply reported on. Incorporating these reflections into my teaching and talking about them with students potentially gives students a different way of valuing their own writing. My research training and background has also impacted my work in the FYC classroom and in the English department in other important ways, from developing a programmatic perspective as well as in my individual teaching.

Professional Knowledge

Graduate training in the history and development of composition can aid in thinking both institutionally and programmatically. I came to my current department with disciplinary knowledge, knowledge of what other people in other places had done, why they had done it, and how it might work here. In many ways, the doctoral process has helped to make me into an expert learner. Academic departments need faculty members who are good learners as well as instructors. If we are wondering about program coherence or some aspect of placement, I have practice in asking questions, looking for resources, and synthesizing those resources to fit our needs. For example, I recently stepped into the role of writing program coordinator (a WPA position) and, among other things, am responsible for overseeing our professionally staffed writing center. When we come together to discuss policy or tutoring approaches, I am not speaking solely from my personal preference or experience, but from a theoretically and historically informed pedagogical perspective.

When I began in the center, some tutors were devoting entire sessions to the use of worksheets and exercises to teach students grammatical structures or rules of punctuation. This pedagogical strategy is of an extremely limited utility. I asked our tutors to read Stephen North's "The Idea of a Writing Center" as well as the National Council of Teachers of English's 2008 "Writing Now: A Policy Research Brief" on the teaching of writing. We also discussed an excerpt from Constance Weaver's *Teaching Grammar in Context*. I was able to successfully argue that it was not simply my personal preference that we not use worksheets, but that over the course of the last thirty years, the field as a whole, supported by empirical and experiential research, had come to this conclusion.

Another example comes out of our attempts to refine the instrument we use to place students into our developmental class or into the FYC sequence. If students score within a certain range on a sentence skills test, they are required to write an essay. The existing essay prompts are designed to be general enough to elicit a response from almost anyone with no preparation. Students can choose from such topics as "Describe someone you admire . . ." and "Recommend or warn people away from a restaurant. . . ." I am, at a minimum, advocating a change in our placement essay topics, to ask students to engage in more complex thinking and incorporate the ideas of others by responding to a written passage. Our current model is about counting errors. Errors are not unimportant, but what we should be looking for is overall structure. This is not, however, a settled question. John Brereton traces the debate about effective placement prompts and the measurement of writing ability back to the 1870s and the beginning of Harvard's writing instruction. Understanding how this debate played out historically allows us to learn from them and not simply reproduce them. Additionally, as Mina Shaughnessy first made clear in 1977, errors are never simply errors. The development of basic writing pedagogy, as in David Bartholomae and Anthony Petrosky's *Facts, Artifacts, and Counterfacts,* shows us that patterns are more important than individual violations of rules, and the patterns are what we need to pay attention to if we are going to help students make lasting changes to their writing.

I would like to echo Jeffrey Klausman's sentiments that a person trained in composition, whether in this role or not, can serve as a point of contact for his or her colleagues with the larger field. Klausman found that many of his full- and part-time colleagues, for a variety of reasons, did not have academic backgrounds in composition. This lack can result in a department in which writing classes are "loosely related by too-often unspoken and, most likely, conflicting assumptions about aims, means, and purposes" (239). I see this play out in my own institution in the sense that composition is something that one does rather than something one studies. While this sentiment may be understandable, the trained compositionist can bring different and useful perspectives into the conversation.

For example, the knowledge of the development of key terms in composition studies can be essential. Take for instance, a word that often gets tossed around in my department, "rewrite." Many faculty will allow or even require that a student "rewrite" a paper if the paper received below a particular grade. While this practice is motivated by the desire to help students improve, developing a shared understanding with colleagues of the principles underlying a rewrite versus that of a "revision" can be very helpful in establishing programmatic consistency across sections. On one level, rewrite and revision appear to be different ways of talking about the same thing, but they are not. A rewrite puts the emphasis on product above all else, essentially focusing on a final grade. A revision, however, places the emphasis on process and the writer herself. Revision, and the necessary support that goes along with it, is about improving the student as a writer by improving his or her grasp of the writing process. The distinction is not merely semantic but implies practices. The fact that I had been formally trained in composition studies allowed me to make these distinctions with my colleagues. Graduate training in composition gave me the ability to put into words ideas that might otherwise have remained inchoate.

With few formal venues for the exchange of ideas in our department, many conversations on classroom practice happen between faculty while they are checking the mail, standing at the copier, getting coffee, etc. In fact, the sharing of tips or lessons between classroom instructors is a fairly common practice. "In my classes we do x, y, and z" should not, however, be both the starting and the ending point of the conversation. For these conversations to be of any lasting value, the participants should be able to articulate *why* they ask their students to do certain things, and *how* these practices fit into the larger framework and pedagogical goals of the class and the department. Robin Varnum's history of Amherst College's collaborative approach to designing writing curricula (before such things as "writing programs" existed) provides one possible model for this work of program creation. Understanding the history of composition provides models and tools to help situate the practices and ideas of individual instructors in a larger context, such as when we face new, departmental challenges in terms of externally mandated program assessment, ongoing curricular development, and the potential links between the two.

Programmatic and student learning assessment (are students learning what we think they are learning in a given class or program?) is always a thorny issue, especially when the mandate originates from beyond the department, and we are given little guidance as to how to carry them out. Many colleagues see assessment as intrusive and a bureaucratic waste of time. A research background gives someone the tools to approach assessment like any complex problem and set about to solve it. I have learned quite a bit about how empirical studies in composition might be designed and carried out, the differences between qualitative and quantitative research, and the advantages and disadvantages of each one when applied to the assessment of student writing (c.f. *Assessing Writing: A Critical Sourcebook* by Brian Huot and Peggy O'Neill). Kathleen Blake Yancey points out that writing assessment and placement testing are reflective of what we value in our classrooms, as an institution, and in our field (144). Through understanding the history of placement testing both locally and nationally, we can better understand our values. In practice, this can be as simple as clarifying the distinction between rewrite and revision with colleagues or as complex as redesigning the FYC curriculum or putting a program wide assessment into place.

Teaching

The fact that most community colleges privilege teaching and classroom performance above all else for tenure and promotion and require faculty to represent that in writing means that we are living out what those like Boyer, the Council of Writing Program Administrators, and others have been advocating for many years. The classroom is, for us, primary. Part of my role as writing program coordinator is to make our faculty aware of the pedagogical choices that they make (indeed to make them aware that they are making choices in the first place), to help them see what other options are available to them, and to understand why it might be beneficial both for them and their students to explore these options.

An instructor approached me because she heard that I do not design my FYC course around weekly units like the "run-on" and "avoiding fragments." She asked me how I teach these things to the students. I replied that I ask students to approach the production of a given text holistically, with sentence-level editing coming late in the process. What followed was a discussion of pedagogical choices, priorities, and how those work together to influence what we ask students to do. While in a norming session during one of our assessment workshops, a colleague and I began chatting about assignment and syllabus design. A successful practitioner in the classroom for many years, she was stunned to hear that one could structure a writing course around a common theme. This conversation opened the door to examining the potential advantages that a theme could bring, such as scaffolding reading and writing assignments across the semester to thereby give students an increased sense of continuity while underscoring the interconnectedness of ideas and knowledge as evidenced in and through their writing.

The kind of work that we ask of and see from our students can determine, to a large extent, our response to the material conditions of our profession. One of the most common complaints of those working in the field of composition is the crushing paper load. Indeed, I have heard professors justifiably complain when they are responsible for only two or three sections worth of student papers. The workload and the requisite energy expenditure increases exponentially the more you teach. Many community college faculty members teach five or more composition classes a semester. Every spare moment could be filled reading and grading. I once saw a woman grading papers in the fifteen minutes between sessions at a conference. Even this part of the job, which I admit can sometimes be daunting and demoralizing, can change depending on how we understand our role as readers of these student-authored documents and what we want our students to do with them.

If you only look for and mark error in student writing, you will quickly become tired and disheartened. If you see your role as that of an editor, you will be crushed under the load. It is a Sisyphean task. Having a working knowledge of the professional discourse around responding to student writing, say the work of Nancy Sommers (e.g., "Responding to Student Writing") or Shaughnessy, gives one insight into how to best mark papers, both in terms of efficiency and helping students. When you are prepared to see student papers as attempts at knowledge creation, however local that knowledge might be, or as attempts to assimilate the discourse of the academic world (Bartholomae, "Inventing"), or as an attempt at finding an authentic voice (Elbow, "About Voice and Writing"), you are in a better position to read the papers. Access to this disciplinary knowledge helps us to see student writing through these lenses as well as analyze and contextualize student practices, giving students a language with which to talk about their writing and thereby the power to alter it for the better.

My background in a PhD program has provided me with another, more subjective way to succeed not just in a teaching-centered career but specifically at a community college. Most people pursuing graduate degrees in English were, I think, good students themselves. I was no exception. For the most part, I did well as an undergraduate and knew that, if I applied myself, I would eventually succeed in school. I had a similar feeling about my Master's and PhD coursework. When I began the dissertation process, however, I did not know this for sure. I almost walked away many, many times. Ultimately, I had to decide that this was something I wanted and could do. My dissertation only began to coalesce once I took ownership of it.

I always share this story with my students, especially my developmental students, saving it for a day on which I think it will be most pedagogically useful. Students may wonder, if they think of it at all, what I have in common with them. I could (and sometimes do) share with them my own family and class background, but I think the most meaningful connection I feel with them is that I know what it is like to be overwhelmed, to be challenged and pushed far beyond my comfort zone, to feel at the mercy of inscrutable academics, and to feel as if my entire fate rests on how this one paper will be received. I have felt, deeply and fundamentally, that I did not belong in an academic setting. I know firsthand the fear and bitter disappointment that comes with the academic life. I also know the exhilaration and the joy of success, even if that success took me ten years to achieve. Some of our students will finish in two years and move on, some take ten years to earn that AA or AS, and some will never finish at all. What I want my students to take with them when they leave my class, in addition to having improved as writers, is a sense that they accomplished something important. Perhaps it will make an impact on the wider world, perhaps not, but they engaged in a meaningful intellectual project and will hopefully see that they can continue doing so.

The Two-year College: Drudgery or an Ideal Site for Composition's Epistemology?

I am arguing, in part, that the field of composition needs to reconceptualize its view of the work of teaching and learning in the classroom generally and the two-year college classroom specifically. The work of teaching developmental and first-year composition all too often falls to those without institutional power, either adjuncts or graduate students. As the ranks of contingent faculty grow, introductory composition courses are turning into the province of the untenured. Too often these courses, the service courses, are the leftovers, the second choice. The community college environment, though, often requires that tenured faculty members teach in the FYC program. The responsibility for developing the program and delivering the classes is shared by all members of the department, full and part time, tenure track and non-tenure track.

I am not a natural born teacher. I work very hard to achieve success in the classroom. Having been trained in the theory, practice, and history of composition as a field allowed me to successfully transition from graduate school to a two-year college environment. Yes, there was (is) trial and error, but I was (am) guided by a set of principles. Some beginning professionals might look at the prospect of such a paper-heavy teaching load as overly demanding or challenging (and, make no mistake about it, it is demanding and challenging). In a very real sense, however, this work is what we have trained for. I would probably elect to teach first-year or developmental composition no matter where I taught. If you have spent years studying the writing process, how to best teach it to students, or how social class, technology, or ethnicity impact writing, you can see your FYC classroom differently. In this light, the FYC classroom is the living, breathing, dynamic space where theories and ideas are put into practice, confirmed, challenged, or expanded. Some may write about their work in the classroom, using it as the basis for published work, and some may not. In either case, every time you walk into the classroom or pick up a student paper to respond to, you are putting theory into practice and, through active reflection, theorizing practice.

So, when students invariably ask me, "Was it worth it?" I can answer "Yes." Entering into the world of the community college with some of this disciplinary knowledge, and the ability to access more of it when needed, puts you at an advantage, especially at a community college where the line between theory and practice blurs. Of course, all of us teaching in colleges and universities today have access to the specialized knowledge of the field of composition, but it takes time and energy to access it. Often, we are short on both. Boyer and others helped lay the groundwork for this conversation for the professoriate generally, but I believe that composition has *de facto* centered around a scholarship of reflective practice for a long while, perhaps since its modern inception. Formal training in the field can help us understand this and make it practical. In this manner, composition is different from other, traditional academic disciplines, and it is this difference that is most apparent and interesting to someone interested in a teaching-centered career. Those of us in the field of composition, and especially those of us in two-year colleges, can take the lead in rewriting not only the history of our field, but its future as well.

Works Cited

Bartholomae, David. "Inventing the University." *Cross-Talk in Composition Theory: A Reader*. Ed. Victor Villanueva, Jr. Urbana, IL: NCTE, 1997. 623–54. Print.

Bartholomae, David and Anthony Petrosky. *Facts, Artifacts, and Counterfacts: Theory and Method for a Reading and Writing Course*. Portsmouth, NH: Boynton/Cook, 1986. Print.

Berlin, James A. *Rhetoric and Reality: Writing Instruction in American Colleges, 1900–1985*. Carbondale: Southern Illinois UP, 1987. Print.

Boyer, Ernest L. *Scholarship Reconsidered: Priorities of the Professoriate*. Princeton, NJ: The Carnegie Foundation for the Advancement of Teaching, 1990. Print.

Brereton, John C. *The Origins of Composition Studies in the American College, 1875–1925*. Pittsburgh: U of Pittsburgh P, 1995. Print.

Carr, Jean Ferguson, Stephen L. Carr, and Lucille M. Schultz. *Archives of Instruction: Nineteenth-Century Rhetorics, Readers, and Composition Books in the United States*. Carbondale, IL: Southern Illinois UP, 2005. Print.

Elbow, Peter. "About Voice and Writing." *Landmark Essays on Voice and Writing*. Ed. Peter Elbow. Mahwah, NJ: Hermagoras Press, 1994. xi-xlvii. Print.

Horner, Bruce. *Terms of Work for Composition: A Materialist Critique*. Albany: SUNY P, 2000. Print.

Huot, Brian, and Peggy O'Neill, Eds. *Assessing Writing: A Critical Sourcebook*. Boston: Bedford/St. Martin's, 2009. Print.

Klausman, Jeffrey. "Mapping the Terrain: The Two-Year College Writing Program Administrator." *Teaching English in the Two-Year College* 35.3 (March 2008): 238–51. Print.

Miller, Susan. *Textual Carnivals: The Politics of Composition*. Carbondale: Southern Illinois UP, 1991. Print.

North, Stephen M. "The Idea of a Writing Center" *College English* 46 (1984): 433–46. Print.

—. *The Making of Knowledge in Composition: Portrait of an Emerging Field*. Portsmouth, NH: Boynton/Cook, 1987. Print.

Shaughnessy, Mina P. *Errors and Expectations: A Guide for the Teacher of Basic Writing*. New York: Oxford UP, 1977. Print.

Sommers, Nancy. "Responding to Student Writing," *College Composition and Communication*. 33 (1982): 148–56. Print.

Varnum, Robin. *Fencing with Words: A History of Writing Instruction at Amherst College during the Era of Theodore Baird, 1938–1966*. Urbana, IL: NCTE, 1996. Print.

Weaver, Constance. *Teaching Grammar in Context*. Portsmouth, NH: Boynton/Cook, 1996. Print.

Writing Now: A Policy Research Brief. Urbana, IL: NCTE, 2008. Print.

Yancey, Kathleen Blake. "Looking Back as We Look Forward: Historicizing Writing Assessment." *Assessing Writing: A Critical Sourcebook*. Boston: Bedford/St. Martin's, 2009. 131–49. Print.

3 Nontraditional Professionals: A Successful Career with a PhD in Rhetoric and Composition?

Ildikó Melis

In *Women's Ways of Making it in Rhetoric and Composition,* three successfully emerging scholars of rhetoric and composition Michelle Ballif, D. Diane Davis, and Roxanne Mountford identified in 2008 what successful academics in rhetoric and composition do or attain: they hold a PhD; they are full-time professors; they are tenured; they are well published and regularly cited; they contribute a "consummate piece to the field"; they mentor others and are invited as keynote speakers at conferences—in this order, I believe. Looking at the list, I need to conclude that working in a two-year tribal community college on the remote edge of Michigan's Upper Peninsula, without tenure, on annually renewable contracts, and with no expectation but an unusual history of publication, the only criterion I meet is holding a PhD in rhetoric and composition. Impressed by the elegance of Ballif, Davis and Mountford's argument, the precision of their supporting details and the supportive, positive overtones of their claims, I wish there were an equally transparent, attainable and encouraging set of standards for success available for those of us who find ourselves on a dazzling array of nontraditional career paths. At this point, I am not sure I can offer an equally compelling set of alternative standards for success other than a general ecological metaphor of academic survival. According to this metaphor, a successful career in rhetoric and composition should include elements of flexible adaptation of standards to the variety and changeability of local institutional settings in which our job of promoting twenty-first century literacy is performed. A successful career and adaptation involves significant modification of the practices of writing instruction that have proven to be effective in rhetoric and composition research, but that may not work in some local settings. On a personal level, success in rhetoric and composition involves a constant rearrangement of priorities and redefinition of success accordingly, accepting the fact that writing instruction is still somewhat of a nontraditional academic career.

Ballif, Davis, and Mountford send a positive message to the women who, they claim—based on Theresa Enos's research—not only constitute seventy percent of the PhDs in rhetoric and composition but also face different and more severe challenges than women in other academic fields due to what Enos calls a dual gender and disciplinary bias. (The latter refers to the inferior status of rhetoric and composition within literary-studies-dominated English departments). Ballif, Davis, and Mountford, however, also admit that their message does not address the majority (estimated eighty percent) of those men and women who teach writing in higher education and who are either in part-time or non-tenure track positions. "Success," I am afraid, is not in the vocabulary of the literature that addresses or describes this majority.

Rhetoric and composition has a spectacular trajectory of disciplinary evolution in the US, which is a success measured in its rising number of graduate programs, professional journals, events, and organizations. However, these developments of the past thirty-to-forty years supported a paradigm that is heavily based on our profession's administrative commitments and a scholarly agenda often removed from a diversity of local contexts as well as from the generally low prestige of literacy and its specialists in society. In addition, this paradigm of success seems to be too simple to serve appropriately the needs of many of us who are struggling to maintain some permanence in our professional standards in a world that is in constant flux. As graduate students, we were enticed by safe prospects on the job market, but what seemed as a boom then is beginning to look like a "university bubble" threatening to burst at a similar scale as the housing market (Ambrose). At the same time, community colleges experience record high enrollment because economic pressures make these institutions more promising alternatives for many students who choose them, at least temporarily, and contribute to a recent phenomenon called "reverse transfer" (Moltz). The trend of four-year college students transferring to two-year colleges to save costs, especially on general classes, including writing, may cause a corresponding upsurge in employment, too, requiring a reconsideration of what looks like a bias toward universities in definitions of professional success in rhetoric and composition. But there is more to the complexity of the rhetoric composition career trajectory than uneven professionalization or economic trends.

Whether a career is deemed to be successful or not is a matter of the cultural standards by which success is measured. Barbara Rogoff offers a definition of culture as a process, in which human standards and patterns of behavior are developed through participation in relevant communities' practices. These practices, claims Rogoff, gain their coherence from the underlying larger processes—modernization, industrialization, or, for that matter, professionalization—and from the economic resources indispensable for their maintenance. Noticeably, all these definitions rely on socio-economic or disciplinary standards, concealing personal factors, like the achievement of a doctoral degree at the age of fifty, after overcoming a personal relationship crisis, raising a family, taking care of ailing parents, or struggling with a life-threatening disease. While I am not suggesting that these elements should be included in professional evaluations, it is good to be reminded that these factors play an important part in the personal perceptions of one's success. The implied fluctuation in these conditions is, however, in stark contrast with the popular ethos of success in US society in general, and with the equally static definition of professional success in rhetoric and composition presented by Ballif, Davis and Mountford in particular.

Many democratic and free societies, especially the US, operate on the principle that everyone can succeed by following the required steps and by applying talent and learning. This meritocratic conceptualization of success disregards changes in larger social or institutional contexts beyond an individual's control, and is, as Alain De Botton points out, one of the main sources of depression and unhappiness. De Botton argues that if success is considered simply a matter of individual effort and talent, those who do not follow the clearly delineated path of success can only blame themselves. Similarly, the assumed equal access to the processes of professionalization Ballif, Davis and Mountford describe suggests that those who do not follow this path are not considered successful.

Disciplines, including rhetoric and composition, are often considered disciplinary cultures, frequently described in metaphors borrowed from anthropological discourses of tribalism or territorialism

(Becher and Trowler; Klein). In accordance with these works' emphasis on variety and dynamic changes in disciplinary cultures—many of which accompany, even if they are not determined by, equally dynamic changes in job markets and the economy at large—the definition of professional success should best be considered a moving target rather than a predictable trajectory.

Rhetoric and composition, in spite of its more than two thousand years of history, is still a newcomer in the modern disciplinary setup of US higher education, and as such, it is troubled more by some of its ailments than are more established fields. These ailments include, but are not limited to, controversial labor conditions and (re)current epistemological crises (including unrealistic paradigm hopes, a gulf between pedagogy and theory, as well as the profession's recurrent trend of self-obliteration). Finally and more damagingly, rhetoric and composition functions in an environment of ill-conceived public perception. These factors, I want to argue, require the reconsideration of a broader range of professional paths in our definition of success in rhetoric and composition than what Ballif, Davis, and Mountford outlined. The problem is not merely that emerging experts in our field get mixed messages about the value of scholarly, administrative, pedagogical, and personal career performance. More seriously, the lack of publicly visible demonstrations of "success"—or rather, a range of possible successes—with rhetoric and composition sends a mixed message about the value of writing, and the expertise involved in it, to our students. Therefore, I would like to promote an analogy between the nontraditional students, whose long and troubled road to success so often starts with working with us, writing teachers, and point out that our profession needs to expand traditional concepts of success to include more of the experiences of nontraditional professionals who work in our field and whose success is shaped by a variety of complex local conditions.

CHALLENGES OF SUCCESS: INSTITUTIONALIZED ANOMALIES

As an emerging discipline, rhetoric and composition faces its graduates with a baffling amount of professional career challenges, which make the definition of success in terms of a full-time, tenure-track job in our field inadequate: Even when the job market is good, Gail Stygall points out, rhetoric and composition positions are prone to elimination and replacement by what is commonly known as "contingent labor"

(379). Bruce Horner claims that work in our field is polarized. On one hand, professionalization entails measuring success rigorously in terms of "specialized knowledge acquired, produced and distributed" (173). On the other hand, several aspects of our expertise, most prominently teaching, are subject to "proletarization" (i.e., degradation to low-paid and invisible work).

Numerous publications acknowledge these institutional dichotomies in metaphors that associate those who teach writing as non- or not-yet traditional professionals with oppression, exploitation, and discrimination. To mention just a few examples, Tracy Taylor and Jennifer Holberg point out that graduate students are regarded as "something Other than faculty" and are represented in academic discourse as requiring surveillance, supervision, and training, which makes them similar to slaves. If graduate students' narratives are told, in Taylor and Holberg's words, as tales of "neglect and sadism," those who work in adjunct positions and who, arguably, are often less qualified to teach writing compared to those who engage in graduate studies, are adorned with even less appealing epithets (614). Although terms like "highway fly-by faculty" and "gypsy academics" (Schell), or "sad women in the basement" (Miller) still suggest some kind of romantic glamour reminiscent of the early euphoria of composition teachers who left their literary studies behind, the more recent metaphors are borrowed from the bare and unadorned discourse of business and economics. Composition classes are said to have been subjected to "adjunctization" (Bauerlein), and "casualization" (Bousquet); "downsizing," and "outsourcing" seem not so far away. For instance, Jaime A. Mejía believes that "if it weren't for English," adjunct positions would soon be filled "by undocumented Mexican workers" (746). I must say that Mejía's metaphor has, in fact, happened already. The graduate program I attended at the University of Arizona had several international students, including myself, from China, Romania, Germany, Turkey, Columbia, India and Hungary. Although we were not undocumented, visa extensions and green card applications added an extra dimension of anxiety to our lives as graduate students struggling with teaching, studying and taking care of family members, often in another country. Most of us started in an ESL program, but because of the politically volatile job market in ESL along with less tolerance for nonnative speakers in ESL teaching, some of us ended up in the rhetoric and composition program, which at that time was particularly supportive. For most of us, staying in this program and earning our degrees were significant achievements similar, perhaps, to the undocumented Mexican's sense of achievement by holding a job and supporting a family at home.

These troubling metaphors are discouraging, especially because many of us who finally earned our degree in rhetoric and composition but who did not attain full-time positions, find ourselves stationed in these nontraditional academic positions longer than expected. In small English departments, faculty with rhetoric and composition degrees are still most vulnerable when it comes to downsizing. I experienced the nonrenewal of four tenure-track English faculty at one small, liberal arts university, three of us with degrees in rhetoric and composition and one with a creative writing degree. In a traditional English department, higher-level classes are offered only in literature and linguistics, and it makes more sense to supplement the workload of literature or linguistics faculty with composition classes, while full-time faculty with rhetoric and composition degrees can feel their positions are relatively more secure only if they do program administration or assessment. However, even the latter position is very competitive and could easily be taken by a social science faculty more qualified in statistical methods; to make things even worse, at a small university, writing program administration is part of the department chair's responsibilities. Realizing these hazardous conditions, our other option was to start a writing major, but we all lost our jobs before these plans could have reached fruition due to a drastic budget cut, which often hits state universities these days.

The persistence of part-time work in our field along with an increasing number of highly qualified individuals who take these positions makes the word "anomaly" a misnomer for this situation, and an increasing amount of evidence suggests that these anomalies have become, paradoxically, institutionalized, especially with recurrent state budget crises and economic downturns. David Smit, who both laments and recommends the end of composition studies, points out a significant shift of focus away from teaching to the administration of teaching composition (29). Moreover, Marc Bousquet's account of the institutional transformations in the US university suggests complicity in the degradation of nontraditional professionals when he assumes that compositionists' (self)-understanding of success involves becoming "managerial intellectuals" since rhetoric and composition graduates assume (writing) program administrator positions in high proportions compared to other disciplines ("Introduction"). According to Bousquet, the power of this managerial minority derives from the exploitation of the non-managerial (teaching) majority.

Bousquet's analysis of what he calls the "corporatization" of the university has several consequences relevant to the definition of success in our field. While doctoral programs in rhetoric and composition fill up rapidly with candidates who, often after many years of part-time teaching, hope to upgrade their position on the job market, few realize that, if Bousquet's calculations are correct, only one in every four PhDs will end up in a tenure-track job. Bousquet also points out that the positive forecasts of the job market publicized by the MLA and other professional sources informing our graduate programs in rhetoric and composition were miscalculated.[1] Consequently, even those who eventually gain those tenure-track jobs will spend more time—and accumulate more debt—getting there.

Bousquet's account highlights a problem with viewing rhetoric and composition through those traditional definitions of academic success that Ballif, Davis, and Mountford review and adjust to promote the success of women who are entering the profession in large numbers. One problem is that this model excessively valorizes research and scholarship and does not prepare graduate students for the administrative responsibilities and economic realities of our field. When I was a graduate student, one important adjustment was made by adding a writing program administration course to our curriculum, and this modification was meant to address, in a small way, the hidden reality that we either end up becoming "composition bosses," or with all our theories and teaching experience, we may not be able to succeed and get a more secure, full-time position. Furthermore, the amount of silence surrounding any alternatives suggested that community college teaching, non-tenure track teaching, let alone continued adjunct status with a doctoral degree, are *not* considered success (or, at least logical steps toward it) in our field. This assumption adds insult to the injury that, if Bousquet's data are correct, at least three out of every four graduates in our field (often with ten to fifteen years of teaching experience) have to endure.

Since these problems seem to be persistent enough not to be considered temporary, it would be helpful to prepare rhetoric and composition graduates for this reality. Too much emphasis on the tenure-track trajectory can have a paralyzing effect on those who do not end up on that path. My anecdotal evidence of this phenomenon is the story of two colleagues whose lives fell apart after their tenure was denied, and who, ironically, while being so critical of the "corporatization" of the university, were unable to see these larger processes at work when their personal lives were involved. While I am grateful for the meticulous preparation for professional life I received in my graduate program, I would have appreciated some preparation for a "second life" after my first full-time contract was not renewed before I was eligible to apply for tenure. With my background in ESL, I felt somewhat prepared to apply to a community college, where writing is often taught together with reading, and where testing, placement, assessment, and curriculum design are higher priorities in faculty work than research or publication. I had no preparation of any kind, however, to teach writing in a tribal community college—one of the thirty-seven colleges controlled by federally recognized Native American tribes in the US. Being a first generation immigrant, ironically, made me more acceptable in this setting where the teaching of reading and writing is still strongly associated with colonialism and oppression. Given the high fluctuation of part- and full-time faculty at this institution, I consider it to be my personal success that after two years of adjunct work, I was finally granted full-time status.

CHALLENGES OF SUCCESS: EPISTEMOLOGICAL TURBULENCES

In addition to being hard hit by the overall and perhaps systemic disadvantages of the university economy, rhetoric and composition scholarship has a long history of epistemological challenges, as expertise involved is labeled as knack, alchemy, lore, or identity politics (Connors, "The Rise"; Braddock, Lloyd-Jones and Schoer; North; Bauerlein). These epistemological challenges can lead to too much reflection, self-doubt, and insecurity, which, in turn, inform some of our scholarship. Without questioning the value of this scholarship, I have to admit that on my nontraditional career path, not much of the critical self-reflection helps me better promote the cause of reading and writing.

In a recent study, Karen Kopelson describes the early years of disciplinary identity formation of rhetoric and composition in metaphors of religious conversion and euphoria. English majors with backgrounds in literature entered the field of teaching writing with a sense of (self)-liberation in the 1970s and 1980s. Success then, so it seems, was measured in the teacher's self-fulfillment rather than in measurable (teaching) outcomes or (relevant) scholarship. Irene Clark's account illustrates this spirit: "Miraculously, . . . with the help of sympathetic colleagues and generous students, I managed to get through that first semester without doing too much harm. Cheerfully, I blundered my way from class to class, relying on my youth, enthusiasm and determinism to carry me through" (xvii). But as rhetoric and composition forges ahead on the path of its own disciplinary identity, "youth, enthusiasm and determinism" are not regarded as sufficient conditions for success, and "not doing too much harm" does not qualify as a measurable outcome of successful student learning in today's higher education climate. In other words, disciplinary culture pressures rhetoric and composition to set for its candidates the same or even more rigorous standards of academic success as exist in any of the established disciplinary fields, yet these requirements did not change the situation that eighty percent of those who teach writing do it in two-year colleges or in other venues where traditional scholarly standards of successful academic careers may not apply. Thinking about my graduate school years, I find some disconnect between the practical problems whose efficient solution is required for my survival in my current environment and my earlier scholarly interest in eighteenth-century textbooks, visual rhetoric, or the subsequent translations of Aristotle's *Rhetoric*. While I do actively engage in research with the purpose of answering practical questions, the kind of scholarship that is required for success in tenure-track positions lacks relevance in my context.

Successful scholarship and research in rhetoric and composition are also complicated by the interdisciplinary nature of the enterprise and by the duality of humanities and social studies in its inherited patterns of inquiry. In addition, the relationship between "English" and rhetoric and composition seems to have moved from an abusive marriage to a pleasureless and isolating divorce. Stephen North in 1987 is concerned that composition "as a knowledge-making society is gradually pulling itself apart" (364); in 2006 Richard Fulkerson is alarmed that composition lacks solid epistemology "other than a vaguely interactionist constructivism" (662). More specifically, Richard Haswell in 2005 argues that our own professional organizations and publications neglect work on three areas that he perceives as demonstrating the most important outcome of expertise in our field: the role of peer reviewing in writing, the measurement and transfer of what students gain from writing instruction, and the teaching of the research assignment. Additionally, Haswell is concerned that the paradigm of RAD (replicable, aggregable, and data supported research) as well as the systematic accumulation of knowledge in the form of regularly published bibliographies are missing from our field. Haswell argues that if we do not value these aspects of our work, it will be impossible to convince our stakeholders, students and the general public, who care about facts, that our work matters.

Working in a tribal college, I feel the sting of Haswell's argument more than I ever thought I would. As the only instructor with a doctoral degree, I often find myself in a situation when administrators want quick and straight answers: they want our graduates to be able to produce error-free documents in a clear and accessible language. Do I know how to teach them to be able to do this? Do I know why our students are doing so poorly on those standardized tests and whether there is anything we can do to make them improve? How much extra time do students with learning disabilities need to be fairly accommodated on their in-class writing? These questions land on my desk on a daily basis and force me to develop a pragmatic attitude to research. Instead of comparing as many plausible answers as possible, I have to come up with something that fits our situation best and has a reasonable chance of persuading our president. Whether reflective knowledge or data-driven research, it only has a chance of informing institutional decisions if it is persuasive enough to gain consensus in the teaching community.

When I was in graduate school, I was fascinated with a recurrent trend of "abolitionist" arguments in rhetoric and composition scholarship whose history traces back to the nineteenth century when first-year composition classes first became a required course at Harvard. This argument, whose very labeling also reinforces unfortunate associations with oppressive social institutions, is particularly troubling because it further increases the gap between scholarship and professional/institutional practice by claiming that writing is teachable; teaching writing requires professional expertise, but the required first-year courses are not effective venues for "attaining the ends we seek" (Connors, "Abolition," 60). Others, like David Smit or Gary Olson, argue that the complexities of writing have never been truly covered by composition studies; in other words, we don't really agree what writing is, how people learn it, let alone how it is best taught. In fact, some of the "post-process" scholarship even suggests that writing is best learned in its functional context rather than being taught in required composition classes. Viewed from the perspective of where I am, these arguments seem to be absolutely counterproductive. Working with a student population that has a conflicted relationship with literacy in the first place, and students who are often less successful in mainstream education than they should be, the whole idea of thinking about why we teach what we teach appears to be completely useless and a waste of time. When I face the emergency of making my teaching more effective and motivating my students to be more successful, the last thing I need is (self)-doubt.

Kopelson's recent study finds that graduate students in rhetoric and composition often feel there is not much in composition pedagogy to research other than "the process method," which to these students at least, seems kind of a given and not very challenging. Cultural studies or critical theories are seen as more appealing for research, yet these areas appear too far removed from the dire realities of the writing classroom, especially in those settings where underprepared students are struggling for academic survival. In other words, some of these theories, which can usefully inform our field and encourage reflection on our work, often distract attention from the mundane tasks of teaching students to write appropriately and successfully in the contexts relevant for their academic and professional fields. In addition, the theories that inform some of our composition programs are labeled by mainstream media as "identity politics" or "subversion of the status quo" and as such, not conducive to the improvement of academic literacy among our students. Teaching in a tribal college, I view this dichotomy from a different perspective: I consider "the process" (or, rather, the multiple processes) that govern my students' writing a valuable instrument of writing instruction and also a subject of further research since there is still a lot more to learn about effective individualized interventions to facilitate "the process(es)" of writing. Critical thinking, analysis and reading of texts, printed or electronic, is a high priority in our general education, but confrontation, controversy, and subversion are considered undesirable in the tribal culture that seeks harmony and peace. Consequently, several texts that stimulated moderate discussion in my "mainstream" classrooms fall flat with my new audience; my teaching materials and approach to analysis require constant revision and modification. The dichotomy between teaching and critical research, considered a potential threat to the success of our discipline, thus, can provide dynamic venues for new approaches to both teaching and research.

One symptom of the conflict or mismatch between the various sources of knowledge that inform our field is that, according to the head of NCTE publications, the books published in our field are not selling well, and this has been going on for about a decade (Mejía 744). Mejía concludes that the epistemological landscape of composition is marred by often conflicting sources of knowledge. In his words, "What the journals and books, both professional studies and textbooks, say— or don't say—about our practices within composition classrooms, . . . does not exactly reflect what's actually going on in many composition classrooms" (744). Symptomatic of this phenomenon, one of my senior colleagues who has been teaching in this community college for thirteen years, and who is an outstanding expert on all levels of "Indian education," told me that she stopped subscribing to *Teaching English in the Two-Year College* and *College Composition and Communication* because she found nothing relevant or useful in them for her work. Since I was hired, I have photocopied a couple of articles for her from these journals, but I can see how many others are less relevant. We are also a hundred miles away from a decent-size library, so our access to many of the standard resources is, indeed, limited. Nevertheless, depending on what practical problem we need to address in our school, we do find some publications relevant and useful. But my priorities in scholarship and research have shifted significantly toward more practical areas of professional knowledge, such as assessment, program evaluation, or contextualized grammar instruction.

The above symptoms of what I termed epistemological turbulences seem to be normal components of disciplinary cultures that, as James Slevin points out, are "multifarious and virtually indefinable" ("Academic Literacy" 201). Slevin adds that the different areas of study, the diversity of methodologies, and "canons" as well as seemingly incompatible theories are all normal in any discipline. Therefore, I also believe that the lack of agreement about writing knowledge should not be regarded as a symptom of crisis, but rather as a sign of growth and increasing awareness of complexity. Being on a nontraditional career path means selecting those areas and paradigms of rhetoric and composition that are relevant to our work, and also, perhaps, replacing scholarly research with administrative research that supports institutional or pedagogical decisions.[2]

Arrogant College Professors, Popular Myths, and Unpopular Chores

The measures of success in a rhetoric and composition career are also influenced by the mixed public representation and evaluation of our work. One major source of the public image of full-time college professors is their representation in movies. William Deresiewicz,, for instance, found a remarkably consistent pattern in the recent movie representations of academics, many of whom are male professors of English: These characters are arrogant, live with a sense of entitlement, neglect their children and family, seduce their students, drink, and, in general, live an embittered and unproductive life, often as a failed writer. (*The Quid and the Whale; Smart People*). More importantly, many regard their students as a nuisance or interference and their academic work as a waste of time. For instance, the professor protagonist of *The Visitor* admits that his scholarly work has been meaningless, and, in fact, abandons his position—full-time, tenured, with benefits—without hesitation or remorse for a more fulfilling enrichment of his personal life through friendship and drumming. The stereotypical arrogance of tenured professors, who, statistically, represent a waning minority of all those who work in college education, sends a mixed message about success in higher education: These characters are successful in achieving tenure, but on a personal level, they are unappreciative or even unaware of their privileged position. Unfortunately, the rest of us who work in higher education under less favorable conditions, but perhaps with more dedication to our teaching assignments, are largely invisible to the public.

What is peculiar about the work of college composition teachers is that our expertise is misunderstood, misrepresented and undervalued. Just as writing is regarded as a "basic skill" that everybody should have acquired before attending college or, on the contrary, is mystified into a unique talent that only a few attain, the public perception of composition teachers' work is often reduced to mere editing and error correction or, on the romantic extreme, is glorified as a subversive redeeming force that is supposed to change lives (*Dead Poets Society*). If the common sense notion of medical doctors was similarly distorted, physicians would be perceived either as simply experts in removing warts or magicians who can resurrect the dead.

To reach a more diverse definition of successful careers in rhetoric and composition, it would be necessary to inform the public about the complexity and depth of our work and change the common sense myths of writing that, in Mark Richardson's words, are "pernicious" and that "poison colleges and universities, affecting the morale of writing instructors, the attitudes of other faculty members, and, worst of all, students' acquisition of literacy" (1). Richardson's tentative list of truths about writing include the idea that learning to write well in one genre does not guarantee success in another genre; that conventions of disciplinary writing are diverse; that writing and thinking are intertwined and develop "slowly and with revision"; that language use is linked to personal and group identity; that rhetorical considerations are crucial in every writing situation; and finally, that writing development is a lifelong process.

As knowledge of what rhetoric and composition entails is gradually accumulating, all evidence suggests that teaching college composition involves a wide range of programs, approaches, methods, and media even if the endeavor ultimately boils down to what Jeffrey Zorn defines as "guiding individual students to improvement as writers of formal expository prose, phrase by phrase, sentence by sentence, paragraph by successive paragraph" (752). My own untraditional professional trajectory has undoubtedly been influenced by what Zorn posits as "local success." As he stresses, students, curricula, and schools' purposes vary widely, and experiences "don't carry over" very well from one institutional setting to another. As I moved from a traditional but ideologically oppressed East-European university to a research I university in Arizona, then taught in a large community college as an adjunct, landing as a full-time faculty member in a small, liberal arts college, finally at an even smaller tribal community college on the Upper Peninsula of Michigan, I had to relearn my profession over and over again.

For example, feedback and peer response, which are considered two important components of helping emerging writers, are given very different roles and emphasis in different teaching settings. In Eastern-Europe, at the time I started teaching writing in an English major program, students were not allowed to revise papers; in Arizona, I learned to incorporate student peer responses in my teaching in a university writing program, and adjusted these feedback processes to the community college environment as well. The liberal arts university where I was hoping to earn my tenure disapproved of revision and peer reviews partly because it was seen as extra work for writing faculty and partly because it was regarded as inconsistent with how writing is done across the curriculum. Finally, in the tribal college, my supervisors expressed cultural concerns about peer reviews, and I had to learn to redesign assignments so that the peer review sessions are less invasive.

Similarly, the five-paragraph essay was a structure the University of Arizona composition program advised its composition teachers to move students beyond. In Eastern-Europe, it is regarded as an important element of cross-cultural rhetoric although it also became the target of critical protests against what was perceived as a "McDonaldized globalization" of academic writing. Teaching in a community college, I found Tom Speer's pragmatic approach to the five-paragraph essay informative, while in my current teaching position, after extensive discussions and explorations, we decided to spend a large amount of course work on developing a five-paragraph essay simply because most of our students had never worked with this structure. It seemed unrealistic to expect them to move beyond a structure they were mostly unfamiliar with. Working myself through these problems with the help of my learned knowledge and exchanges with colleagues who have more extensive local experience takes me years, and accurate measurement of the success of this work poses an added challenge to this process.

WHAT HAS SUCCESS GOT TO DO WITH IT?

US society is very much success oriented, and success is often expressed in terms of material possessions and power. In addition, success is frequently perceived as a rapid change from "rags to riches," or, "from adjunct to WPA." In fact, our whole higher education system is based on a success-oriented ethos: we are telling our students in no uncertain terms that going to college and earning a degree are indispensable for their success in life as measured in average pay rates.

How does writing feature in this dream of success? As writing program administrator Diane Chin reports bluntly in Gerald Graff's article, "If writing is so damn important, why are the lowest paid, least secure, most overburdened people in the 'academic community' made responsible for teaching it?" (3). When many instructors in writing are still unqualified and hired on the assumption that anyone can teach writing, and those who are successful both in terms of pay and position are either administrators or scholars with their successful professional activities far removed from the majority of classrooms, I am not sure how we can give a clear and unmixed message about the importance of writing in society. How does it reflect upon our discipline and the profession of teaching composition that instead of Irene Clark in 1964 "miraculously managing through" her writing classes "without doing too much harm," in 2008, Gerald Graff reports his teaching experiences in these words: "when my colleagues hear that I teach first-year composition, they figure I must be a saint, a masochist, or a victim of blackmail. It's axiomatic in our trade that established academics do not voluntarily teach comp unless they have a Mother Teresa complex" (3).

Rhetoric and composition predominantly looks upon current changes in the university in negative terms, sensing a shift of power and control moving away from faculty toward administration. Yet, it is possible to look upon these processes as a crisis that, according to Chinese wisdom, is also a window of opportunity. Namely, the universities' more businesslike behavior includes increasing emphasis on their "customers," or "clients," who are the students. Learner-centered teaching, emphasis on measurable outcomes, and reliable, data driven decision-making in program direction are not necessarily evil. As Terry Doyle states, teaching is difficult work, and it is especially difficult work in higher education where success of faculty is measured in terms of research and scholarship. I believe that it would be a mistake to view changes in higher education simply in material terms without noticing that these processes also encourage innovative, learner-centered pedagogies, the building of learning communities and learner-centered environments, and the involvement of new media which, if they become the measures of success for faculty, should match the ideals rhetoric and composition scholars and practitioners have endorsed all along.

Notes

1. Bousquet's criticism rests on two main propositions. First, the MLA analysis assumed that, just like any market, the PhD job market will also

operate in a cyclical manner, with the alternation of bear and bull periods. Second, Bousquet emphasizes that this analysis underestimated the greed factor that makes giving up the more profitable part-timers for full-time faculty financially less appealing. Kim Clark's article from *US News and World Report* provides these figures:

> On average, traditional professors, who have tenure (or lifetime job guarantees), benefits, and campus offices, cost colleges the equivalent of about $8,000 per three-credit class, one recent study found. Adjuncts, the vast majority of whom teach only one or two courses at any particular college, cost their employers an average of about $1,800 per course. Schools not only pay adjuncts less per classroom hour but often don't offer benefits or support such as offices or secretaries. (par 4)

2. At the time of working on this draft, I was the recipient of an American Indian College Fund—Mellon Research Fellowship. Working on a literacy profile project for a year was a challenge, and I am still facing the challenge of publishing my nontraditional research conducted in an unusual setting, using very small samples, and coming up with findings whose significance is hard to demonstrate beyond their local context.

Works Cited

Ambrose, Jay. "University Bubble Bursting?" *The Washington Times*. 28 November 2009. Web. 10 January 2010.
Aristotle. *Rhetoric*. Trans. W. Rhys Roberts. New York: Dover Publications, 2004. Print.
Bauerlein, Mark. "Where Are Rhetoric and Composition Going?" *The Chronicle of Higher Education*, 28 Jan. 2008. Web. 11 November 2010.
Ballif, Michelle, Diane Davis, and Roxanne Mountford. *Women's Ways of Making It in Rhetoric and Composition*. Mahwah, NJ: Erlbaum, 2008. Print.
Becher, Tony, and Paul Trowler. *Academic Tribes and Territories: Intellectual Inquiry and the Cultures of Discipline*. Philadelphia, PA: Open UP, 2001. Print.
Bousquet, Marc. "Tenure Bosses and Disposable Teachers." *The Minnesota Review* 58–60 (2003) Web. 2 November 2008.
—. Introduction. *How the University Works? Higher Education and the Low-Wage Nation*. New York: New York UP, 2008: 1-54. Print.
Braddock, Richard, Richard Lloyd-Jones, and Lowell Schoer. *Research in Written Composition*. Urbana, IL: NCTE, 1963. Print.
Clark, Irene L. *Concepts in Composition*. Mahwah, NJ: Erlbaum, 2003. Print.

Clark, Kim. "Does It Matter That Your Professor Is Part Time?" *US News and World Report* 11 Nov. 2008. Web. 10 January 2010.

Connors, Robert J. "The Abolition Debate in Composition: A Short History." *Composition in the Twenty- First Century: Crisis and Change.* Ed. Lynn Z. Bloom, Donald A. Daiker, and Edward M. White. Carbondale: Southern Illinois UP, 1996. 47–63. Print.

Connors, Robert J. "The Rise and Fall of the Modes of Discourse." *College Composition and Communication* 32 (1981): 444–55. Print.

Dead Poets Society. Dir. Peter Weir. Perf. Robin Williams, Robert Sean Leonard, Ethan Hawke, and Josh Charles. Touchstone Pictures, 1998. Film.

De Botton, Alain. "A Kinder, Gentler Philosophy of Success." *Technology, Entertainment, Design, Ideas Worth Spreading.* July 2009. Video. Web. 13 January 2010.

Deresiewicz, William. "Love on Campus." *The American Scholar.* Summer 2007. Web. 10 November 2008.

Doyle, Terry. "Helping Students Learn in a Learning Centered Environment." *A Guide to Facilitating Learning in Higher Education.* Sterling, VA: Stylus, 2008. Print.

Enos, Theresa. *Gender Roles and Faculty Lives in Rhetoric and Composition.* Carbondale, IL: Southern Illinois UP, 1996. Print.

Fulkerson, Richard. "Composition at the Turn of the Twenty-First Century." *College Composition and Communication* 56.4 (June 2005): 654–87. Print.

Graff, Gerald. "Bringing Writing in from the Cold." *MLA Newsletter* (Summer 2008): 3–4. Print.

Haswell, Richard. "NCTE/CCCC's Recent War on Scholarship." *Written Communication* 22 (2005): 198–223. Print.

Horner, Bruce. *Terms of Work for Composition.* Albany: SUNY P, 2000. Print.

Klein, Julie Thompson. *Crossing Boundaries: Knowledge, Disciplinarities, and Interdisciplinarities.* Charlottesville: U of Virginia P, 1996. Print.

Kopelson, Karen. "Sp(l)itting Images; or Back to the Future of (Rhetoric and?) Composition." *College Composition and Communication* 59.4 (June 2008):749–80. Print.

Mejía, Jaime Armin. "Interchanges. Responses to Richard Fulkerson, 'Composition at Turn of the Twenty-First Century.'" *College Composition and Communication* 57.4 (June 2006): 738–51. Print.

Miller, Susan. *Textual Carnivals: The Politics of Composition.* Carbondale: Southern Illinois UP, 1991. Print.

Moltz, David. "The New Reverse Transfer." *Inside Higher Ed.* 14 February 2010. Web. 11 November 2010.

North, Stephen M. *The Making of Knowledge in Composition: Portrait of an Emerging Field.* Portsmouth: Heinemann, 1987. Print.

Olson, Gary A., ed. *Rhetoric and Composition as Intellectual Work.* Carbondale: Southern Illinois UP, 2002. Print.

Richardson, Mark. "Writing Is Not Just a Basic Skill." *The Chronicle of Higher Education.* 55.11 (November 7, 2008): A47. Print.

Rogoff, Barbara. *The Cultural Nature of Human Development.* Oxford: Oxford UP, 2003. Print.

Schell, Eileen. *Gypsy Academics and Mother-Teachers: Gender, Contingent Labor and Writing Instruction.* Portsmouth, NH: Boynton/Cook Heinemann, 1997. Print.

Slevin, James F. *Introducing English: Essays in the Intellectual Work of Composition.* Pittsburgh: U of Pittsburgh P, 2001. Print.

—. "Academic Literacy and the Discipline of English." *Profession 2007* (2007): 200–20. Print.

Smit, David. *The End of Composition Studies.* Carbondale: Southern Illinois UP, 2004. Print.

Smart People. Dir. Noam Murro. Perf. Dennis Quaid, Thomas Haden Church, and Sarah Jessica Parker. Miramax, 2008. Film.

Speer, Tom. "Reconceiving the Five-Paragraph Essay in an Era of Uncertainty." *Teaching English in the Two-Year College* 22.1 (February 1995): 21–29. Print.

Stygall, Gail. "At the Century's End: The Job Market in Rhetoric and Composition." *Rhetoric Review* 18.2 (Spring 2000): 375–89. Print.

Taylor, Tracy, and Jennifer Holberg. "Tales of Neglect and Sadism: Disciplinarity and the Figuring of the Graduate Student in Composition." *College Composition and Communication* 50.4 (1999): 607–25. Print.

The Squid and the Whale. Dir. Noah Baumbach. Perf. Owen Kline, Laura Linney, and Jeff Daniels. Sony Pictures, 2005. Film.

The Visitor. Dir. Thomas McCarthy. Perf. Richard Jenkins and Hazz Sleiman. Overture Films, 2007. Film.

Zorn, Jeffrey. "Interchanges. Responses to Richard Fulkerson, 'Composition at the Turn of the Twenty-First Century.'" *College Composition and Communication* 57.4 (June 2006): 751–56. Print.

4 Opportunity and Respect: Keys to Contingent Faculty Success

Sue Doe

Success in academic settings need not be defined by the kind of position a faculty person holds but can be understood as the control that a faculty member has over the terms and conditions of her labor. This claim is made in the context of widespread diminishment of support for tenure lines that are well established: tenure-track positions across the disciplines rose seventeen percent from 1976 to 2005, while both full-time and part-time non-tenure-track appointments more than tripled (228 percent and 214 percent, respectively) over the same period ("What" 16). While it is beyond the scope of this essay to rehearse the full history of this trend or attempt to explain its causes, the implications of this cultural retreat from the tenure-line appointment form the context for my research and this chapter. In short, I argue that in the liminal space between the gold standard of tenure and the willful use of an untenurable underclass lie well-supported non-tenure-track faculty positions that, for the foreseeable future, offer a productive faculty space. These positions will require particular kinds of support to make them viable, however, and the question of what constitutes such support is the subject of my research.

Two key factors—opportunity and respect—appear to have the most significant effect upon contingent faculty sense of control. These factors often overlap and are by no means exclusive of other factors. My research suggests, however, that if we focus our efforts on improving the working conditions of non-tenure-track faculty in these two areas, we can build departmental cultures that work collaboratively toward professionalism. The key to constructing opportunity and conveying respect involves opening the doors of faculty governance to non-tenure-track faculty so that they are able to develop understanding of institutional mechanisms for advancement.

My understanding of contingent faculty perspectives derives from two sources—my own experience off the tenure-track and a year-long qualitative study of twenty-two non-tenure-track faculty from across the disciplines in the local setting. I worked for over twenty years as a non-tenure-track faculty member before moving to the tenure track in 2007, and my nontraditional career supports the idea that there are multiple ways to define success as well as varied paths for pursuing it. While I experienced many of the indignities that are associated with life off the tenure track, including annual hire and fire processes, the repetitive anxiety of routine budget cuts, and dismissive responses to my own scholarly and creative output, I was also afforded opportunities within the units in which I worked. For instance, I was able to develop my teaching skills, author curricula, and represent my fellow contingent faculty members on committees. No matter how token the governance opportunity, I took advantage of it so that I might learn how faculty participation in university structures works. Then, in the months leading up to my first national search for a tenure-track position, I received high levels of support from tenure-line colleagues who offered advice on the job search. Moreover, they supported my need for opportunity and worked proactively to demonstrate their belief in me. Their experience suggests a model of faculty mentorship, as it shepherded me through a process that built my confidence and altered the course of my career

Second, my research on contingent faculty involves participant-observation, which has afforded me insights and access available only to someone from inside the community. Of course, my participation is now complicated by my movement out of the non-tenure-track ranks. However, it is widely understood by my non-tenure-track research collaborators that I am still very much a contingent hire, and they are invested in my success as well. Ours is a land grant Research I institution in which research is the coin of the realm, and my research collaborators were drawn from all areas of the campus. Data collection included interviews, observations, document analysis, and the facilitation of cross-disciplinary discussions among contingent faculty from seven of the university's eight colleges. I recruited participants across the whole of the campus because I suspected there were wide differences in contingent faculty experience unit to unit, college to college, and my suspicions were confirmed. For instance, in most of the science, medicine, and engineering departments, both rank and promotion opportunities existed for non-tenure-track faculty, while these practices were far less common in the humanities. Two participants in the study, who came from colleges associated with the sciences, were even able to convert to tenure-track positions shortly after the close of the study, an occurrence that was not unusual in their colleges but was virtually unheard of in the liberal arts. The conversations that occurred across these divides were instructive to everyone; the marked differences across disciplines provided opportunity for modeling, encouragement, and critical assessment of disparities in institutional opportunity.

My findings are distilled here into four short, representative case studies involving two contingent faculty members from English and two from the sciences, all of whom have been given pseudonyms. These four faculty members' experiences represent the two fundamental motivations that I observed generally among the contingent faculty and suggest directions for our efforts as we work toward academic workplaces that improve the lives of faculty off the tenure-track while also maintaining professional standards.

THE MOTIVATION OF OPPORTUNITY

Among the faculty in my study who were primarily motivated by opportunity, Olsen, from the liberal arts, and Felicity, from the natural sciences, offer representative examples. For Olsen, a new scholar with a terminal degree, contingent teaching afforded opportunities to extend her curriculum vitae and develop her capabilities in the areas of teaching and scholarship. In fact, prior to coming to our campus, Olsen had left a full-time position at a community college to reduce her workload of committee work and administrative responsibilities. Felicity, who also possessed a terminal degree in her field, sought opportunities within her immediate geographical area. A well-established researcher and teacher, Felicity was well known and respected in her department, but she had been passed over for its tenure-line positions.

Olsen

As an instructor of composition, Olsen hoped that her terminal degree and expanding teaching experience would one day qualify her for a better academic appointment. Like others who were new to the department, she was assigned an office in a location some distance from the main English department and down a rundown hallway that had been inhabited by a steady stream of transient academic workers—graduate students and contingent faculty—over the years. There was a computer in her office but no printing capability. For that she would need to hike to the department. In what became a metaphor for both the conditions of her position and her response to it, Olsen abandoned her office, established a paper-free classroom, and set up shop between classes in the front foyer of the library. There she conducted her office hours—laptop, water bottle, and books in hand—and students would grab a cup of coffee before sitting down to discuss their papers. Olsen's official position was that she liked this improvised setup and the freedom it afforded her. The only hint of disappointment she conveyed was when her laptop needed a new internal battery and she observed, "If I were on the tenure-track, I would just call tech support."

Olsen seemed to use her personal laptop and the table she claimed to assert her independence from departmental resources. She became a kind of "library squatter," embracing the terms of her freelance status by claiming a common area as her own. For the onlooker, her homesteading in the library telegraphed a message of resistance or opposition to untenable working conditions, and her cheerfulness was not to be misunderstood as satisfaction. Instead it suggested a survivor's approach to difficult circumstances.

Further, Olsen was thoroughly focused on the future and was open to the possibility that it might exist right here, although she was not sanguine about her chances. In fact, roughly a year into her work at this university, when Olsen had sufficient seniority to move to a better office located in the heart of the department, she began to use both the department-supplied desktop computer and her assigned office for all of her meetings with students. She no longer spent time in the library foyer, which seemed to confirm that Olsen's early library use was less a matter of preference than a physical statement of her agency in the context of her marginalized status. Lacking support, she had inscribed herself onto the campus landscape. Then, when offered an office in the central hallway of her department, she took it in the hope that dedicated office space validated her professionalism and might create new opportunities in the local setting. However, those opportunities did not materialize after a second and third year, so Olsen came to believe she would likely remain part of the instructional flex-force, nothing more. Rejecting what she felt to be a summary judgment of her capabilities, she headed off to law school; although she was excited about this new direction, her departure was a loss to her personally and professionally, and her department lost a highly motivated and talented teacher-scholar.

Felicity

A seasoned veteran of both the classroom and the laboratory, Felicity was once tenured in the natural sciences in another country but followed her partner to the U.S. where she took a non-tenure-track position to keep herself current and wait for a faculty position. However, Felicity was understood to be "geographically bound," a notion that she came slowly to understand was pejorative in the U.S., unlike in her home country. By all accounts, however, Felicity successfully maintained her value to the department. A dozen years into a position that was renewed annually, she maintained a thriving lab and had participated in many successful grant proposals. She taught upper-division courses in her department, served on graduate committees, and oversaw a multi-year National Science Foundation project involving undergraduate research. Her student evaluations suggested that students were engaged by her dynamism in the classroom and the relevance of her research. In every way, Felicity was living the life of a professor and had a workload distribution only slightly different from that of her tenure-line colleagues. For Felicity, opportunity meant one thing—conversion onto the tenure-track, which would signal her importance to the department and the department's commitment to her in return. However, when she competed for advertised positions in her department, she was passed over on two occasions. Over time, she became vocal about practices that subordinate or even ignore the applications of local non-tenure-track faculty in favor of outside applicants.

Discussion

Olsen and Felicity, as representatives of opportunity-motivated contingent faculty, might be said to have inhabited opposite ends of the opportunity spectrum. Olsen was just starting out and looking for opportunities that would drive the next step of her career. She was mobile, able to fairly easily relocate at this early stage of her career even though her departure represented a significant loss to herself and her department. Felicity, on the other hand, lacked mobility, which meant that her options were more limited. As a fixture in her department, her age, gender, and geographical inflexibility played into her department's low assessment of her potential to become a fully enfranchised colleague. Felicity's situation reflected the traditional view of contingent female faculty, as suggested by both Eileen Schell and Theresa Enos, who have argued that the professional identities of female contingent faculty are often absorbed into a local economy that conflates personal circumstance with professional capability. Describing the domestication of such faculty, Schell points out that women often encounter a chilled response in their professional settings since their professional lives often follow "fluid, discontinuous, and contingent career trajectories that were interrupted by childbearing, childrearing, and family responsibility" (58). Similarly, Enos describes the phenomenon of "the battered wife" of departments, or the underemployed non-tenure-track faculty member who tries again and again for the elusive tenure-track position, only to be rejected. We may wonder why Felicity kept returning to that battering household, but it is important to note that Felicity had begun to vocally object to the hiring practices of her department. She was not sitting quietly by, accepting without challenge the limitations that were placed upon her. So while she may seem to have had much in common with historic examples of non-tenure-track female faculty, her rising level of critical awareness of academic workplace inequities made her an emblematic example of contingency-in-transition. Felicity's example suggests that mature contingents need local advocacy and aggressive policies that protect current employees, while new scholars like Olsen need professional development tied to opportunities for either local promotion or employment elsewhere. Both of these contingent faculty suggest the need for powerful role models, conscious mentoring by tenure-line faculty, and a commitment by departments to pay attention to the career direction and progress of contingent faculty.

Like Olsen and Felicity, other contingent faculty in the study group sought opportunity and in many cases were actively testing the waters of alternative work outside the academy that might sustain them. One participant ran a home-based counseling practice, while another published chapbooks. Still another had a full-time government position and taught at the university only at night. In all of these cases, there was a sense of readiness for opportunity. However, this mindset should not be misunderstood as an indicator of low commitment to the current position. Rather, contingent faculty in this study would have happily accepted both a greater commitment and a greater demand from their university employer. Even the participant with a full-time government job approached the chair of her department to see if her role might be expanded. Had there been opportunity, she would have given up her day job where she enjoyed seniority, the professional application of her disciplinary background, and full-time job security. This instructor hoped to more fully engage in academic work, but she understood the context well enough to proceed carefully. She would only leave her existing job if a faculty position were offered as a real job opportunity.

Further, the opportunity faculty's extracurricular commitments were focused on career enhancement. Most were positioning themselves for the next step, whether at this location or another. As a group, they were consciously grooming themselves for new opportunity. In fact, at the conclusion of the study period, two of the other opportunity-motivated faculty competed for and won tenure-line positions in the local setting, a practice that the American Association of University Professors (AAUP) recommends and celebrates on its website, as with the conversions achieved at St. John's and Western Michigan ("Teaching and Teaching-Intensive"). Administrators might consider the goals of opportunity-motivated faculty like Olsen and Felicity as they contemplate how best to support such faculty and pave the way for their future success while also protecting the institutional investment universities have already made in their academic talent.

THE MOTIVATION OF RESPECT

Of the many faculty motivated by efforts to obtain respect in their organizations, Prudence, from the humanities, and Bob, from the sciences, stood out as representative. While many in this group pointed proudly to their work, most carefully distinguished their work from the conditions of their work. Most also took some degree of personal responsibility for what they understood to be their underemployment, but their calls for respect sprang from the recognition that they were not alone in bearing responsibility. One study participant put her sense of persistent workplace injustice this way: "I could have done better . . . but there were no chances to progress . . . the pay was poor. . . . Now I am too old and I don't see anything else I can do. You know, no one else is going to hire me." Another contingent faculty member described it this way:

> I don't mind the isolation I experience with teaching, but I do have concerns about the university's perspective on what is valued. I don't think that the work itself, the teaching, is valued. . . And I find it ironic that the research I do doesn't matter either. Even this committee work I do, it doesn't hold any weight. . . . Sometimes it seems the university looks elsewhere and sees all of these social issues and injustices, and yet in their own backyard, doesn't recognize the plight and the poverty level of the adjuncts.

Prudence

Among the instructors from the humanities, none was more capable of bridging the gap between the tenured and the non-tenure-track than Prudence. Her doctoral work in rhetoric and cultural studies equipped her for institutional critique, and her ability to conceptualize and contextualize issues of contingency positioned her as a key informant to faculty of all ranks.

ABD for now many years, Prudence had once held a teaching position in the public schools (where, as she put it, "a person knows success because she grows in the job"), and she recognized that the career she had given up for her new one had led to a "loss of social capital." However, she became an established instructor in the university setting and had worked effectively there for over a decade. She had no plan for how to complete the doctorate at this point; thus, while she might once have focused on opportunity, she now focused on respect. She became increasingly involved in governance efforts, accepting responsibility virtually anywhere it was offered. Also, while she had an alternative plan in mind for a future outside of academe, she wanted to leave things in better order and so worked collegially to improve working conditions for her fellow contingents. Her efforts gave rise to two distinct policy changes in her department. First, she accomplished a unanimously supported change to the department code, creating standing committees for non-tenure-track evaluation and hiring. To make this happen in a faculty meeting where she was not authorized to make a proposal, much less vote on it, she used her tenure-track contacts to get the proposal on the table. She also authored the evaluation criteria that were adopted by the committee charged with reviewing the annual files of contingent faculty in her department. This document was later adopted by her entire college. Additionally, she prompted departmental authoring of a narrative explanation of the evaluation tool for contingent faculty. In these ways and others, Prudence gave voice to calls for contingent faculty control over the terms of their labor and the valuing of that labor.

Bob

Like Prudence, Bob, a doctorate-holding scientist in the veterinary school, made a significant impact on the way his labor and that of his contingent peers was understood by his department and college. He lobbied for contingent faculty representation on committees and, as he put it, "gained a seat at the table" for contingent faculty in department and college-level governance. The challenges he faced in accomplishing this were substantial since he was functioning within the context of a research-dependent discipline. Here, where distinctions among faculty were made by how much funded research they brought in, Bob made an improbable case for himself as a classroom instructor and surprisingly obtained not only rank but opportunity for promotion. By the conclusion of the study, Bob had gone even further, successfully making a case for his conversion to the tenure track through a uniquely constructed workload distribution that became a model for other departments and colleges.

Bob's respect-motivated agenda occurred over the course of several years, during which he successfully engaged his department in a variety of actions aimed at improving the conditions of his contingent colleagues' employment and his own visibility. For example, he completed a survey of all faculty members in his college, established an annual retreat for non-tenure-track faculty and research associates that his dean regularly attended, and created a contingent faculty handbook explaining the opportunities and limitations of life off the tenure track. Additionally, he established new understanding among faculty at all levels about the specific inclusions and exclusions of contingent faculty in the faculty manual, where, as he pointed out, "faculty privileges" applied to all faculty unless otherwise stated. Perhaps most remarkably, Bob remained on good terms with both non-tenure-track and tenure-line faculty during this process.

Discussion

For most of the contingent faculty whose primary goal was respect, their recognition that their non-tenure-track positions were likely "permanent" led them to seek greater respect from local environments. Consequently, the respect-motivated contingents were generally interested in changing the conditions of employment, not just for themselves but for others and the future. This interest in collective self-advocacy suggests that respect-driven faculty resist what Dana Cloud in *Control and Consolation in American Culture and Politics* has called the privatization of shame and guilt in the workplace, or "turning workplace uncertainty and owners' ruthlessness into ... psychological phenomena rather than effects of decisions and actions made by business owners" (xiii). Such privatizations of workplace uncertainty, in which the individual is held responsible for failure, undermine collective agency, locating both problem and solution within the individual. Respect-motivated faculty like Prudence and Bob actively rejected this mindset and were unwilling to see themselves and their particular circumstances as isolated or the result of their own inadequacies. They worked proactively to improve working conditions and they often needed the support of like-minded tenure-track faculty to gain access to streams of power.

Most respect-driven faculty are not considering alternative careers, using their positions as stepping stones, or weighing their options. Instead, they consider their contingent positions the livelihood they are committed to, a career. At the same time, they are often open to opportunity, and so the distinction between the motivation categories needs now to be revisited. It is not that respect-motivated faculty are unmoved by opportunity, nor that opportunity-motivated faculty are disinterested in respect, but rather that they begin with different priorities. It seems that those seeking respect have developed a healthy skepticism about the probability of opportunity. As such, they seek structures and frameworks, codes and language, and constraints on managerial freedom to ensure more stable policies in the future. They seek participation in faculty governance, knowing that without a voice and representation, contingent faculty have little say about the terms of their work. Their priorities suggest connection to economic theorist Amartya Sen, who challenges commonplace linkages between income and happiness. Sen, winner of the Nobel Prize in Economics (1998) argues in *Development as Freedom* that people seek capabilities, not just to earn more money or have access to more privileges, but so that they can be involved in the decision-making that impacts their lives. Among respect-motivated faculty, there is broad understanding that participation is the key. As Bob put it, "a seat at the table" is the only way to be counted, to have one's ideas counted. For these faculty members, then, respect often translates into calls for participation in all areas of faculty life but particularly in faculty governance where the terms of work are negotiated.

SUMMARY OF FINDINGS

This study suggests that we need not endorse the idea that the tenure-track is the sole mechanism to professional fulfillment and success in the academic setting. Instead, it may be that the working conditions and control that academics of any rank have over their labor and the valuing of that labor are factors as important as the type of appointment they hold. This finding is not meant to challenge the wisdom of converting non-tenure-track faculty to the tenure-track, nor to suggest that the variety of "exemplary policies" for full-time non-tenure-track faculty that have been identified through studies like that of Roger Baldwin and Jay Chronister should be ignored. Rather my findings suggest there that there is much departments can do to create an inclusive environment where today's contingent faculty can achieve the potential for a promising future.

Further, the findings of this study bring issues of contingency from the macro to the micro level, suggesting that contingent faculty seek opportunity and respect more than they seek specific enhancements to, for instance, salary and benefits. More important than income, Sen argues, is freedom; more essential than wealth is an enhancement of capability and opportunity or what Sen calls "social opportunity," which are those societal arrangements (for education, health care, etc.) that make it possible for an individual to live better and participate more fully in the life of the community (39). In university settings, the overarching appeal of tenure can be understood as the composite effect of all those capabilities and opportunities associated with the tenure track—freedom to speak and research freely (academic freedom), freedom to manage one's daily working life, freedom to participate in decision-making, freedom to develop curriculum alongside colleagues, freedom to choose one's leaders, freedom to be respected for one's scholarship, freedom to expect investment in one's continued success and professional development. While tenure provides the clearest path toward controlling the features of a satisfying academic work life, it may not be the only path if we open the doors of participation more fully to those off the tenure-track.

It may also be useful to consider Sen's description of "unfreedoms," such as economic insecurity, famine, and lack of civil liberties, which he sees as obstacles to happiness. Sen argues that those who participate in the determination of the type of society they live in are better able to control "unfreedoms" and, as a result, enjoy a higher quality of life than those who do not have such control (24). Sen's point suggests that increasing the opportunities for non-tenure-track faculty participation in the construction of their workplace conditions will enhance their sense of success, which in turn may translate back into enhanced personal investment and professionalism. This is quite pointedly an argument for wider contingent faculty participation in governance and other features of academic responsibility. This theoretical notion seems to be confirmed by Adrianna Kezar and Cecile Sam's 2010 study, which found that contingent faculty inclusion in governance paves the way for them to "shape their working conditions" and help create a culture that "values and expects their inclusion" (90). In other words, when contingent faculty are included in curriculum development, governance, and other core activities, working conditions improve as do levels of satisfaction. The professional futures of our departments depends upon our ability to reconcile ourselves to more inclusive policies, especially given decreases in tenure-track lines.

Implications

The insights offered here into the motivations of faculty whose professional lives occur off the tenure track have implications for the future of the profession and the careers of our graduate students, suggesting that at-will faculty are far from being passive participants in bad jobs undertaken in inhospitable environments. Most are persons with agency who vigorously seek to understand their circumstances, contribute to their campuses, and make informed decisions about the future. Collectively, they seek alternatives for themselves, inscribe upon their institutions the integrity of their work, and generally seek fuller participation in the life of their academic units. Further, while the contingent faculty in my study may seem to lend themselves to generalizations about "traps" and "potholes" in the academic career path, they actually are not so easily categorized. While contingent faculty careers do not conform to traditional trajectories of success, their nontraditional paths have become the norm.

Additionally, the study itself seems to have had an impact on non-tenure-track faculty capability, suggesting that contingent faculty often support each other while also responding well to support from institutional entities. Participants in this study reported that the cross-disciplinary discussion groups helped them develop new awareness of conditions across the campus and approaches they might take for their own benefit. Bob's work in developing a college survey, a college retreat, a contingent faculty handbook, and faculty manual clarifications, for instance, had a galvanizing effect upon contingent faculty from other parts of campus. Bob's success suggested that contingent faculty as a whole may have more agency than they realize and might construct many of the conditions of their professional lives. In turn, Bob learned from Prudence that tuition dollars in core courses in the humanities actually subsidize research in science colleges like his, not the other way around. As a result, Bob and others in the sciences developed an increased appreciation for the role of those teaching the core curriculum. They understood in new ways that there are more institutional obstacles to progress and success for some contingent faculty than for others. In general, the cross-pollination that occurred in these discussions resulted in some contingent faculty becoming activists, in others more actively seeking professional support and mentoring from their departments, and still others seeing a rationale for involvement in governance.

However, this study also suggests that it is not just a matter of contingent labor taking up arms but of those inside the system helping contingent faculty gain agency. Instead of speculating about why contingent faculty choose such a bleak line of work, implying that unlike them, those on the tenure track rise through a kind of providential natural selection, tenure-line faculty and administrators could more purposefully integrate contingent faculty, advocate on their behalf, and acknowledge that academic careers are constructed. Such construction is precisely what I had the good fortune of experiencing rather late in my professional life. This collaborative effort consisted of a series of steps that made it possible for me to make the move from the contingent ranks to the tenure track after over twenty years in the trenches. Specifically, I was assisted in my first national search by tenure-line faculty who partnered with me on scholarship; invited me to undertake increasingly complex service and administrative functions; opened the doors to participation in faculty governance by inviting me to participate in varied forms of curriculum and program development; talked with me at some length about those governance experiences to awaken me to the policy implications of committee work; recommended me for increasing levels of responsibility and visibility in my own department; and assisted me with the reading of job applications and the writing of cover letters and CVs. In general, the approach they took communicated belief in me, building a sense of both opportunity and respect for my work but it also educated me about processes that had become out of reach and were in fact alien to me until I was fully integrated.

A Specific Role for Rhetoric and Composition

Particularly within composition, we might re-envision the roles of adjunct faculty by acknowledging and even embracing the job specializations we have had a hand in creating. We can develop clarity about the different roles that have evolved for contingent and tenure-line faculty in our discipline and elsewhere throughout the university. Then, rather than see these roles as fixed and unwavering, we might see them as changing genres of work, emergent and constructed, not static.

Our clarity on this matter could go some distance toward shaping the positions we take not only within our own departments but with our fellow university citizens who also employ contingent faculty. We might convey to others that we believe in what our contingent faculty do as they teach our small classes and pay close attention to student work, especially in the context of the large, public university. To make a strong teaching ethos possible, we might proudly assert that we entrust our classrooms to highly qualified non-tenure-track faculty in the belief that they are capable classroom practitioners. Our ability to convey such belief in the quality and importance of this instruction could situate us rather more fully at the center of larger institutional discussions on the relationship between faculty-student connections, the retention of undergraduates, and the relationship of these important goals to a highly professionalized teaching faculty. We could see our role as one of informing other faculty across our campuses about the value of this work in the context of tenure-line workload distributions that marginalize the teaching mission. Such clarifications would counter inflammatory positions like those forwarded by Kevin Eagen and Audrey Jaeger, who claim that adjunct faculty undermine student retention due to inaccessibility. Characterized by Eagen and Jaeger as faculty who are too often unavailable to students, contingent faculty are singled out as perpetrators of behaviors for which tenured faculty have long been faulted (182). As John Curtis and Monica Jacobe point out, such critiques would be better directed at institutional failures or "lack of support structures" (6) that would make it possible for contingent faculty to avoid becoming freeway flyers.

It may be that no group is better able to offer this kind of framing than are we in rhetoric and composition. For instance, as I have interviewed and observed contingent faculty, I have become increasingly convinced of the relevance of community literacy theory to this discussion, especially as that work addresses deliberation among local publics. Like community literacy efforts, which require a consideration of "the situatedness and materiality of literate practices" (Higgins, Long, and Flower 11), so, too, work on contingent faculty issues involves an acknowledgment of material differences in opportunity while also suggesting diverse stakeholders who "rarely share common perspectives on problems, much less a sense of what constitutes the common good" (11). Why would we do this? Because somewhere between "cheap labor" and the expensive and increasingly rare tenure line is a good non-tenure-track faculty position that reproduces most of the benefits of life on the tenure-track, and because doing so raises the professional profile of those off the tenure track.

This argument suggests that faculty success can be understood to involve individual opportunity through which a person "grows in the job"—to use Prudence's words—as a scholar, developing institutional agency and becoming part of disciplinary, programmatic, and university processes. For contingent faculty, then, becoming involved in university governance affects the contingent's knowledge of place and comprehension of opportunity. Further, participation in governance makes discussion and debate possible as it provides structures for defending or challenging the benefits to which faculty have traditionally been entitled and the responsibilities they hold. Participation in faculty shared governance, moreover, is the central mechanism by which individuals not only bear the burden of programmatic decision-making but also become functional contributors in the conduct of their disciplines and the functioning of their colleges and universities. Further, as contingent faculty gain governance experience, they make themselves more useful to their institutions and more marketable for secure positions.

Assisting the contingent faculty cause is a project that rhetoric and composition scholars are especially well suited to undertake. If Sen is right and people measure success more in degrees of freedom than in the particular outcomes of that freedom, then composition has an opportunity to inscribe upon our campuses new definitions of success. Rhetoric and composition might become the argumentative center of efforts to enfranchise the contingent ranks in governance circles, paving the way for their new opportunities. Our success in this endeavor might be measured in terms of expansions to contingent faculty capabilities and opportunities through efforts such as these:

Support for Governance Participation

- creation of non-tenure-track standing committees at every level of faculty governance, more-than-token non-tenure-track representation on all existing faculty committees
- voting rights for contingent faculty on all committees, especially those related to curriculum
- assured presence on search committees and task forces at all levels of the university
- workload distributions and evaluation processes that reward contingent faculty service

Mentorship by Tenure-line Faculty

- inclusion in programmatic design and revision
- professional development in job search processes, including analysis of job advertisements, construction of the cv, feedback on cover letters, and mock interviews
- co-authorship of articles and collaboration on research

Structures for Contingent Faculty Self-Advocacy

- support the building of non-tenure-track capability by creating contingent committees and charging them with the accomplishment of specific goals

- provide social opportunities so that non-tenure-track faculty can meet one another and collaborate on curricular and governance projects
- provide mechanisms for the report of non-tenure-track committee work
- seek the advice of non-tenure-track committees for department, college, and university policies
- provide material support for the creation of handbooks and the organizing of professional development retreats
- co-author a bill of rights that articulates fundamental goals for the development of non-tenure track faculty capability, opportunity, and expectations for workplace respect

As this list suggests, a variety of policies and approaches can improve the working conditions of contingent faculty, helping to construct well-supported non-tenure-track faculty positions that are situated in productive faculty spaces. Whether motivated by opportunity, respect, or both, these faculty members serve in essential roles that should be compensated more fully through the building of faculty capacity. Rhetoric and composition, which has heavily depended upon those off the tenure track to support its many curricular innovations, should lead the way in this effort.

Works Cited

Baldwin, Roger G., and Jay L. Chronister. *Teaching without Tenure: Policies and Practices for a New Era.* Baltimore: Johns Hopkins UP, 2001. Print.

Cloud, Dana L. *Control and Consolation in American Culture and Politics: Rhetorics of Therapy.* Thousand Oaks, CA: Sage Publications, 1998. Print.

Curtis, John, and Monica Jacobe. "Consequences of an Increasing Contingent Faculty." AAUP Contingent Faculty Index. *American Association of University Professors.* 2006. 5–16.Web. 23 June 2012.

Eagan, Kevin M., and Audrey Jaeger. "Effects of Exposure to Part-time Faculty in Community College Transfer." *Research in Higher Education* 50.2 (2009): 168–88.Print.

Enos, Theresa. *Gender Roles and Faculty Lives in Rhetoric and Composition.* Carbondale, IL: Southern Illinois UP, 1996. Print.

Higgins, Lorraine, Elenore Long, and Linda Flower. "Community Literacy: A Rhetorical Model for Personal and Public Inquiry." *Community Literacy Journal* 1 (Fall 2006): 9–34. Print.

Kezar, Adrianna J., and Sam, Cecile. "Beyond Contracts: Non–Tenure Track Faculty and Campus Governance." *NEA 2010 Almanac of Higher Education*. 2010. 83-91. Web. 23 June 2012.

Schell, Eileen E. *Gypsy Academics and Mother-Teachers: Gender, Contingent Labor, and Writing Instruction.* Portsmouth, NH: Boynton/Cook, 1998. Print.

Sen, Amartya. *Development as Freedom.* New York: Knopf, 2000. Print.

"Tenure and Teaching-Intensive Appointments (2010)." Report of the Committee on Contingent Faculty and the Profession. American Association of University Professors, 2010. Web. 23 June 2012.

Welsh-Huggins, Andrew. "Leader of Nation's Biggest Campus Wants to Change Rules That Govern Granting of Tenure." Cleveland.com. 4 February, 2010. Web. 23 June 2012.

"What Are the Priorities? The Annual Report on the Economic Status of the Profession, 2007–2008." *Academe* 94.2 (2008): 9–18. Print.

5 Disclaimer: "Professional Academic on a Closed Course: Do Not Attempt this at Home."

Heather Graves

Most of us who work at the college and university levels do so for our own reasons. In my case, I could have taught high school in Southwestern Ontario and made more money sooner in my career, but what I most enjoy about working at the post-secondary level—and what is not available at the high school level—is the opportunity to conduct research to create new knowledge in the field. Conducting research is an integral part of many (but not all) post-secondary university and college positions. The amount of research required varies, of course, with the institutional mission and the nature and kind of programs being offered. There were two things that I didn't understand when I secured my first position at a university: the first was the extent to which the nature of the place where I worked would frame a context for my career; the second was how difficult it could be to craft the kind of career I sought: one where research would play a central role.

The profession, as an individual experiences it, depends almost entirely on what is valued at the institution where the individual is employed, the type of position held, the nature of the work that consumes the day-to-day activities, and the culture in which that individual pursues that profession. During the past five-year period I have moved out of a tenure-track job at a teaching university, spent three years writing intensively at home as an independent scholar, and then moved back into a tenured position at a large research university, a transition that I understood to be impossible. Based on my experience, while teaching can be an important site of research, teaching itself can also keep one from being a researcher. At the same time, creating new knowledge and sharing the insights from our research and experience is integral to the field. Without this work, people in the field cannot grow intellectually. For those of us teaching in graduate programs, creating new knowledge is even more crucial: how can we adequately supervise/assist the work of newcomers to the profession if we don't do much research ourselves? If we don't publish, how can we help our students learn to negotiate the perils of reviewers and editors? Through my narrative, I question the status research has within our profession and how we may, unwittingly, be undercutting our own efforts to produce knowledge about writing by not balancing it with our commitment to teaching as the center of our profession.

The amount of teaching that we, as rhetoric and composition instructors and scholars, generally shoulder as an accepted part of our academic appointments often overwhelms our ability to complete much research. For example, at previous institutions I taught six classes per year on the semester system and seven classes per year on the quarter system. Half of these were writing classes; the other half were graduate courses. At these institutions faculty were to spend forty percent of their time on research, forty percent on teaching, and twenty percent on service (This is fairly standard, I believe, at institutions with graduate programs).

Many members of our profession, both tenure track and non-tenure track, work at institutions with higher teaching loads than I have experienced. Rhetoricians and compositionists who accept the administrative duties of directing a writing program or center also find there are precious few hours in the term to progress with research projects. Yet without some kind of research output (i.e., publications) many of us cannot earn promotion in the profession (or even remain in it). The choices are to relegate research to a few weeks in the summer (resulting in a slender output) or stay up a few hours later at night or rise a few hours earlier in the morning to do this work, an option that is physically very difficult to sustain over the long haul. I know.

In 2005 after twelve years of sixty plus hour work weeks (during which I published several articles and one academic book), I burned myself out and quit as a tenured associate professor at a private teaching/research university in the Midwest. Over the five years since, I have inadvertently transformed myself from a purveyor of other people's knowledge at a tier-two university in the U.S. to an initiator and facilitator of knowledge creation across Canada and around the world.

The way I did this was to quit a teaching-heavy job to write for three years. It cost me $200,000 in salary alone to gain a publishing profile that enabled me to move to a position at a research-based university that has a lighter teaching load (four courses per year instead of seven) and presumably more support for research. I am not recommending this as a course of action; most people are not in the position to give up such salary. Instead, what I seek to share is how this experience helped me re-examine the priorities of teaching-heavy positions in a way that was difficult if not impossible when I was in one myself. Based on my experience, I would argue that people don't have to be defined by the institution that offers them their first professional position, nor do they have to become mired in an institution that doesn't suit their individual strengths when they hit mid-career. It takes hard work and planning, but a person can take control of his or her work life and shake it up. Of course, we can't always foresee or control the way our lives will change, but my experience has demonstrated that change always has positive aspects to it that make it worth the original effort. I should also acknowledge that sometimes it can take a while before the positive aspects make themselves known; sometimes, a person has to craft those positive aspects him- or herself.

Purveyor of Knowledge, Not Creator

When I accepted a position at a teaching university with masters and doctoral programs in English and rhetoric and composition in the Midwest in 1993, I expected to continue the research agenda that I had begun in graduate school. In fact, I did continue it, while also teaching six classes per year in a semester system that ran from mid-August to mid-May and serving on the committees of (or directing) numerous graduate students (thirteen in four years), but only by working fifty or sixty hours per week. Even so, my publication output was meager. In six years I had two articles published based on my dissertation research, plus a couple that I worked on during graduate school, and two others that evolved out of my teaching. During this time I also switched institutions, a move that required developing a whole new set of courses in technical and business/professional communication and teaching seven courses per year in the quarter system. When I met with the then-chair of my department in 1999 to discuss my prospects for tenure, she suggested that if I could get a contract for an academic book, my case for tenure would be quite strong (I know now that I would have gotten tenure at that institution with my existing publication record at the time [four or five articles]: others had been tenured with less). However, I took the chair's advice to heart and considered my options for producing a book. In six years, I had taught forty-three classes and received two course releases from the standard load: one at the first institution to help me further my research agenda as a junior faculty member, and one at the second institution to help me develop my courses for their programs. I had used this time and the summer months to draft the three or four articles that had been published. But nowhere had I had time to develop a new research project that might provide a foundation for a book, so I returned to my dissertation data to see what ideas lay there untapped.

In 1999 I envied my younger self who had had four months available to conduct the ethnographic study that yielded my dissertation data. It was these notes and transcriptions that I used in 2000 to develop a book proposal and then as the basis for *Rhetoric in(to) Science*. The challenge of that book was developing and applying a more sophisticated conceptual framework to the data than I had used in the dissertation. I had to develop the book proposal by working evenings and weekends and the next summer because regular work hours were consumed by class preparation and grading. I earned tenure, and the book proposal was accepted by Hampton Press. The issue then was how to find the time to write the book. It was one thing to write journal articles and the book proposal in small pieces of time scattered across weeks and months, but writing a theoretical discussion of the epistemological and ontological roles of rhetoric in scientific discourse was not going to be possible without sustained and coherent time to think. I applied for two quarters of leave starting in January, 2001, with the goal of starting to write when the grading was finished in December.

I was granted the leave (at three-quarter pay) plus the summer to generate a three-hundred-page book manuscript. This manuscript was a complete rethinking of the data; even the chapter on analogy was rethought and rewritten completely from the two articles that were published earlier on this topic. After receiving extensive reviewer comments on how to improve the manuscript, I rewrote it again, but this time in two months in summer 2002. After minor revisions in the summer of 2003, I finished it. The book, *Rhetoric in(to) Science: Style as Invention in Inquiry,* appeared in print in 2005.

Coincidentally, 2005 was the year that I also quit my job as a tenured associate professor of English. During those twelve years, I had worked between fifty and sixty hours a week all year round and shared the raising of our two children, the youngest in the last year of high school and the other a university undergraduate when I walked away from institutional employment. I quit for two reasons: I was exhausted, and I was spending too little time each week doing things I loved. The main reason that I had become a university professor was to do research, and after the book came out, I felt like that was the end of what I had to say. It was not clear how I might manage a new study with so much time consumed by teaching. The problem of how to find time to analyze and interpret new data was discouraging. I could (and did) do some fairly simple research that grew out of classes I was teaching. Another alternative might have been to change my area of research from rhetoric of science to something better suited to the minimal time I had to spend on it.

Prior to 2005, my experience in the profession was confined mainly to purveying others' knowledge. My days were so consumed by course preparation and paper grading that I never cleared headspace to think beyond, "What do I *have* to do today?" It was time to make a change when I received my teaching schedule for the following year: seven courses taught on *three* different campuses and at least three of them taught at night. For me, the travel between campuses, coupled with the grading and preparation, meant that I would get virtually no research done during the teaching year, and it was the research that kept me going, year to year. I asked myself, "What would be a better schedule?" It struck me then that there wasn't one. No configuration of classes, days, times, terms, or subjects could make this worth doing. At that point it was clear that I had to make a change. My response had nothing to do with the course assignments and everything to do with the fact that I was burnt out. A sabbatical was out of the question: I only had one quarter of leave left to me after taking two quarters three years earlier to write *Rhetoric in(to) Science.* One quarter of leave might allow me to sketch out a plan and begin reading, but it would not allow me to launch a research project that involved the kind of intense research and writing that produced the book.

Actually, I didn't need a temporary break so much as I decided I didn't want to spend my life like this anymore. Viewed dispassionately, I had achieved as much as an academic as I could given the employment circumstances. It had taken ten years of hard slogging to write that academic book. My course evaluations regularly exceeded the department mean. I had given three-dozen presentations at numerous national conferences. While I would leave the knowledge-making aspects of academic life with regret, I felt satisfied: I had met or exceeded the professional goals I set for myself when I graduated with a PhD in 1992.

I considered my options. What was my dream job? That's easy: writing. In fact, that's why I entered the profession in the first place. I wanted to create knowledge, and it seemed clear that there were several ways to do this. Conducting research and writing about it, as I had in *Rhetoric in(to) Science,* was one fulfilling option; in addition, teaching over eighty courses over twelve years, I had gained a vast knowledge of a broad range of writing curriculum that could be shared to help others become better writers and teachers of writing. I didn't know it at the time, but I had decided to mobilize the teaching knowledge that I had developed.

In Canada, the latest buzzword from humanities funding agencies is "knowledge mobilization," that is, taking the knowledge gained from research and experience and translating it into products that transfer outside the academy. Researchers in medicine, engineering, the sciences, and social sciences have been disseminating their research products for years, but for humanities people this is a relatively new concept: how do we make our knowledge accessible to the general public? Scholars in composition and rhetoric (writing studies in Canada) are uniquely situated to do this because writing is essential for success in contemporary society. An obvious way to mobilize our knowledge in rhetoric and composition is to translate our experience in teaching writing into teaching materials that will benefit others, both instructors and students.

The course preparation and grading had turned into a grind. I didn't want to continue and was having increasing difficulty continuing the fifty to sixty hour workweeks. It seemed like a good time to change careers. Two factors made quitting possible. The first one was that my partner and I had figured out a way to manage on only one income. We relocated to a city that was much cheaper than the large city we were living in. My partner got a job at a research university in southwestern Ontario that would allow us to pay our bills. The second factor was that we had signed two contracts for books: one, a technical communication textbook for Broadview Press, and the second, an edited collection of essays on teaching writing in Canada. Between the two of us, we didn't have the time to write either book if we were both teaching full-time. Our plan was that once we moved, I could write the bulk of the textbook and oversee the editing of the collection, while we looked for other book-related opportunities. Perhaps I could become a full-time writer, and if our books were successful, maybe I could supplement his salary (and at least partially replace my professor's salary) with income from the books. In June 2005, I finished grading my last paper, submitted final grades by mid-month, climbed into bed and slept for days, and then climbed out again sometime towards the end of July. Although I was still physically exhausted, it didn't take much effort to sit in front of my computer. It turned out I wasn't intellectually exhausted at all, so I started writing.

Yes to the Writing Life

It only took a few weeks to edit and format the academic book before sending it off to the publisher. The technical communication book took longer. After eight years of teaching many sections of technical communication, the chapters rolled off my fingers. The technical communication book was developed from a variety of source materials adapted to the needs of the students who showed up in my previous classes. My partner and I traded the course back and forth from year to year, both of us improving it each time we taught it. It started in 1994 with a course packet of thirty pages of lecture notes, and six or seven years later had burgeoned to 150 pages. Since existing textbooks all took the same largely theoretical approach to the practice of technical communication, we had developed our own, heavy on applied strategies and practical advice. We wanted to turn our extensive course packet, lecture materials, classroom exercises, and assignments into a book that took a rhetorical and applied approach to technical communication. Finally, after leaving the profession, I had the time, energy, and headspace to transform the lesson plans, handouts, and assorted PowerPoint presentations into intellectual capital that someone else could use. Ironically, this writing was an act of scholarship that could not be accomplished while actually teaching the material I was writing about. Many of the pedagogical techniques we had developed for teaching technical communication were innovative and a lot of fun for students, I realized as I worked on my chapters of *A Strategic Guide to Technical Communication*. In fact, most of my students had, against their own expectations, thoroughly enjoyed taking technical writing. Although those students who sit in the room can benefit from good instruction if they so choose, an individual instructor's reach is quite modest even over several decades. Writing a textbook to present these new ideas allows the opportunity to reach a larger number of students in addition to actually changing the pedagogy of other instructors and perhaps eventually the whole field. This is one reason why I like creating textbooks—to help instructors who are not specialists in the area (and many of the instructors who teach technical communication are not specialists when they start) create a strong course that will benefit their students.

When my partner and I were three-quarters of the way through the technical communication manuscript, we took on a new project: a Canadian edition of Lester Faigley's enormously successful *The Brief Penguin Handbook*. The combination of text and visuals made this handbook more appealing and eye-catching than traditional handbooks. Pearson also gave us significant scope in adapting it. This meant that we could add or expand or excise sections according to their usefulness and applicability to Canadian students and academics. For example, we expanded the chapter on "Writing About Literature" and added a new chapter on "Writing about Film and New Media." Adapting someone else's book is a completely different exercise from writing your own from scratch. In an adaptation, you focus on the enjoyable task of improving on the original as appropriate and inserting equivalent examples better suited to the culture and values of the new group of readers. Of course, you don't make nearly as much money from an adaptation either.

While living and working in the U.S., it never occurred to me that I was amassing a wealth of knowledge about the subtle differences between the two cultures. Some differences, of course, are obvious, but others arise out of cultural values and expectations. I didn't realize that this dual vision would enable me to distinguish fine differences during the process of revising this book. For example, Canada is a country of two official languages (English and French). In addition, some cities include street signs in languages other than English or French—for example, downtown Toronto has street names in Mandarin and English. A chapter that begins by discussing the "English Only" movement requires significant revision, if not rethinking, when placed against a Canadian assumption of multilingualism.

This book, the Canadian edition of *The Brief Penguin Handbook*, has been enormously successful. It has been the bestselling handbook in Canada ever, and we are currently negotiating a third edition with Pearson. *The Strategic Guide to Technical Communication* has also been successful: this past year we wrote a second edition, which is now in production with Broadview. During the past six years we have also created the Canadian edition of *The Little Penguin Handbook*, which has run to a second edition. We are also in the process of negotiating a contract on a fourth textbook on business and professional communication. From the perspective of creating successful writing-related textbooks in Canada, my decision to step out of the profession to write full-time worked; from the perspective of generating income, it was less successful. Mobilizing academic knowledge in the form of publishing textbooks takes an enormous investment of time both in the lead up that enables someone to have the knowledge and experience to write the books (in my case, twelve plus years of teaching and research) and in converting that knowledge and experience to significant income (after the first year, about three percent of my professor's salary; after three years about twenty percent of my professor's salary). In fact, the timeline for converting the manuscripts to income was so extended that full-time writing was not ultimately sustainable.

Something More?

Although I was busier than ever working on fascinating and important projects, there were some serious drawbacks to life as an independent scholar and researcher. Lack of income was a major one, but I also found that I missed the research aspects of being an academic. Opportunities came along for me to work on grant-funded academic research projects because of my expertise in rhetoric and writing, but I could only play a peripheral role without an institutional affiliation. This affiliation was addressed fairly easily by establishing an adjunct research position at the nearby university (without pay or building space), but it was hard to justify spending more than the minimum time on research projects that would not generate income when we were in straitened financial circumstances. I could oversee travel reimbursement for conferences that I organized, but I could not submit my own receipts for reimbursement. At the same time I was learning so much that would contribute to the learning of others if I could more immediately share it. For example, I was invited to participate in a $150,000 Social Sciences and Humanities Research Council (SSHRC) collaborative grant proposal to study doctoral writing education in Canada, and we began collecting information about nation-wide writing resources for graduate students. But I didn't have a forum for using this information or developing new resources without being more directly affiliated with an institution of higher learning. I now (ironically) had the time to do research but not the resources. I started to see ways that I could contribute to the profession in Canada that had not been available to me at earlier points in my career. When I quit my university job, I believed that I was stepping out of academia altogether. However, after three years we had a co-edited collection of essays, three completed (and successful) textbooks, and a half-finished manuscript on business and professional communication. I had also written by invitation a chapter for an academic book and was a collaborator on two funded grant proposals. Although it was not my purpose, all of the writing and other work-related activities that I did while on this alternate career path also served to change my academic CV in fundamental ways. It made me a viable candidate for a position at a research university.

In late 2007 we saw an advertisement for a director of writing across the curriculum at a large research university in western Canada. When my partner inquired about the position and whether the institution might be interested in hiring an academic couple in rhetoric and writing studies, the chair of the search committee responded in the affirmative. It turned out that they had searched unsuccessfully for someone to fill the director position the previous year, and the chair was already familiar with some of my research on gender and writing. In addition, the faculty of science was interested in my work in the rhetoric of science. The university hired my partner to direct the WAC program, and they created a position for me. Had I not been so productive during my three years as a full-time writer, I doubt the administration would have been interested in recruiting me. At any rate, my new academic position was to teach two courses per year and the equivalent of two more courses in workshops on writing to graduate students in science and consultation with faculty in science to improve undergraduate writing instruction (in Canada, a standard load at a research university is 2/2). I took this position because of the reduced classroom time and the greater flexibility it offered outside of the classroom for getting more research done. With less time required for course preparation and grading, I expected I would be able to continue writing the textbooks while also pursuing more challenging research projects.

Although I signed a five-year contract to teach a 1/1 load plus alternative teaching a year, the then-dean changed it to the standard load (2/2) within eight months of my arrival. While I was not happy about this change, there seemed to be little I could do about it. While four courses per year is a significant reduction from the six and seven courses a year I was teaching at previous institutions, it's still time and energy consuming, especially when they are four writing classes. The quantity of grading constrains the kind and amount of research that can be done. However, instead of having one day every two or three weeks to work on some research during the term, in my current position I have at least one day per week (most weeks) to work on analyzing data or reading the literature around the subject matter, and to draft a page or two on an article presenting the results. It's still difficult to undertake time-intensive research such as the ethnographic-type study of a physics laboratory that I conducted as a graduate student. Interdisciplinary research that requires a reasonable level of knowledge of a specialized area is also difficult when teaching a standard load. It takes a significant investment of time to learn the second (or third) area during which time research productivity tends to stall.

After three years at a tier one-research institution, I have found that the opportunities and support for faculty who want to do research are far greater at this kind of institution than at second tier ones that focus on undergraduate teaching but maintain some graduate programs as well. For example, graduate research assistants (GRAs) are plentiful at my current institution; that is, I can apply for one to work twelve hours per term for me during the fall or winter terms, and I can employ a second one for six to twelve hours for two months during the summer. I have also been successful applying for grant funding, both within the institution and government-funded, that enables me to employ additional graduate students to work on my research projects. At the same time, the application process is time-consuming; reviewers are not always members of the discipline of rhetoric and writing studies; and the process is fiercely competitive. With a GRA, some of the work of data collection and analysis can proceed without me during the teaching semester. At this institution, I have the novel experience of some of my research getting done without me having to do every step. Previously, I would have had to work every evening and most weekends to get this work done (At the same time, I should point out that the GRAs don't train and direct themselves. In some cases, it takes more time to help them learn what to do than it would to do it myself). However, this work does contribute to the production of what the government calls "highly qualified personnel." These possibilities exist to me as a faculty member at a research institution that were not available to me at the teaching institutions with graduate programs.

While there is abundant help, there is not abundant time. Support for teaching release for faculty is not readily available. Data collection and analysis can proceed during the term while I am grading papers, but the process of converting the data and analysis into a manuscript depends on me, so it goes slower. While reaching the point of writing is a lot of work, the actual writing process is equally time and energy consuming. Nonetheless, this extensive support apparatus means that I have opportunities that I did not have in the past to help me become more productive as a scholar. This support also means that I can tackle more projects—and ask more complex and important research questions—than I have been able to since I finished my graduate work in 1992.

Role of Research in Composition:
Institutional and Professional Contexts

The only way that I achieved the somewhat meager productivity (read "publications") that I did manage between 1992 and 2005 was at the expense of any pretense of work-life balance, that is, by working far in excess of the hours for which I was being paid. Even with this prodigious effort, I could not have jumped from the second-tier teaching institutions to a tier-1 research institution because my output was, as one grant reviewer has described it, "limited." It's not that I was incapable of doing more extensive and significant scholarship (as the reviewer seemed to imply), but that the resources of time and energy were exhausted primarily through doing the main work of teaching many classes and interacting with many students. And, in fact, the teaching loads of six and seven classes per year that I was assigned were regarded as reasonable—generous even—because they were less than the nine or more classes that constitute the standard load at many teaching universities and two-year colleges. And it does not compare to the workloads of those instructors without secure employment who teach "part-time" while also traveling between campuses and institutions to generate income to feed themselves and their families. These individuals work in excess of full-time hours for part-time pay while hoping, in many cases, to secure a full-time position somewhere. To secure a full-time position, many instructors also have to work research into their evenings, weekends, and holidays.

All of this is not news, of course. But it does seem that many people in the academy, including rhetoric and composition, regularly work hours in excess of what they are paid. Many of us work these hours because we love what we do, but others work like this because they are afraid—afraid they won't be offered courses next term or they won't get tenure. Whatever the goal, reaching it doesn't alter this dynamic. Once tenured, more publications are required to gain pay raises or be promoted. The expectations for performance remain high so that the only way for many people to meet them is through working in excess of 40 hours a week.

At the same time, faculty and instructors are not victims. We choose to participate in the system, and we choose this line of work among many other choices. We can also create other options for ourselves if we want to, although this takes time and the outcome is always uncertain. But the outcome of any venture, including work in higher education, is always uncertain. The question becomes whether it is worth it to work these hours to achieve those goals. For some people, who do achieve their goals, it probably is worth it (providing they have managed to retain their sanity, their health, and the people they love). But what of those who don't? When I left my job in 2005, I had achieved many of my goals, but I was putting in long hours and wasn't getting far in the areas that mattered to me. I couldn't keep working those hours so I was going to have to cut somewhere. The teaching couldn't be cut so it was going to have to be the research, at which point it was no longer worth it. And now? Without meaning to, I reached what I thought was an unattainable goal (a position where I can do more research and less teaching), and I no longer work fifty or sixty hours per week.

It worked for me to walk away for three years, but it won't work for everyone. And I'm not suggesting that it will or that it should. What

I am suggesting is that all of us should take a step back from time to time to consider whether our current situation is working for us. And I'm not just talking about whether a given situation is working for us personally; we should also consider whether it is working for us as a profession. Many institutions say they value teaching performance while they then award pay raises based on research and publication performance. Other institutions devalue research, which puts academics who want to pursue scholarship in a bind because they have heavy teaching loads and little support or encouragement for research. In these cases, an instructor must work extra hard to get small amounts of research done, and he or she may find it difficult to change institutions because of a meager publication record, won at great cost. Still other institutions require a respectable scholarly output while also requiring significant teaching. In these cases, instructors are forced to choose between earning tenure (i.e., achieving excellent teaching evaluations as well as publishing some articles) and having a life. I think scholars in composition occupy a worse position in the teaching/research dichotomy because the field privileges teaching to the point where many members pour hours into their teaching to ensure that students have a valuable learning experience, leaving themselves with reduced time to meet their research commitments. Some members of composition who value research can also find themselves marginalized in a field where an underlying assumption is that the needs of the student are paramount.

Although I have framed the exigence for excessive workloads as coming from "institutions," that sets up an "us-them" opposition that is inaccurate. Institutions are constituted by the individuals who work there, just as professions are constituted by the individuals who join them. Is this the kind of working environment that we all want to perpetuate? We might consider whether we should continue to encourage and welcome newcomers (those graduate students and newly-minted PhDs) to our profession, knowing that many of them can only be successful if they work far in excess of the hours for which they will be paid. This is a conversation that we should be having within institutions and within our profession; we should be looking for a way to balance teaching and research in a way that still leaves a few hours left over in the week to have a life and that accurately reflects our goal of valuing both research and teaching.

6 Coming to Terms: Authority in Action and Advocacy

Moira K. Amado-McCoy

For more than two years, out of both choice and necessity, I have been asking myself a set of questions I believe are central to the purposes of this volume. First, I have struggled with the question of "success in rhetoric and composition," both within my professional life and in regards to my own professional identity. If achieving tenure is the mark of success, how should our professional activities be measured? And as a fully credentialed professional, what will serve as markers for my own sense of success? I have also had to come to terms with an even more preliminary concern: within the sometimes still essentialist boundaries of an English department in North America, what is it that we rhetoricians do best? In the process of our own professionalization, this seems a rather overlooked question. But it is a question we have to face more directly outside the walls of the academy; we'll certainly have to be better at both asking and answering this question if we are to encourage students to venture out and persuasively "sell" their unique credentials to what can only be, at the moment, largely skeptical audiences.

For me, one of the best ways to approach the question of the usefulness of an art of rhetoric for the many professional worlds outside the academy is to begin to articulate the factors that link the teaching of language so closely, and unavoidably, to politics. My work as a community advocate is helping me understand more precisely why training in language studies is also training in politics, in public service, and ultimately, in advocacy. Our important theoretical work about language and power can (and probably should) be used to intervene directly in the political economy. Here at the turn of the 21st century, it seems worth reinvestigating why and how university-trained rhetoricians are well suited to serve as professional public advocates.

I won't rehearse the complex relationship between writing, identity politics, and pedagogy here. This is a conversation with which my readers are already familiar, and one that continues to hold in thrall the general public and those pundits hoping to anoint themselves arbiters/saviors of culture. For the most part, those of us who teach writing for a living would find any remaining claims that culture can be productively or ethically separated from politics an especially strange proposition. Identity issues bear directly upon the teaching of writing, reading, and research because they bear directly upon the acts of writing, reading, and research.

In this essay I suggest reasons—theoretical, historical, practical, and professional—we should be confident in encouraging students to pursue careers in the public and nonprofit sectors as professional advocates. In attempting to explain why I see this work in its most distilled form as "professional advocacy," in the second half of this essay, I use examples of the experience I've gained as the executive director for a nonprofit LGBTQ organization. The threads that seem to hold all of this together for me are two related facts. First, pedagogy has always been of utmost importance to rhetorical education. So much so, in fact, that study and teaching are parts of a single trajectory. Likewise, the majority of advocacy work, as I've experienced it, revolves around education. Second, rhetoric education trains scholars to be particularly sensitive to the complications of multiple audiences, and this is a rhetorical competency that nonprofit executive directors of all sorts must have in spades. About the first critical thread I will have fairly little to say. It is simply a fact that of all the research degrees (except, perhaps, Education itself), rhetoric and composition programs take the preparation of teachers most seriously. Bearing witness to this fact: the wide range of pedagogy theory courses, pro-seminars, teacher mentoring, classroom support, and assistant WPA positions filled by graduate students present in even the most humble English department. The teaching of writing is itself a research agenda in our field. It's not a radical claim to suggest that historically, methodologically, and theoretically, pedagogy defines our field. Unlike other academic fields, "rhetoric and composition" (sometimes pointedly articulated as "rhetoric and the teaching of writing") implies the teaching of composition, not merely the study of composition. The examples I provide here will suggest that acts of teaching are also central to the work of the executive director of an advocacy organization.

To the question of our expertise in identifying, analyzing, and "writing-to" multiple audiences, I devote a much greater portion of this essay. In each of the examples I provide, proficiency with multiple audiences is paramount. In fact, identifying expertise in this area as central or even constitutive of the work—the "what we do best"—of the professional rhetorician may be the real contribution of this essay. The idea that rhetoricians make good professional advocates is important, but the ability to analyze and write to multiple audiences is what ultimately makes a good advocate. The arguments I make about the value of "competency with multiple audiences" may expand classical notions of "audience awareness," and it may also help explain how community work both constitutes rhetorical knowledge and expands our understanding of rhetorical knowledge in ways that "teaching the conflicts," or "service learning," or "cultural critique," or even "community internships" cannot.

My current answer to the question about why the study of text is always political has become very simple: reading and writing are always political because reading and writing are always rhetorical. If I didn't know it before (by way of teaching technical writing, for example, or through service learning projects, or teaching literary theory as an examination of the development of English departments in North America defined by controversies "before and after 1968"), what I know for certain in transporting this knowledge into the public realm as an activist and advocate is that rhetoric is the study and application of language in action. Differentiating rhetoric from other types of textual analysis (by way of action and change, or more simply—politics) makes rhetoric a study of language and power, which makes it a study of ethics. To study ethics in/of language is to study the ways language both harms and heals, and there are no more pressing ethical issues at the turn of the 21st century than those dealing with identity and healing. To put it another way, there is simply no way (in a world where the word "text" itself has become a verb) to approach ethical issues without an eye to language, identity, and translation. This, as I see it, is not only a good definition of the work of rhetoric, it is also a very good definition of politics.

Terms of Employment

My first job, with a shiny new PhD in hand issued by one of the finest rhetoric and composition programs in the country, was one my peers and mentors considered a "good job." Although certainly not a prestige job, I was proud (and relieved) to have landed a "2/3" where I was appreciated for the scholarly and pedagogical work I loved. I was also encouraged to use my full professional toolbox to create courses and programming (being invited to teach a literary theory course, for instance, and add to the gender studies curriculum). In addition, because the department was relatively young, small, and quite "bottom-heavy," I would immediately be given a voice in departmental governance.[1] In my ideological commitment and my optimism (and, it must be admitted, my smart-graduate-student-with-a-new-job hubris), I didn't recognize problems lurking in the very material circumstances I initially judged as pure opportunity.

It wasn't long, however, before I began to wonder precisely how a rhetorician best fits into a traditional literature-based English department, why this department was radically bifurcated between literature and rhetoric, and how I was to safely define and develop my own work—including the advising of graduate students—in such circumstances. Unnervingly, I found myself in the peculiar position of holding the terminal degree in a field I suddenly wasn't quite sure how to describe, especially to colleagues who, perversely or not, claimed not to know "what rhetoric is exactly." Or, more accurately: I didn't seem to be very good at articulating why we did what we did in the face of criticism that found rhetoric and composition lesser work than the other specialties the department provided. This criticism went so far as characterizing the field as disposable (lobbying to cut all rhetoric and composition from the department) and discouraging students from taking courses associated with "rhetoric" or theory courses taught by one of the "compositionists." I also seemed to be under the gun to answer why a "comp/rhet person" seemed to know and care so much about race, gender, and sexuality. My questions-to-self became refined thusly: why did rhetoricians often come specially equipped with agendas dealing with identity and political subjugation? And why did I find it so easy and so compelling to wade into the murky waters of interdisciplinarity, when some colleagues seemed to feel that working across the disciplines made me a jack of all trades, master of none? I soon understood that these questions were questions of expertise:

questions of who gets to say what in which arenas and with what degree of authority.

Naturally, I was compelled by these questions partially because I was building my own sense of scholarly identity. But more importantly, I discovered powerful exigencies to provide strong articulations of the breadth of textual study. This was especially true because, as our faculty struggled to define ourselves as a department, we were being closely observed by our graduate students. I was sensitive to those who looked to us as models as they considered their own possible careers in the academy. We few rhetoricians were of particular interest to students as we seemed to offer an additional but largely undefined option, and yet we were clearly on the low end of the power and prestige spectrum in the departmental political schema (with which they seemed very familiar). Although they also seemed acquainted with the horrifying statistics representing the ratio between literature PhDs and available jobs, these students wondered out loud about what their education at the hands of a rhetorician might imply about themselves as scholars and, in turn, what that might suggest for them as professionals seeking employment.

The answers these curious and job-hungry students were receiving from English department faculty were, to be generous, mixed. These mixed messages, as I read them, seemed to hang again on questions of interdisciplinarity and expertise. For a rhetorician, the very nature of our profession requires broad and interdisciplinary approaches to language study, yet the traditional English department often has not incorporated the means by which to reward the breadth inherent in interdisciplinary and community-based study. Many traditional English departments are still organized to suspect civic work as representing a lack of rigor and to encourage the belief that depth and breadth of study have an inversely proportional relationship to one another. In our case, the department had been fairly liberal in using the language of interdisciplinary study in job descriptions and job advertisements and yet had not worked through the problems of providing structures for recognizing proficiency and expertise in such study. This mismatch of intent and capacity manifests the sorts of mixed messages that faced our students. As so many have pointed out, the arbitrary systems of dividing the work of reading and writing by genre, canonicity, and/or historical period presents real conundrums for rhetoricians working in departments that support this current-traditional model. I wonder if it might also afford real opportunity.

The nonsequiturs between the immediate needs of the young women and men who study with us and our own ideas about the value of what we do isn't always a result of intradepartmental conflict. Sometimes it is a result of the real gap between our assumptions that what we teach will have a positive effect on the way students face the "real world" and their own questions about how this could be so. It's certainly true that university faculty tend to take the value of a liberal arts education for granted (after all, we have jobs), while students increasingly ask us to make the case for them in practical terms. As a whole, I think we have often been negligent in articulating this value for our students. I believe, for instance, that useful answers can be provided in drawing out the underlying interdisciplinarity that makes our work possible but which we seem slow to make explicit: the root relationships between the disciplines. Consider a closely related example. Anyone who has ever looked at "the numbers" to justify a Women's and Gender Studies program, or a Latin or Greek course, or even a philosophy department, has had to grapple with the fact that students want to know "what they can do" with their degrees. This has been the experience of Alison Phipps, the Director of Gender Studies at the University of Sussex, who also remarked that students seem increasingly prone not only to reject majoring in gender studies but also in philosophy and history. Phipps traces this trend to the fact that in determining their degree program, students most often ask "what sort of job they can get with this degree." Interestingly, however, Phipps also reports that this same concern did not seem to deter students from seeking degrees in media or film studies. Further she reports, "the politically active students now seem to be interested in International relations, peace studies, and sexuality studies."

So, what distinguishes these newly successful programs from those that are failing? For me, the difference lies between what we might call "pure" study and study paired with one or more "active" discipline/s: business, say, or computer technology, or in the case of "sexuality studies," medicine, psychology, and/or sociology. In the case of rhetoric—historically, theoretically, methodologically—it is always already paired with "active" disciplines: the law, diplomacy, marketing, economics, even medicine and the sciences. Successful programs are distinguished by their willingness to name and articulate not only the relationships between fields of study, but the theoretical and material debts one department or specialty has to the other(s). Once again, the distinction lies in doing, in action and articulation and collaboration. That which distinguishes fields may not lie in the object of study, but rather in the articulated—in the sense of being connected in such a way that flexibility of movement is achieved—methodology. For many years, as a student, I almost subconsciously marked that the literary criticism I read did not necessarily emerge from English studies, but rather from philosophy, economics, psychology, the sciences. I wasn't able to explicitly articulate that relationship, however, until I began teaching rhetorical theory, literary theory, and feminist theory out of an English department myself. I quickly realized how my own scholarly experience working within the history of ideas would be put to best use in the classroom. Concepts became clearer, more meaningful, and infinitely more useful to students when I invited them to explore the background within which the theorists worked and how and why their work was borrowed for use in textual analysis. Rhetoric makes these relationships explicit even while literary study tends to obfuscate its debt to other scholarly traditions. This is the opportunity I'm claiming for rhetoric education: we'll reject any fantastical claim to purity in favor of demonstrating rhetoric's gritty past and its collaborative and eminently useful future.

Rhetoric is by nature multidisciplinary/interdisciplinary and constitutively political (action and ethics based). When I was a member of a traditional English faculty, I had an ongoing disagreement with one colleague about whether or not we, as teachers, should concern ourselves or our students with questions of what is done with texts, or what students do with what we teach. He made the (to my mind, unapologetically essentialist) argument about the "beauty" of literature—the importance of the English department on purely aesthetic grounds. He rejected out of hand the notion that art is always political, a claim I often make both inside and outside my own classrooms. Even so, the time is ripe for English departments to call on their rhetoric concentrations in ways that will directly benefit enrollments and retention. Why shouldn't a rhetorician expect that her education will lead to a prosperous career? Perhaps more to the point, why are some within English departments still loath to suggest such purpose?

The second half of this essay will demonstrate one such purpose by illustrating some of the points of contact between training in rhetoric and composition and the work of community advocacy. The experience I call on involves my own transition from the university to a position as executive director for a nonprofit agency and as a professional consultant, although I think many careers could be considered through the same lenses. It seems certain that avoiding productive comparisons between job requirements and academic credentials is, in one move, to dismiss the history of rhetoric and to avoid its future.

Suitable Terms

Let me begin by saying that while it is true that careers dealing with "advocacy" today demand excellent trained readers of text and culture, writers who can identify and write to multiple audiences, professional communicators able to work in multiple formats/venues, and a facility with research methods and with theory, it is also risky to step away from the university for work that may not ultimately prove a more suitable match.[2] My own transition from university faculty to nonprofit leadership began with my commitment to interdisciplinary work at the university. I use the word "transition" here quite self-consciously. Moving from faculty status to, well, probably to anything else, but certainly from faculty status to an action-based (or political) career or to a career in business/commerce, is a serious matter of identity morphing, so much so that I find it reasonable to compare academics who leave the academy to Kate Bornstein's idea of the "gender outlaw." When we break the unspoken rules, "queer" the idea of the scholar, one of the results is a certain struggle to find a place on the spectrum between blurring identity and taking on entirely new personal, professional, and social identities. The second point of contact I want to make between being gender queer and my professional "transitioning" is that approaching academic work interdisciplinarily isn't a choice. It's a requirement for intellectual honesty. The complex acts of reading, writing, and analyzing "text" simply cannot be accomplished through one literature, one body of knowledge, one disciplinary lens.

There is more to be said about the identity issues involved in this sort of transitioning, but the remainder of this essay must be devoted to the transition itself and to providing a few salient examples of how students trained in rhetoric might put their educations to good and satisfying use in the nonprofit sector. But, as with most stories I can tell about my professional life, the seed for the as-yet-unforeseen transition from full-time tenure-track faculty member to executive director for a struggling LGBTQ center in the North American Deep South began with the classroom, when a group of students approached me in my second year on the job and asked me to teach a course in feminist theory. As far as I knew, there had never been a course at our university devoted to feminist thought, but several women and men across campus taught at least some feminist theory (I was on the gender studies committee with many of them). My first response was to encourage students to recognize other feminist faculty members and other feminist work going on across campus. I asked them to explore the professional websites of other professors, read proposed syllabi before enrolling in any class (one art history class, I explained, was not necessarily like another), and in these ways familiarize themselves with feminist theorists and jargon so that they could spot feminist presence when they saw it.

Then, with student collaboration, I developed the first course on our campus devoted entirely to "feminist theory." My second "teachable moment" with these students was to let them know that with so many brands of feminism to learn about—due especially to scholars across the disciplines working with their own problems, theories, and methodologies—I wouldn't be solely responsible for course content. I wanted student exposure to extend beyond my own understanding and technical repertoire, and a radically interdisciplinary course was born. Twelve to fourteen scholars from across campus were invited to speak about their work and/or "the single text you find indispensable in teaching the meaning of feminism."

That was a successful course, and largely because of the rich connections I'd made with faculty across campus in the process, I subsequently developed a program, *AfterWords*, in collaboration with the department of dramatic arts. *AfterWords* is based on the theoretical, historical, and practical connections between literature, theatre, and the plastic arts. There are several major stakeholders or "audiences" for this after-talk roundtable program, namely members of the audience from the four main stage productions dramatic arts offers each year, theater students and majors, and various faculty who collaborated on the project. Depending on the show, English department faculty were also featured at each event, with the intention of building a useful pedagogical bridge between English and dramatic arts, and also to showcase the diversity of the work in English studies. Finally, this program earned the interest of individual members of the board of directors of a nonprofit agency designed to support an LGBTQ community center. Individual members of this board gravitated toward themes of identity politics and art-as-activism, and with their support, I developed a film series for the Center, organized around the histories and theories of civil rights activism. The department of dramatic arts agreed to let us use their black box theatre and projection technology for the film series, and a new and vital bridge between the university and the community became material.

I was next invited to serve as an advisory board member for the Center, and within the year I was asked to take over the "LGBT Community Center" as its first executive director. The agency was failing by most measures, and though I didn't think of myself as a natural administrator, I was identified by the agency as a good fit for this job largely because I was familiar with the literature in feminist, queer, and postcolonial theory, and because the film series was attracting more people and having a greater positive effect on their mission than any of their other programs. The individual members of the board who hired me may not have articulated the "fit" in the way I just have, but I know they saw me as a vetted professional who was able to articulate the weaknesses in their organization and had studied the historical trajectory of civil rights movements and the place of LGBTQ organizing within it. I think they probably also recognized someone with the potential ability to articulate a vision and compose a mission that would face discriminatory and homophobic ideologies head-on, was willing to build an organizational structure from the inside, who could lead them to raise funds by communicating their vision passionately and rationally with various stakeholders, and might even be able to write grants for sustainable funding.

From my perspective, each of these possibilities springs directly from my training in rhetoric studies. The partnership had emerged from my commitment to the intersections of textual study, interdisciplinarity, and experiential pedagogy. Six months into my tenure as executive director, I can say that we've made significant progress in each of these areas and also that each challenge also remains an uphill battle. The following are illustrations of these challenges, the progress we've made in meeting them, and some explanation of how and why I believe that professionally trained rhetoricians might be well equipped to meet the day-to-day challenges that face nonprofit agencies.

Unfamiliar Terms

When I stepped into the executive director's position, the organization I took over was known as Bay Area Inclusion, or simply "BAI." Because I'd had many conversations with individual board members about their understanding of the work of the agency, and because I'd been observing the agency for two years before I'd begun the film series, I had identified three significant problems going into the job. The first problem would have been immediately recognizable to any careful observer: the board members were not able to articulate a clear mission for the agency (and I'd heard that the larger community felt that lack of cohesion almost instinctively). I asked individual board members about the agency's history and their own ideas about the need for a "community center" in general. Some recalled that the agency was first created as a place where gay individuals could socialize without fear. As I read through seven years of meeting minutes, I discovered that in 2002 the founding members were reacting to threatening language used by politicians in Alabama about "the gay lifestyle." But in my conversations with board members and other community members, no one mentioned the possibility that a LGBTQ-focused agency could also work to overcome ideological misinformation to promote full social and political enfranchisement of LGBTQ individuals. No one reasoned that such work would also make the community safer for all citizens. No one spoke of safety, actually; not a single person I spoke with mentioned the idea of homophobia. In fact, in writing workshops I moderated with the objective of creating a working mission statement, it was a struggle to convince board members that homophobia needed to be addressed at all, much less addressed as the problem—the agency's central problem.

The second easily-identifiable challenge related to something each board member did offer as a principal goal of the organization as it was initially articulated: full inclusion. Individual board members explained that the "inclusion" in Bay Area Inclusion meant that they wanted to create spaces and programming "where everyone is welcome." For me, this important goal would mean creating a culture of true diversity, but diversity was lacking in the organization itself. The key players were sincere in their desire to achieve diversity, but they had made little effort to actually cultivate diversity in a place where social segregation still largely ruled the day. When I signed on as executive director, the agency was serving a completely white, almost exclusively female, Christian, lesbian, and middle-class population, most of whom were in their mid to late forties or older. I guessed that this was probably a result of the fact that the central organizing figures in the agency coalesced around this identity profile as well. One of my first acts as executive director was to challenge the board on their own terms. Desiring inclusivity is one thing, I argued, but it's a completely different thing to cultivate it. Why, I challenged them, would people of color, men, and straight allies, want to attend any of their events? What would draw them? What aspects of the agency were designed for people unlike themselves? And what, primarily, were the power and identity structures that were keeping difference out?

Finally, I had my doubts about the idea of a "center" itself. In the case of an "LGBTQ center" which seemed to look inward at the expense of looking outward, I worried that this particular version of a center—a place around which people gather and which provides a safe haven by virtue of its distance from the rest of community—may have run its course. My academic training had taught me the danger of declaring a center where no center existed or obtained, especially where diversity or inclusivity was a concern. I recommended an approach that would decenter the center. I thought we might more productively pursue a diverse and diffuse network of ideas that radiated outward instead of seeking inwardly. Ideas of outreach and networking began to inspire and direct our writing as we articulated an updated vision for the agency. Under my directorship, then, the agency would not continue to worry about finding a brick-and-mortar center (a goal they had been unsuccessful in achieving for six years). We could then drop the idea of a capital campaign in favor of building a war chest for programming that targeted ideological change within the larger community (suggestions included a billboard campaign, a community garden, a theater-based after-school program and a writing program for at-risk youth). The change from an inward-looking center to an outward-seeking network would underscore our mission statement, and thereby, our daily work. And once we began to see our mission as deep ideological change, we were able to focus on formalizing such a mission statement.

I began by providing two pages of potential language to the board, and then we came together in what I can only describe as a writing workshop. We gathered around my kitchen table where we reviewed the working language, brainstormed, wrote draft language, carried out peer reviews, engaged in vigorous debate, drafted again, worried about language, threw out sentences, brought them back in, crafted language, reviewed, argued, and ultimately emerged with a final product we found productive. It was a good start: most of us approved the vision statement and the new mission statement enthusiastically (though not all to the same degree). The important thing was that we were able to identify homophobia itself as the problem, one we could help "eradicate" through "education, service, and dialogue." We believed education and the cultivation of dialogue would lead to more informed wellness choices, and we hoped to bring the entire community to our cause, not just LGBTQ people. We began transforming a rather exclusive social club into a civil rights service organization through writing.

Less than a year after the board approved our new outward-seeking mission statement, we were in a position to revise that mission statement for clarity and purpose ("Dedicated to exploring misunderstandings about gender identity and sexual orientation especially as those misunderstandings lead to violence and other recognized social ills.") It will be clear to readers of this volume that the application of feminist theory, postcolonial theory, and Freirean pedagogy, (in short, continental philosophy) to the specific ideological problems this agency faced has been the primary launching pad for our community work. Likewise, my experience with student writers managing peer review, drafting thesis statements, stressing the importance of asking good questions, and practicing consequence-driven prose helped me to negotiate the importance of process and drafting. It was important for the board to understand, for instance, that our first draft of the mission statement made it possible for us to redraft for clarity of purpose and strategy. After only a year of experience as a civil-rights oriented agency, we were in a position to more precisely identify the problem we wanted to attack ("misunderstandings about gender identity and sexual orientation") and to suggest a set of solutions. (*Exploring* became our key word once we could see that in addition to programs designed to educate, serve, and cultivate dialogue, we required a research component if we were to be truly effective.)

We have come to understand our mission statement as a living document open to revision as we continue to identify our precise niche within a very complex equation, to target funding already earmarked for social problems, and to gather in more stakeholders. As a rhetorician (and a Whitmanian pragmatist), I understand that our evolving mission and vision are testaments to the fact that we are working (and that to be working means to be writing). I understand and can teach that we are necessarily using language to create reality, not the other way around. Very early on I recognized that one of the most important aspects of the executive director's work is that of visionary (and this recognition was validated in the many nonprofit management books I subsequently read). The visionary is the surprisingly metaphysical language used by contemporary thinkers in business administration which describes a leader's ability to see the complexities of routes toward long-term change paired with the ability to translate this insight for the purposes of inspiring and motivating multiple stakeholders (Carlson and Donohoe, Sand, Wolf). It is also, surprisingly, very much like the work of writing and of writing teachers.

I would also describe my work with a volunteer professional designer to redesign the agency's look and branding as collaborative writing.[3] The fact that page design itself is part of the professional domain of the rhetorician reflects the reasons a university rhetorician is capable of teaching Technical Writing classes even if s/he is not up to date with the latest technology and/or new media. All of the rhetorical principles obtain when form meets function as it does in page and logo design. An educated sensitivity to the way readers read a page is crucial when designing branding that will not only represent your agency but even suggest the ethics, attitudes, and exigencies of the agency, sometimes even before any one-on-one human interaction takes place. Branding requires that the page (paper or electronic) and the design speak for themselves.

BAI required a complete redesign in its media, presentation, and Web presences. Its logo was common and outdated, there had been little effort to pair the rather opaque symbolism in the logo to the work of the agency, and the website had been pieced together in bits with sporadic volunteer help (a common problem for nonprofits). When we began the redesign, BAI was represented by a logo that spoke to geographical location (a water symbol) and a somewhat transcendental, if currently trite, symbol of peace and harmony (the dragonfly). The redesign used color to create a bridge between the old and the new. We translated the blues and greens of the old logo to a more muted, contemporary and almost industrial feel, while also suggesting depth and professionalism. We then created a completely new logo, one we hoped would speak to growth, change, wellness, and life. The open circular organic form of the new logo (the old design had been linear) suggests fullness and inclusivity while also speaking to ongoing change, and it incorporates our new full name: BAI Community Action Alliance. In addition, the full logo subtly mirrors the tripartite nature of the key terms upon which we would build our programming platforms. Those graphic features underscore the byline now used with our new name: "Cultivating well-being through education, service, and dialogue."

I have no doubt that many nonprofit agencies grow under similar circumstances (in bits and pieces, fits and starts, with the revolving-door of volunteer help) and would benefit tremendously from the clear attention of writers and theorists schooled in the arts of cultural critique, textual analysis, and the symbolic mediation of language. Moreover, it has become clear that my ability to work with—direct even—professional page and Web designers comes from my training in both textual and visual rhetoric as well as emerging simply from my ability to teach. My training in English departments has taught me that teachers must be able to translate complex ideas with which they are well acquainted for use by individuals unfamiliar with that content but fully imbued with ideas of their own. The executive director must be constantly aware of what rhetoricians would call "audience" issues, but in ways that the rhetorical triangle only begins to explain. They must know that the way to animate logos, ethos, and pathos is to enclose or float the entire model within the driving force—the exigency—of the writing situation.

Terms of Endearment

The idea of rhetorician-as-translator, or at least agent-of-translation, who must be adept at recognizing multiple stakeholders and speaking to different audiences at once, may be the most direct link to using professional rhetoricians in both the corporate and nonprofit workplaces. We learn quickly that much of what a technical writer does is translation—translating technical material for the end-user in a user's manual, to draw on the most common example. Working as a writing consultant for faculty in a prestigious school of business administration that was serious about the value of writing-intensive curricula, I experienced first-hand how complex and multi-layered the technical writer's tasks could be in the workplace. I once consulted, for instance, with a professor in decision sciences and management information systems who assigned a workplace task to his students: they were to take up the role of professional systems analysts and write up technical specifications for a client who develops software. In this case, the student would have to look both "downstream" to the software developer's customers and back "upstream" to how the system analysts translated the technicians' specifications. This sort of real world writing not only requires finely tuned translation skills, but also the ability to recognize secondary and tertiary audiences both upstream and downstream from the writer herself.

In my advocacy work, perhaps no rhetorical knowledge is called on more often than the ability to write to multiple audiences. This is true for all sorts of professionals who do executive director-type work (business management folks, public relations specialists, media professionals, etc.), although they may not address this capacity quite as explicitly as a trained rhetorician. In advocacy work, attention to multiple audiences both upstream and downstream is always a critical need. This understanding became more pronounced for me with each task I took on. Grant writing is a common example of work that must be carried out with close attention to audience. Most obviously, each grant must speak to the concerns of both the requesting agency (the writer) and the granting agency (the reader) simultaneously, as the defining goal is matching agency need and mission with the grantor's own mission and desire. But what I've also discovered on the ground is that any given grant may be seen by multiple stakeholders outside the grantee-grantor relationship. I have found it useful to share a grant and/or specific language from a grant with other interested parties, for example. I'd share language taken directly from a grant with folks who were new to our mission and wanted to know more. I might send a copy of the full grant to potential private donors. I also used language from the grant, sometimes full paragraphs or full sections, for other purposes (content for the Web page, for instance). Grants are written with both upstream and downstream audiences in mind.

In my position as executive director for this LGBTQ organization, I have found it necessary to witness full court proceedings, about which I then report back to the local community. Writing about a complex court case is never a simple matter, but subtleties and subtexts are rife when the case involves gender diversity and sexual orientation. Because I hoped to get the reports out to as wide an audience as possible, my interpretation of those events was sent to our community email list (individuals who had voluntarily signed up to receive our notices), our board and advisory board, and to others outside the initial address list (the attorney, for instance, and her clients as well). It must also be acknowledged that my evaluations of the courtroom would be further distributed to multiple audiences' scrutiny, with possible wholesale lifting of electronic content when they were posted to various new media such as Facebook Causes (or just cut-and-pasted wholly or in bits and pieces). I obviously could not write to each potential audience specifically, but my professional training in these complexities made me a more likely candidate for such work than a person with a background less based in critical textual analysis.

This same professional preparation carried me through verbal discussions with various stakeholders as well. When I spoke with a Catholic parish priest, I needed to be aware that it was important to reach him individually but also that his superiors would be the final decision makers if we were to progress far enough to ask for material help from the Church. I was also acutely aware that everything he said to me had to be measured in his multiple roles: as a conscious keeper of his own individual ethical standards, as a school administrator, as a spokesperson for his congregation, as a theologian, as Director of Child and Youth Protection Services for his diocese, and as a model of behavior and obedience under the archdiocese as well. To those multiple audiences, I had to add my own constituencies when I considered my rhetorical contributions to the conversation. In advocacy work, rhetorical credentials and proficiencies might be thought of as necessarily intensified because of the human cost that is potentially at stake (although the Space Shuttle Columbia disaster certainly demonstrated that even in the most sterile of technical situations, there is always a human cost at stake).

To more finely demonstrate what is at stake, I want to take the final few pages of this essay to flesh out the example of my conversations with the Catholic Church about LGBTQ issues. It was important to me that I maintained respect for the integrity of the advocacy agency I was representing and the advocacy entity I was addressing as I tried to make progress with (at least the local) Church. Without rehashing the old arguments for and against the sophists, a good rhetorician must—as Abner Mikva has anecdotally said about Barack Obama—

learn "how to appeal to different constituencies without being inconsistent" (Weisskopf).

In the Deep South, if one wishes to reach the citizenry, one must accept that "church" constitutes an important part of individual and community identity. Through our InView film series, BAI had already begun the process of cultivating dialogue about the complex subject of reconciling spirituality with sexuality. In that forum, we were working almost exclusively with our direct constituency: on any given night most of our audience were LGBTQ people and the families and friends of LGBTQ people. This meant that, for the most part, our dialogues were also between people familiar with the struggles LGBTQ individuals face when trying to retain their own religion or discover another church that might be more tolerant. Given my own directive that we would be more than inward gazing and work instead to network outward (especially in my goal of increasing diversity through cultivating straight allies), I knew we would approach mainstream churches with our agenda.[4] I chose to begin with the Catholic Church for personal reasons, and because I respect their theological training, their tolerance for radical priests, and the room they make for radical and intellectual church centers. (I grew up attending Newman Centers, the places most likely for liberal minded priests to be assigned.) When I went to speak with the Catholic church about supporting our work fighting homophobia and advocating for the safety of the LGBTQ population, I knew that there would be certain arguments to which the priest I spoke with (and his superiors) would be most sympathetic, and I knew that other arguments had the potential to completely undermine the possibility of a working relationship. As a trained rhetorician, I knew that the principles of kairos and "occasion" must determine my approach and that stasis theory would serve almost as a methodology in these talks. My training in argument theory helped insure that I at least arrived prepared to frame my arguments in ways that were safest to the Church.

I chose the parish priest I've been working with because not only is he Director of Child and Youth Protection in our local diocese, but because he publicly and actively pursues goals that mirror our own mission statement. For instance, writing an article to be used in the 2008 annual Retraining for Religious and Employees (required by the archdiocese), he wrote, "It is vital to our children's health and well-being that adult ministers . . . provide safe environments where every child is treated with dignity and respect" (Archdiocese). Likewise, our extended mission statement includes a sentence about transformation based in respect: "We come together as individuals and as a community to do what we can to eradicate the culture of silence, violence, hubris, and apathy and in its place to build a culture of tolerance, modesty, creativity, and productivity" (BAI: Community Action Alliance). As such, I approached him with our agenda from the perspective of safety and inclusivity, while refraining from the fraught connection I could have made (and may yet make) to "dignity and respect for life." In conversations with this priest I have cited suicide rates, homelessness rates, disenfranchisement from the church, and refuge for the downtrodden. I spoke about a broken foster care system and the horrifying numbers of children needing adoption, both of which could be radically alleviated by allowing and even encouraging adoption into gay-parent families.

It has not been difficult to discover powerful moments of stasis with this churchman. He is worried about the same things we are worried about, and he doesn't have ways to reach the population I can reach. He and I both understand the double and triple disenfranchisement of the LGBTQ population. In the heart of the Jim Crow South (though law forbids discrimination based on race, our area is still very much socially segregated, including a segregation of churches; in the same way Mardi Gras in our area is defined by white balls and black balls, white parades and black parades, the majority of churches are also casually defined as either black churches or white churches), I argued that the sort of misinformation based on fear of difference and resulting in faulty media representations about gay life is the same sort of misinformation which caused so much (often sexualized) violence against African Americans in both the 19th and 20th centuries. I demonstrated with stories, statistics, and other research that LGBTQ folks are misrepresented and targeted for violence because of misunderstandings about the differences between sex, sexual orientation, and gender differentiation. I explained that homophobia is often a product of misunderstanding about gender diversity as opposed to a problem with the choice of sex partners.

He said he was unfamiliar with any distinction between sex and gender. He asked me to teach him, to tell him more about gender theory. Not something they cover in seminary, apparently, but of vital interest to the ministry nonetheless. What a great discovery for me. I found myself in a productive conversation about gender, queer theory, and bullying with a Church representative devoted to protecting children and youth. At his suggestion, I hope to put together a presentation for the Archbishop. At our second meeting, he and I together began to strategize about how to get me "in front of" this decision maker. We both believe that there are ways to creatively garner resources from the church "without bringing all the baggage the full church will bring with it" (his words, not mine). He knows that the wellness and safety work to which BAI is committed needs to be carried out. For reasons that are obvious (though I still hope, temporary) the church would rather we carry it out for them. We're better equipped.

What has been most surprising to me as I walk this fine line between the work of the scholar and the work of the activist is the discovery that scholars of rhetoric have much to teach major stakeholders about gender and sexuality; about ideology and identity; about language and power; about drafting, writing, and critical analysis. Perhaps this teaching function isn't surprising after all; it turns out that most of what we have to offer in advocacy is educational. It is true to the art of rhetoric that rhetoricians use this training about literacy and power and the skills to teach about it to intervene directly in the political economy. Given rhetoric's own history and the first-hand experience I've had applying my education to civil rights and advocacy work, there remains no good reason to withhold this information about our students' credentialing from our students themselves. We identity scholars have something to teach the larger community even as they have something to teach us. Imagine if there were hundreds of us spread across the country, talking, learning, persuading.

Notes

1. The department hadn't granted tenure for nearly ten years, so there were only four senior faculty members when I was hired in a batch of five assistant professors.

2. I was told by two of my academic mentors that a move away from the academy could be dangerous to my prospects within the university system in the future. One wrote to say that although the opportunity to direct a nonprofit seemed an "interesting prospect," he also wanted me to know that "academics are weird. They hold suspect anyone who dares 'leave our ranks' and goes into the public/private sector for a while" (personal email). Although I believe in the transformations this essay may suggest, I am ethically compelled to pass this warning along.

3. The cross-disciplinary bridges I helped to build during my time at the university were instrumental here, too. I got to know the terrific graphic designer who designed our website through the collaboration I did with her colleagues when assembling the *AfterWords* speakers for the play *Bobrauschenbergamerica* produced by the department of dramatic arts.

4. Although there is a Metropolitan Community Church in our area, which a few of our constituents attend, we at BAI had resolved to work for long-term ideological change. We weren't interested so much in a "gay church" as we were in working to assure that all people of faith would feel welcome at any church of their choice.

WORKS CITED

Archdiocese of Mobile. Office of Child Protection. "Article Number 3: Appropriate Boundaries When Working with Children and Adolescents." *Workshop Handout*. Jim Cink. 2008. Print.

BAI: Community Action Alliance. "Who We Are." *Mission Statement*. 2009. Web. 19 June 2012.

Bornstein, Kate. *Gender Outlaw: On Men, Women, and the Rest of Us*. First Vintage Books ed. NewYork: Routledge, 1995. Print.

Carlson, Mim, and Margaret Donohoe. *The Executive Director's Survival Guide: Thriving as a Nonprofit Leader*. The Jossey-Bass Nonprofit and Public Management Ser. San Francisco: Jossey-Bass. 2003. Print.

Cink, Fr. Jim. "Appropriate Boundaries When Working with Children and Adolescents." Mobile Archdiocese.org. Article 3 for Religious Employees. Archdiocese of Mobile. 2008. Web. 11 October 2009.

Phipps, Alison. "RE: Guardian: Postfeminist Passions/The Demise of Women's Studies Has More to Do with Changes in the Job Market than Lost Battles." Women's Studies Listserv (WMST-L) Archives. Center for Women and Information Technology. The U of Maryland, Baltimore County. 27 March 2008. Web. 27 March 2008.

Sand, Michael A. *How to Manage an Effective Nonprofit Organization: From Writing and Managing Grants to Fundraising, Board Development, and Strategic Planning*. Franklin Lakes, NJ: Career Press. 2005. Print.

Wolf, Thomas. *Managing a Nonprofit Organization in the Twenty-First Century*. New York: Fireside Books-Simon & Schuster. 1999. Print.

Weisskopf, Michael. "Obama: How He Learned to Win." Time.com. Time Inc. 8 May 2008. Web. 11 October 2009.

7 Ten Ways English Studies Contributes to User Experience Research, or: How to Retrofit an English Studies Degree

Dave Yeats

When I was about fourteen years old, I decided I wanted to become an English professor. I imagine that my desire was motivated by my love of reading and writing topped off with a healthy dose of *Dead Poets Society*. Naturally, at the time I had no idea what an English professor did, but a job revealing the world of literature to students appealed to me. Today, twenty years later, I find myself on the other side of that goal. I worked through degrees (BA, MA, and PhD) in English departments until I earned the coveted tenure-track position in an English department at a major public university. Much to my disbelief, and despite the fact that I liked a lot of what the position called for, being an English professor ultimately wasn't for me. After two years, I decided to leave my job and return to what some academics call "industry" or "the corporate workplace."

What finally drove me away from academics is probably something that draws some people into it: security. Academic work is safe. Upon entering my job as an assistant professor, everything that was expected of me was defined, and the path to tenure was clear. Within this rigid structure, I was informed that I had some autonomy when it came to my teaching and research, but my full participation in the department wasn't expected for several years. To me, this level of security was stifling. I was a young assistant professor interested in doing things—practical things—to improve my students' job prospects and workforce training. I was informed that my ideas for program development would be welcome after I had achieved tenure.

Now, my pendulum swings to the opposite end of the safety continuum. Working in a small consulting firm as a user experience (UX) researcher, I can't say today that I know where my next project (and paycheck) will come from. I struggle to invent my own roadmap to success, and I even find difficulty in defining what success really is in the business world. Where the academic career path provides clear boundaries with explicit goals, the corporate workplace does not have the same explicit structure. I am comforted, however, by the fact that my work is practical and valued by my clients. It is that practicality in the business world that I find most rewarding. I bring my clients answers to questions that they cannot answer on their own. And I do this work with a small, agile group of like-minded individuals who have the ability to invent new and creative ways of working and thinking. There is no hierarchy or tenure and promotion ladder; there is only us, and we are equal. I've spent a lot of time grappling with the perceived "failure" of my academic career, but in retrospect I have come to terms with how my particular journey represents one alternative of many available to PhDs. My goal for this chapter is to provide specific insight into how training in English studies has served me well in my consulting work.

As a user experience researcher, I conduct studies designed to discover how people experience a particular device, interface, product, or service. Companies come to me when they have questions like "How can we help our customers install our DSL service on their own without calling technical support?" and "What are the essential and best features for a retail website viewed on a mobile device?" In what I do, I employ practices common in the fields of market research, cognitive psychology, anthropology, human-computer interaction, and others. Above all else, however, I see my work as a product of my training and experience in a spectrum of fields within English studies.

This chapter addresses ten elements of English studies and explains how I use each of these elements in my work. To set the stage, I should explain that I moved from a BA in literature to an MA in creative writing to a PhD in technical communication and rhetoric. In my mind, the shift works this way: I moved from textual analysis to production, and then I moved from the artistic to the practical. I hope that the following sections will give readers a different perspective on English studies and will encourage more creative ways to use degrees in English.

LANGUAGE AND LITERATURE

For me, English studies begins with language and literature. However, as the rest of this chapter shows, I do not stop at language and literature alone. Even though I believe that language and literature does provide the beginning to English studies, I also believe that it can often unfairly inhibit other fields within English because of its perceived dominance. As such, it is the origin and often opponent of other areas. As Isabelle Thompson and I wrote in "Mapping Technical and Professional Communication," "some programs find themselves at odds with their host departments, and the arrangement can have serious negative repercussions for the ability of technical communication programs to innovate, thrive, and achieve the level of success . . . that they would otherwise reach" (226). Because of this misalignment of programmatic goals, I believe that many English studies fields like technical communication, linguistics, and composition will eventually find themselves working outside of English departments. In fact, many already have.

In his "Positioning Programs in Professional and Technical Communication," Sam Dragga argues that programs "institutionalized in departments of English . . . encourage[s] the privileging of textual studies (i.e., teaching and research likely to be appreciated by colleagues in literary fields)" (221). Despite the fact that a focus on textual studies can limit what contributions are valued in departments of English, I'm not ready to discredit the lessons I learned in this core area of English studies. The idea of narrative almost daily informs what I do. Everything from Freytag's dramatic arc (115) to Campbell's study of archetypes (13) surfaces in my work in sometimes surprising ways.

In business, I have to understand my role as a consultant in terms of interrelationships between myself and others. In many cases, I find myself identifying with a particular type. I ask questions that may be part of a literature course: What are the power relationships at play between the characters? What are the characters' motivations—what are they trying to accomplish? How does what the characters do or say clarify or obscure these motivations? In resolving conflict, I have to answer these questions using both interactions with others and by interpreting texts, including emails, proposals, contracts, and statements of work. Most of us, I believe, consciously or unconsciously understand ourselves as a character involved in a narrative. Kenneth Burke went so far as to suggest that literature (or "critical and imaginative works" as he called them) is, in fact, a series of "strategic answers" that "size up situations, name their structure and outstanding ingredients, and name them in a way that contains an attitude towards them" (1). It's my opinion that literature's ability to shed light on the human condition is a valuable tool to wield.

In delivering information to a corporate client, I sometimes overtly use my sense of narrative for dramatic effect to make my findings have more impact. In particular, many UX consultants deliver a *customer journey map,* or *touchpoint story,* which essentially tells the story of a customer—sometimes real, sometimes only based on real people—to help companies understand what their customers must go through to engage in services. Telling a story (with a beginning, middle, and end) about a person trying to install DSL in their home and facing sometimes insurmountable obstacles gives my clients an appreciation for what they ask of their customers.

I will take a moment here to recognize that the simplistic, modernist view of storytelling above does not address what our postmodern experience in the world tends to teach us. Specifically, all narratives are more complicated than they first appear, especially in the corporate world where stories are re-shaped and re-told in ways influenced by the storytellers and the corporate environments and cultures within which those storytellers reside. It isn't unusual, for example, for me to revise a report on the advice of a client who wants to avoid some of the "political quicksand" or "landmine" some of my findings could uncover. I will admit that remaining culturally and strategically aware of the complications inherent in storytelling is crucial to successfully relating a story.

CREATIVE WRITING

As with language and literature, the skills I developed when studying creative writing (fiction, in my case) apply directly to my work. My training led me to a kind of writing that tended to be highly direct, active, and stark. Some might call it the Hemingway school. Experiencing this approach to writing led me to think about things like the difference in impact between Germanic and Latinate words. I began to attend to the craft of writing more than I ever had before, making sure each word carried the most accurate meaning. In my client communication, I tend to be brief and direct as well. In an environment where writing about business or the psychology of customer relationships can be full of passive construction, I try to give my clients a clear sense of agency and action in my writing. In fact, giving voice to my clients' customers even involves using dialogue in the form of verbatim quotes from research studies.

Using the tools of creative writing can help me reach clients in a medium they can immediately connect with. When I deal with clients who are distracted, clarity and familiarity can help focus their attention. The ability to write in clear, precise language with the most immediate impact allows me to deliver memorable messages with great efficiency. Whether I'm writing an email clarifying a particular aspect of a project or writing a presentation that contains a recommended course of action, I draw from my experiences learning how to hone language down to its essence.

It was also in my creative writing training that I began to understand writing as a craft rather than a talent. I had often given lip service to "the writing process" in the abstract, but I had rarely put much of that model into practice. When I started attending creative writing classes based on the Iowa writers' workshop model, I began to realize that I could put a great deal more effort into my work, which (I think) resulted in better writing. Today, I find myself more aware of my writing process and even catch myself running through a draft-revise-proofread process with the simplest of client emails. It has saved me from making mistakes on several occasions.

Discourse Communities

Another piece of my training that still strongly guides what I do is the ability to quickly understand and adapt to different discourse communities. When I entered the master's program at the University of Missouri, I was overwhelmed. Though I had been a literature major in the past, I felt as though the people around me were speaking some strange foreign language. I came to realize that it wasn't much different than a foreign language. Communities have their own ways of talking that simply exclude outsiders from being able to fully participate until they, too, learn the ways in which specific terms are applied. This includes not only specialized terms and jargon, but also common words that are applied differently by a specific community.

Understanding the ways in which language can be adapted for specialized use was an eye-opening experience for me, and it's a lesson I never truly forgot. Today, I interact with a wide array of companies in many different industries. In a given week, I may interact with a creative advertising/marketing firm, a computer hardware manufacturer, a department store retailer, and a telecommunications company. Even within those different industries, I may talk to a project manager, a researcher, or a software developer. All of these clients have developed a discourse community based on the industry or role and (in many cases) based on idiosyncrasies within their own company. When switching from community to community, it's essential that I stay actively aware of new jargon and new ways to use familiar terms so that I can immediately begin talking to clients in their own terms. It's my goal to become closer than simply a vendor my clients use. I want to become a partner who understands their business. Language awareness gives me the tools to accomplish that goal.

Nondirective Tutoring and Composition

Interpersonal techniques I learned while working as a writing tutor help me with my current work as well. Most of the research my clients ask me to do is based on gathering information about how their customers (the "users") experience their products, services, or interfaces. One of the best ways to do this is to arrange one-on-one sessions with representatives from their target customer group. These sessions often center on the guided use of a product while a facilitator gathers data about where users have problems and brainstorm ideas about how designers and programmers can aid users in overcoming (or avoiding) those problems. For example, if a company wants to know if their mobile e-commerce website is designed effectively, I would recruit people to come into a market research facility and ask them to perform shopping tasks with their phones. I would watch to see how they search for products or browse categories, whether they can add items to their cart, and if the checkout flow is easy to follow. Throughout this process, my goal is to guide them while interfering as little as possible with the participant's natural inclinations and instincts.

The approach of guiding without interfering is one of the most important things a good facilitator understands. Good data requires a neutral approach toward the one-on-one user sessions. In other words, a facilitator cannot "help" a participant find the correct link or series of commands that will make the program or website complete the task they are hoping to accomplish. Showing users how a program works or letting them know that the "Cancel" button they're looking for is really called "End" on this particular interface would skew the results of the research. While it seems like a simple matter, learning to be nondirective is difficult for most moderators. Because it's also important to be friendly and set participants at ease during a test, it's natural to want to be helpful as well.

I draw most explicitly on my experience as a writing center tutor when I'm moderating one-on-one sessions. For a few years, I spent time every week helping students with writing assignments of all kinds, from remedial composition through graduate theses. In each case, the pedagogical approach to our writing center was to be nondirective. The thought was that if you simply fixed the comma splice or article agreement error, then the students would never learn how to improve their own writing. While my current use of some of these techniques is not aimed at helping participants to learn, they still succeed in putting people at ease and understanding how to offer their own opinions without interference from what I may already know.

Practical Writing Training

It was during my time as a Master's student that I was first exposed to the field of composition. I enrolled in a course required of all composition instructors, and soon afterward I was teaching my own class. I was struck immediately by how practical the course seemed. Even though I was essentially preparing students for academic writing rather than workplace writing, giving students the fundamental tools they would need to form complete and coherent thoughts seemed to me to be the most essential kind of instruction a person might need to become successful and productive in any endeavor.

I was so enthralled by what I saw as the "practical" nature of teaching writing that I asked to teach a technical writing course. My first attempt at teaching that class was rudimentary, but it included teaching reports, memos, presentations, résumés, and other essential business documents. I was energized by the prospect of helping students create the kinds of documents they would use for a lifetime—documents that accomplish the work of business.

I came to realize that my passion for language was beginning to shift away from the literary training that brought me to English studies in the first place. I had a strong desire to teach practical workplace skills, and, later, to practice those skills. I was more interested in the kind of writing and documents being used to directly influence the working world rather than those documents aimed at furthering an academic discussion. While I often use the shorthand of saying "practical writing" when referring to writing in the workplace, I don't intend to somehow discredit or devalue writing done in an academic setting. This writing has a purpose and achieves certain goals, but to me it isn't "practical" in a mundane sense. While many academics may be bored with workplace writing, I find it to be satisfying to produce documents that others need to accomplish work goals.

At the moment I began to find myself drawn to workplace writing, I started to look for ways to earn a paycheck for writing. I wanted desperately to test my hunch that what I had learned could be applied to a practical, business-friendly endeavor. Fortunately, I completed my MA during the dot-com bubble, and the high-tech industry needed writers of all stripes to write documentation. In retrospect, I had very little trouble finding a position at a software company and I quickly made the transition into a new career. Rather than finding that people had explicit training in technical communication, I discovered that my fellow technical writers were former journalism, history, or sociology majors.

I will always look back at my training in composition and the opportunity to teach as the primary reasons for my initial interest in applied areas of English studies. Unfortunately, I think there are many cases in which applied teaching and "industry" work are undervalued in English departments. My experience tells me, however, that a good writer who understands how to communicate is a valuable asset for any organization.

Rhetoric

The most important lesson I draw from rhetoric is the ability to understand the needs and desires of my audience. Because I know the importance of taking time to analyze the needs of my audience, I know that they don't understand the term "rhetoric," which means I rarely share that rhetoric is a part of my doctorate. In my experience, it's more to the point to say that I'm an expert in audience analysis, persuasion, or argumentation theory. Introducing the term "rhetoric" is counterproductive in that it muddies the value of what I can offer to clients.

If the readers of this chapter remember nothing else, I hope they will remember this piece of advice: *convincing a potential client or employer that English studies offers a worthy set of marketable skills is not important.* Your goal in a situation where you must persuade your audience that you're marketable is not to make them understand the value of an English major. Instead, the goal is to make them understand that *you* have the qualifications necessary for the job. I encounter many current and former English majors who have an inferiority complex when comparing themselves to engineers or business types. They want to enter into conversations that help others understand that they're worth as much as others professionals. While I am sympathetic to those who bemoan the plight of people who wield language for a living, I also would encourage a different approach: reinvent yourself. The interpretation of rhetoric that most strongly resonates with me in the workplace is Aristotle's view that rhetoric is the art of persuasion. Who better than a rhetorician to write a compelling résumé and cover letter? I encourage anyone to employ the "available means of persuasion" (Aristotle, qtd. in Bizzell 181) to create a persona that will cause employers or clients to sit up and take notice.

TECHNICAL COMMUNICATION

While technical communication as a discipline has grown into a complex field with many different specialties, I most commonly approach technical communication as applied rhetoric. In other words, I see my work in technical communication as rhetoric training put into practice. A keen awareness of the audience is critical, but a good technical communicator must go a step further than simply knowing his or her audience. Technical communicators are advocates for their audience. They empathize. Good technical communicators understand that their readers are actually trying to accomplish a goal other than reading the documentation.

When I teach (as I occasionally do), I tell my students that one of the most important lessons a technical communicator needs to learn is that no one wants to read what a technical communicator writes. In fact, the audience of technical communication is trying to accomplish a goal that (for the reader) does not include "read the manual." The documentation is not an end in itself; it is a means to an end. When I was writing online help or technical documentation, I always tried to understand first what my readers were trying to accomplish and do my best to give them the ability to move quickly past the documentation to complete their goal. From a reader's perspective, true satisfaction can only be achieved when the goal is achieved, not when the documentation has been read.

Technical communication, then, led me directly to my current field. Technical writers recognize the gap between the users' understanding and the product or interface they're writing about. They close the gap by creating training or procedural writing. In my work, I research the gap between users and technology, but instead of writing to users about it, I write to the designers and developers of the technology. Rather than helping users to use an awkward, unintuitive interface, I work to make the interface less awkward and more intuitive. The gap, then, is closed not by better documentation, but by better design.

NEW MEDIA

Many English departments are now hiring scholars in new media. Similar to the way English began to examine films as texts, the wide variety and sheer volume of media produced for both artistic and practical purposes provides abundant new avenues for research and instruction for English studies. The danger, however, is that some departments approach new media in traditional, literature-based ways. English studies' approach to film has traditionally been film-as-text. The same kinds of analyses that apply to literature can be applied to film criticism.

As with film, one approach to new media studies has been scholar-as-critic. New media instructors analyze and interpret new media artifacts much as a literature scholar analyzes and interprets nineteenth-century novels. Another approach might be in new media production in which new media instructors approach the production of new media artifacts much as a creative writing instructor approaches the art and craft of writing. In this case, the emphasis is on more *avant garde* or artistic uses of new media. In some cases, however, new media scholars focus on practical instruction about how to generate media applicable to the task of getting business done.

My experience with new media during my graduate training was balanced between the theoretical/critical and the practical. In a theory-heavy course about artificial intelligence, for example, my final project included creating a "bot" (short for "robot") that could chat with people through an instant messenger interface. In that way, I had the opportunity not only to learn the theoretical approaches to new media design but also to apply those theories to a real-world, working example. My classroom work could also serve as a professional portfolio for potential employers.

In my consulting practice, I produce all kinds of media. While I still enjoy writing a well-crafted report, I often find myself creating presentations, video clips, websites, or other media-rich artifacts that suit the situation. I will be the first to admit that I am not a filmmaker, nor do I aspire to be. Instead, my goal is to communicate clearly using the most applicable channel. As new tools become available, I use them judiciously in providing valuable services to my clients.

Usability

While there are many definitions for the term usability (sometimes referring to a technique, sometimes referring to a quality), the most important aspect of usability is its inherent worldview. Usability begins with a belief in user-centered design. As Donald Norman and Stephen Draper state in *User Centered System Design,* "the emphasis is on people rather than technology" (2). User-centered design is "about the design of computers, but from the user's point of view" (2). The foundation of usability depends on the assumption that difficult interfaces can be improved by incorporating an understanding of users into the development process. I was fortunate enough to be exposed to both the theoretical and practical aspects of usability evaluation during my PhD coursework.

Today, unfortunately, usability is a field that is undervalued in the marketplace. Specialists in usability like Steve Krug and Jakob Neilsen emphasize that usability evaluation can be easily learned and practiced by anyone. Their practices involve training others to practice usability research rather than practicing usability research themselves. Because usability is undervalued, I tend to avoid using the term when talking about what I do. The ultimate goal of UX research is to improve the usability of a product or interface, but the term has begun to lose its luster.

Again, I have to lean on my understanding of rhetoric to recognize that it's not my responsibility to restore the field of usability to a higher level of esteem in the business community. I do, however, continually try to show my clients how much broader a usability evaluation can be when it is practiced by someone who has been extensively trained in both techniques and theoretical approaches.

EMPIRICAL RESEARCH METHODS

While all of the aspects of English studies mentioned above have helped me get to the place I am today, I believe that the most relevant and practical lessons I received came from my training in empirical research methods. Empirical research isn't ubiquitous in English studies. Literary scholarship often relies more on applying a theory to the interpretation of texts or arriving at a research question only by serendipitous means rather than a specific agenda. But empirical research remains an important aspect of composition and technical communication research. Through training in empirical research methods, scholars can learn to develop research that systematically gathers valid data.

More specifically, my training allowed me to gain experience in a wide variety of methods. In any given research study, I may combine methodological elements of interviewing, surveying, observation, task analysis, discourse analysis, or heuristic evaluation. The strength of using multiple methods to gather data about a single research question is that the data from each method can contribute to a convergence in the findings, granting additional support for any recommended courses of action. While my clients may believe that they're paying me to gather data and produce a report, I believe that the most important thing I can offer is empirical research design. In fact, the data collection and analysis, while important, would not stand up under scrutiny if it were not supported by the foundation of solid empirical research.

There are many ways that empirical research methodologies and design come into play in my everyday work, but one such example is counterbalancing the order in which participants are exposed to a specific design. For example, if a client wants to know if users prefer webpage A over webpage B, then it's a mistake to show all of the users webpage A before they see webpage B. That ordering effect has an influence on how users experience the page. Therefore, it's important to account for (but not eliminate) ordering effects by showing half of the users webpage B first and half the users webpage A first. Understanding the implications in every decision in research design allows me to be confident in the findings I deliver to clients.

Conclusion

Reflecting on it today, I am happy that my journey through English studies has led me here. While I still maintain close friendships with colleagues who are professors in English departments all over the country, I feel truly valuable and engaged when operating in the private sector. I hope that the story of my experiences will inspire others to examine ways in which they can apply their skills in a new endeavor.

Works Cited

Bizzell, Patricia, and Bruce Herzberg, eds. *The Rhetorical Tradition.* Boston: Bedford/St. Martin's, 2001. Print.

Burke, Kenneth. *The Philosophy of Literary Form.* Berkeley, CA.: University of California, 1973. Print.

Campbell, Joseph. *The Hero with a Thousand Faces.* Novato, CA: New World Library, 2008. Print.

Dragga, Sam. "Positioning Programs in Professional and Technical Communication: Guest Editor's Introduction." *Technical Communication Quarterly* 19.3 (July) 2010: 221–24. Print.

Freytag, Gustav. *Freytag's Technique of the Drama: An Exposition of Dramatic Composition and Art.* Trans. Elias J. MacEwan. Chicago: Scott, Foresman, and Company, 1900. Print.

Krug, Steve. *Don't Make Me Think, 2nd ed.* Berkeley, CA: New Riders, 2006. Print.

Nielsen, Jakob. *Designing Web Usability.* Berekley, CA: Peachpit Press, 1999. Print.

Norman, Donald, and Stephen Draper. *User Centered System Design.* Hillsdale, NJ: Lawrence Erlbaum Press, 1986. Print.

Yeats, Dave, and Isabelle Thompson. "Mapping Technical and Professional Communication: A Summary and Survey of Academic Locations for Programs." *Technical Communication Quarterly* 19.3 (July) 2010: 225–61. Print.

8 Establishing a Writing Curriculum at a Law Firm

Benjamin Opipari

Incivil. Bloodless. Infirm. Rambling. Incoherent. Words used to describe a tyrannical dictator, perhaps? On the contrary. These are words used in one nationwide survey to describe legal writing—a survey, surprisingly, of judges and attorneys.

Faced with such daunting superlatives, at least one big firm has taken a stand by hiring their own in-house writing consultant. Litigation firms, after all, place writing skills near the top of the list of key competencies for successful attorneys. In August, 2006, I was hired at Howrey LLP to design and implement a writing curriculum for our 800 attorneys worldwide. The firm, based in Washington DC, advertised for the position in the *Chronicle of Higher Education* because they wanted to hire an academic, not an attorney, for the position. Their logic was simple: why hire someone with the very skills and habits that they were trying to eliminate? They wanted an outsider, someone who could objectively assess a piece of writing, someone who was not tainted by the genre.

When Howrey first advertised my current position of in-house writing instructor, I had just finished my dissertation and was only a few months from my defense. At the time I was the director of the writing center at Colgate University. I took the position when I first began writing my dissertation, and at the time I didn't know if this was a transition job between being a full-time graduate student and an assistant professor in my field (dramatic literature), or if writing center work was my future. Regardless, I jumped at the position when it was advertised.

My writing center directorship was an administrative position in the department of writing and rhetoric. Before this, I had been the director of the writing center at The Catholic University of America, a position I held as a PhD candidate there in English language and literature, where I worked with both undergraduate and graduate students. Save for a brief stint in radio, I have been a career educator; I have a Master of Arts in Teaching and was a public school teacher before getting my PhD. And I have always enjoyed coaching, whether indoors or out, having been a head high school track coach for ten years.

My wife and I were miserable in the environs of upstate New York, and we missed our hometown of Washington, DC. We decided that moving back home to friends and family was more important than staying in academia.[1] Still, as I was preparing for my dissertation defense, I was on the academic job market. I recognized quickly, however, that the job market in English was soul-crushingly bleak. We knew that we had to leave upstate New York, but the odds of finding a job in my PhD field were slim. And any job I might have had would most likely have been for less money than I was making at Colgate, where the cost of living was low. Taking a job for less money in an area with a higher cost of living just did not make sense—especially with a growing family.

Then, one day Howrey's job listing appeared in the *Chronicle*. From the placement, it looked like the firm's leadership wanted to hire an academic. The job description looked strikingly similar to the job I held at Colgate. Howrey wanted someone who would "develop and deliver a writing curriculum for junior to senior level associates, enabling associates to think rigorously, write clearly, and edit efficiently" and "develop associate's ability to produce written work product with the appropriate organization, style, and tone." Furthermore, they mandated that "curriculum design should include grammar, style, persuasion, paragraph structure and a strategy for approaching the writing process. Curriculum delivery will likely include lectures, workshops, and one-on-one coaching." The writing instructor, they said, would play a critical role in understanding partner requirements for documents and briefs and would tailor associate instruction around these requirements.

For weeks, I had been telling my wife that "it would all work out," that we would end up back in DC somehow. Of course, I had no plan, and not one DC area school had openings in my field. So my reassurances were rather brazen—though "blind" might be a better word. When I saw the *Chronicle* ad, I was vindicated. Literally hours after it appeared, I sent in my cover letter and resume. (Note to those transitioning from academia to the corporate world: cover letters are short, and resumés should be one page, maybe two. They are not CVs. There is a big difference.) I knew an attorney at the firm, so I asked him to put in a good word to my future boss. I called her a couple of days later to set up an interview. Five months later and a few interview rounds later, I was offered the job. In fact, the phone call with the job offer came only ten minutes, literally, after I passed my dissertation defense.

Telling people I coordinate a writing curriculum at a law firm, teaching attorneys how to write better, requires a bit of comedic timing: I usually have to wait a beat for the laughter to subside. However, to litigation attorneys, bad writing is nothing to laugh about. Associates who are weak writers have a dim future, and partners stand to lose millions of dollars when on the wrong end of lawsuits. Litigation attorneys often spend their entire day writing. In fact, one attorney I know tells people he is a writer, not an attorney (cue joke about public perception of lawyers here).

The public's view of legal writing is not a good one. In fact, even among lawyers, it is not a good one. Legal writing is often criticized for its impenetrability. And it is a perception that has held constant for several hundred years. In 1596 an English chancellor ordered a hole cut through the center of a one-hundred-twenty-page document and made the author walk around in public with his head through the center. Thomas Jefferson once lamented that fellow lawyers were accustomed to "making every other word a 'said' or 'aforesaid,' and saying everything over two or three times, so that nobody but we of the craft can untwist the diction and discover its meaning" (490). Charles Dickens complained about lawyers' "liking for the legal repetitions and prolixities" (9). And Jonathan Swift said that lawyers write "in a peculiar Cant and Jargon of their own, that no mortal can understand" (297).

Ask any lawyer about the state of legal writing, and you will hear a list of problems. They know the genre needs fixing, that it is seen by most as painfully verbose and often incomprehensible. A good legal brief should follow one guiding principle: it must be understood by everyone, attorney or not. Some judges tell attorneys, for instance, to write as if their reader is a smart high school student. Others tell attorneys to write as if their parents will be reading. At one legal writing conference I attended, Judge P. Kevin Castel of the U.S. District Court, Southern District of New York told the audience that as writers, "attorneys should imagine their reader as a Martian, descending upon the earth for the first time and reading a brief cold."

Legal writing also needs to be clear and concise for no other reason than judges and their clerks are flooded with written documents. They can read upwards of one-thousand pages per week—on top of court time. They often read at night, when they are tired and hungry. As a matter of efficiency, judges demand concision; many tear off and throw away all offending pages over the limit mandated by the court.

Lawyers also write for other people besides the court, and each audience has different expectations. For example, lawyers write letters to their clients that explain the merits of a case or the likelihood of success if they were to pursue litigation. Sometimes these clients are not attorneys, so lawyers must be able to take a complicated legal concept and explain it in plain English. Lawyers also write to opposing counsel, and these adversarial documents must be coolly argumentative without resorting to histrionics. And lawyers write memos to other lawyers in their own firm. Partners will often ask associates to write a research memo designed to apprise partners of the background of a case, or these partners might ask associates to research the answer to a question, usually one involving whether it is a good idea to take on a new case or client. Because partners are always busy, with papers seemingly scattered all over their offices, memos are not the time for literary flair. They must be concise and on point.

Clarity is also important for the simple fact that persuasion becomes rather crucial when millions of dollars are at stake. Attorneys are not in the business of ambiguity. Furthermore, attorneys and judges usually do not share a similar background. An intellectual property attorney with a doctorate in biochemistry might be writing for a judge with a background in political science. If the attorney wants to win, she must explain her case in plain English, not a toxic combination of legalese and scientific jargon.

And herein lies the irony: every attorney will tell you that legalese is bad, that legal writing deserves its reputation for being "heavy-handed, ponderous, overblown, misleading, and dull" (more words from the aforementioned survey). In this they are unanimous. Yet the writing still persists, even from those who decry its existence.

My role was created by a group of partners at the firm who recognized the value of a full-time instructor. Most firms hire outside vendors to conduct one-off programs and to coach attorneys (what academia calls "tutoring") on their writing. These outside consultants, however, only visit firms once or twice a year, and they are not invested in a firm's success.

Because I was Howrey's first hire for the position of writing instructor, and the only person at the firm with my educational background and academic experience, I was given a simple charge: develop a writing curriculum from the ground up. I decided to play on my academic experience—six years as a writing center director and ten years teaching writing—to simply envision Howrey as another university and to structure my curriculum in this manner. For one, law firms are similar to universities in their hierarchy. Just as students write for their professors, associates write for partners. Associates submit briefs to the partners, who read them and return them for revision. And just as poor students can be kicked out of school, bad writers are often exited from firms. From my perspective, this makes for a motivated group of students—albeit because their careers depend on good writing. I am even a member of an academic department of sorts: Howrey's professional development department, a group responsible for the training of attorneys. My colleagues are academics. One has a PhD in organizational behavior, while another has a PhD in organizational and industrial psychology. I began teaching my writing seminars only two months after starting at Howrey. I knew nothing about legal writing, but I soon realized that partners stress the same writing issues to associates that teachers stress to students. I hear the same themes: thesis statements, topic sentences, organization, paragraph structure, concision, vivid verbs, and classical argumentation, all hallmarks of good writing. So what I teach associates is identical in many ways to what I taught undergraduates.

Still, it was not easy at first to get up to speed on a genre with which I had no experience. Like most people, I thought that legal writing was supposed to be filled with jargon, was supposed to be obtuse, was supposed to be understood only by those in the rarified air of *juris doctors*. This is often what the lay public believes, and they—correctly—express frustration with lawyers who write with no awareness of audience. To be sure, some attorneys believe that obscure legalese will make for a happy client. At first blush, I can see how someone might feel this way; if, as a client, I am paying a lot of money to a firm to churn out motions to the court, I want my attorneys to write something that I am unable to write. That's why I am paying them.

But others create such convoluted prose because it's the only way they know how. They need help learning what it means to be a good writer. And what I realized quickly, as I tore through stacks of legal writing texts, written for both law students and attorneys, is that good writing is good writing, regardless of the audience or genre. Still, because I am not an attorney, I needed to familiarize myself with the discipline. I read legal writing texts, became an active member of the Legal Writing Institute listserv (consisting of legal writing faculty), read legal writing academic journals, and even attended legal writing seminars. I read countless memos and motions. Most importantly, I asked several Howrey partners what they considered to be the characteristics of both good and bad legal writing. We talked about bad habits they wanted me to address and good habits they wanted me to emphasize. (After all, they *are* paying my salary.)

I manage my curriculum around three premises. One, I work with attorneys to help them produce clear and concise writing that can be understood by anyone, even those outside the legal industry. Two, legal writing should be interesting because at its core it is about tension, a guiding narrative principle of a good piece of writing. This means that even the driest antitrust case should aim to be engaging. Third, I am not a lawyer. I do not offer expertise and guidance in areas unique to the genre of legal writing, such as the use of case law and other nuances of court documents.

I am Howrey's WAC coordinator/writing center director/writing professor all in one, with two primary duties. One, I visit each of our offices worldwide twice a year, teaching seminars on writing-related topics. As associates progress through the firm, their writing assignments become more complicated. They require more advanced writing and cognitive skills, just as undergraduates' writing assignments do. For example, first year associates are often charged with writing memos (either factual or argumentative), client letters, or small sections of larger court submissions. They do not write the advanced argumentative documents, such as appellate briefs, that more advanced associates do. This progression mirrors that of the undergraduate experience, where students are asked to tackle more challenging writing assignments as they go.

During each office visit, I conduct three separate seminars, one for junior associates (first and second year associates), one for midlevels (third and fourth year), and one for advanced associates (fifth year and above). Some seminars are unique to the associate level and their writing on that level. For example, junior associates take a seminar on memo writing, a common assignment for their level. Midlevel associates are given a basic course in writing motions. And advanced associates are offered a seminar on appellate brief writing. Other seminars are not as specific to the associate level, but they are offered on a two-year cycle, ensuring that associates take every course as they progress through the firm. For example, junior associates take a course on editing and proofreading for style and another one on punctuation; midlevel associates take one on constructing stylish sentences and another on constructing persuasive paragraphs, while advanced associates take a seminar on creating powerful first impressions in their briefs and another on how to explain complex scientific topics to a lay audience.

One of the most satisfying parts of my job is the freedom I have to construct my curriculum. I have learned to become creative with my courses and to develop them based on the areas that need addressing in our attorneys' writing. For example, because we have a large intellectual property practice, many of our associates have PhDs in the sciences. They have been exposed to—and in some cases, written—journal articles in their areas of specialization. But the attorney with a PhD in biochemistry might be writing for a judge with a background in history. So in one of my seminars, we take articles from periodicals like the *Journal of Biological Chemistry* and the *Journal of Electrical Engineering*, rewriting selected article excerpts for an educated, non-scientific audience. We also use as examples articles from magazines like *The Atlantic, The New Yorker,* and *The Economist,* noting how they take complicated topics and rewrite them for a general audience.

Furthermore, I am even able to use my dissertation specialty in one of my seminars entitled "Using Narrative Theory to Write a Statement of Facts." Legal briefs contain two main sections: a statement of facts and an argument. The facts section is a description of the events of the case: a narrative of whatever brought the two parties to court in the first place, or, if the case is ongoing, whatever conflict caused the writer to submit the current motion to the court. A good narrative is subtly persuasive, taking a side without using argumentative language. In the ideal brief, the judge will read the statement of facts, be persuaded to rule in the writer's favor, then look to the argument section for historical precedent that will give him the rationale for his ruling. In my narrative theory seminar, I use elements of story such as conflict, tension, homeostasis, and character development to teach attorneys how to write a statement of facts that will win the judge over.

But my seminars are not limited to legal writing. I hold a monthly "Great Writing" series, in which we examine writing from outside the legal genre. These are usually magazine pieces. They are not deliberately argumentative—one piece from *The New Yorker,* for example, was a feature about a man who may have been wrongfully executed in Texas for a crime he did not commit—yet they are all unquestionably persuasive. We examine the authors' stylistic devices—everything from tropes and schemes to the rules of style in Joseph Williams's classic text *Style: Ten Lessons in Clarity and Grace*—so that attorneys can apply them to their own writing.

One challenge I face in my seminars is that because we are an international firm with offices in London, Madrid, Paris, Amsterdam, Munich, and Brussels, I work with attorneys whose native language is not English but who write in English. Many of my coaching sessions with these associates address common ESL concerns, such as the propensity of our German associates to write interminably long sentences. Furthermore, these attorneys in our European offices write in British English. Given the differences between British English and Standard American English in issues of usage and punctuation, I modify my seminars accordingly. I work with speakers of Dutch, German, Spanish, Flemish, Greek, Swedish, and Portuguese, among other languages.

Besides teaching, I have other writing-related roles at Howrey, chief being Howrey's writing coach. Lawyers of all levels of experience come to me with drafts of briefs they are writing; I work with everyone from first year associates to experienced partners. Some of my coachees come on their own, while others are referred by more senior attorneys. Writing is one of our key core competencies at Howrey.[2] Attorneys who have deficiencies in their writing skills are told to seek me out for coaching. If their writing does not improve, they are not long for the firm.

I model our coaching sessions after my experience working with undergraduates. The goal of both professional coaching and undergraduate tutoring is identical, at least in the long term: produce a better writer by making the writer do the work. My ground rules are similar to those in university writing centers. We work together for forty-five minutes, and we schedule follow-up sessions on the same draft if needed, because legal briefs can be long—in some cases upwards of fifty pages. Furthermore, drafts go through several revisions, so I will often work with an attorney several times on the same brief.

I hold coaching sessions at a round table in my office, where we sit side by side. I never coach at my desk. I do not copy edit, and all sessions are collaborative with a healthy exchange of ideas. These attorneys recognize that if I do the work for them they will learn nothing, so getting them to participate in the process is easy. I will certainly work with attorneys to correct patterns of error, but ours is a process of discovery, not immediate correction. I might ask the writer to read a passage aloud so that she can listen to how confusing or awkward it sounds, for example, or I might ask the writer about her rationale for using commas in a particular fashion. I might also model correct comma usage in one sentence, then watch as she goes through a paragraph and makes the corrections herself. In addition, I often field phone calls or emails from attorneys who have usage or punctuation questions or who want to run a sentence or two by me to test its euphonic qualities.

Coaching at a law firm comes with two challenges. One is the perception—shared often on college campuses, unfortunately—that equates coaching with remediation. That is, only weak writers need assistance. This probably prevents some writers from seeking me out, and it also exposes an irony: those who see the value of coaching are often the best writers in the first place. I combat this perception by working from the top down, by reaching out to partners and reminding them that coaching is available even to them. This is how word gets around: those partners with whom I work, then, will tell all the associates under them to avail themselves of my services. The voice of one, in other words, falls on the ears of several, and this is the best way to advertise.

The other challenge of coaching can be summed up by what one partner asked me when I interviewed for the position. He said, "We are a blue chip firm. We recruit from the top law schools, and these students went to the top undergraduate institutions. We spend a lot of time during the recruiting process puffing these students up and telling them how great they are. How do you think they will react to someone telling them that, in fact, they are not as great as we said they were, and that they need help on their writing?" Admittedly, coaching can be difficult in a profession known for its egos. Fortunately, I rarely have such encounters. My students are both bright and motivated. Because of this, our coaching sessions are energizing for both parties. This is no editing session, where the attorney watches me suggest changes and then dutifully makes them without hesitation. Instead, this is a thoughtful exchange of ideas, of questions, of comments. In short, it's the ideal writing center session. Attorneys want to become better writers in the long term, which is why so many are even eager to go over a motion that they submitted weeks earlier. So I watch and comment as they create and revise on the spot.

Of course, there is one major philosophical difference between university writing center work and corporate writing center work. At the university level, the honor code rightly prevents the tutor from doing any work for the writer. In this setting, the goal of the tutor is to change the writer, not necessarily the writing. Here at Howrey, my goal is also to help create better writers. But we are a litigation firm, where cases involving potentially tens of millions of dollars are at stake. Consequently, it is absolutely my responsibility to help make what is on the page better—immediately. If I don't, we could lose the case, we lose money, and the firm suffers. Litigation is a competition. I am part of a team, and I want to win. To that end, I collaborate with the attorneys to improve their writing, an act that in a university setting would be academic dishonesty.

In other capacities, I perform duties similar to that of a WAC coordinator or writing center director. I write a monthly newsletter called *Lucidus* that is packed with practical tips on clear and concise writing. This newsletter is great way to publicize my services at the firm. I also consult with partners on how they can give effective feedback to associates. I have begun to create an online writing center with resources to make our attorneys better writers: archived issues of *Lucidus,* links to writing-related web sites, an annotated bibliography of writing-related texts, and PDF handouts on improving almost any aspect of their writing.

I am also called on to resolve grammar and usage issues in patent infringement cases, which are all about language; one side sees the patent claim as meaning one thing, while the other side sees the claim language as something else entirely. It's the job of the judge to rule on what the claim construction language actually means, so in patent cases, punctuation, grammar, and sentence structure are critical. I have been involved in several cases—even conducting my own legal research—in which I have cited rules from grammar texts to prove that a sentence in a patent claim construction means, according to the precepts of English grammar, what our client intends it to mean.

There are many significant differences, naturally, between a law firm and a college. One is the dynamic between writer and evaluator. When partners return briefs to associates for revision, associates are often given little guidance on how to proceed with the next draft. Partners return these drafts to the associates with instructions like "rewrite," but without guidance or suggestions on how—or even what—to improve ("Some of your sentences are too long. Consider shortening them by lessening the distance between your subject and verb," would be a concrete suggestion, for instance). Too often, associates make the change that the partner requests without bothering to ask why the partner requested it. The law firm argument against feedback, of course, is that it wastes time: the billing hour prevents any type of sit-down discussion about writing. The illogic in the thinking is that it is faster for partners to either make the corrections themselves or to redline their changes and ask the associates to accept them under Word's track changes feature. This makes little sense. Time invested working with the associate early in the process, though it might seem inefficient, saves a great deal of time and money: the associate will become a better writer and will not repeat the same mistakes. But because drafts are almost always returned electronically, there is little opportunity for partner and associate to discuss next steps in the writing process. This is where I come in. And if I have had a chance to sit down with the partner beforehand to understand what she deems to be "good writing," I can be sure to stress those points with the associate.

Another difference is that in the law firm climate, writing styles vary widely among partners. One partner's pet peeve can be another partner's preference (for example, the unhealthy obsession with striking *that* from every line). Aside from issues such as verbosity and jargon, good writing is often a murky proposition. One partner might believe split infinitives to be the root of all evil, while others see such a debate as nothing but an impediment to concentrating on matters of good style. This makes for a tenuous line I must walk. An associate will sometimes say that while he agrees with my advice, the partner to whom he must submit his assignment likes it another way. And in this case, all I can do is tell the associate my view and explain my rationale.

Next, law firms are a for-profit business. Partners, unlike professors, understandably are not interested in improvement for the writer's sake unless it also coincides with improvement in the firm's revenue stream. On the college level, faculty strive to improve student writing both as an end in itself and so students might learn skills that will help them after they graduate. Neither goal is an unrealistic proposition.

The greatest challenge I face, though, is the insistence by some on slavish adherence to rules: some useful (commas, semicolons), others made up (split infinitives, beginning a sentence with *and* or *but*). Brock Haussamen, in *Revising the Rules: Traditional Grammar and Modern Linguistics,* writes that rules like the split infinitive and final position prepositions have achieved "grim fame" because "the errors are exceptionally easy to spot. Finding them requires almost no knowledge of grammar; one need only scan the word order to find a word between *to* and a verb, or a concluding preposition. For those over the decades who have worried that their grip on grammar is not what it should be, these are two rules that have been easy to grasp and easy to wield" (138). What Haussamen is saying is that teaching grammar and punctuation is a safe proposition: violations of the rule are easy to spot and are easy to teach. Style, a more nebulous proposition, is hard.

But one can be a wonderful writer who pays only minimal attention to rules (like Ernest Hemingway). Conversely, one can also be an atrocious writer despite flawless punctuation and grammar. Unfortunately, some attorneys believe that good writing is measured by adherence to these rules. As Haussmen says, because these rules are easy to spot, they provide a black and white template to evaluate a writer. With these rules, there is no grey area. You are either a good writer or you are not.

It's easy to understand why attorneys, perhaps more than other profession, enjoy making rules the hallmark of good writing. Attorneys' lives revolve around precedent, which are nothing more than rules established by courts. If they persuade their readers to follow precedent, they win cases. This logic can also be applied to writing. In their view, someone who follows the rules—precedent established long ago—is a good writer.

Of course, legal writing is different from writing in the university setting. Documents must often be produced in a short time span, sometimes in a day or two. Writers who work under such intense deadlines do not have the luxury of sitting in a sun-drenched quad, listening to the birds chirp as they ponder their words. They also often do not have time for substantial revision, and this is no fault of their own. When I coach attorneys in a time crunch, I must do so in the context of time management. What are the three most pressing issues that they can improve, for example? Given that it's 10 a.m. and they must submit the document by the close of business, what would be the most efficient way of editing this document? With procrastinating undergraduates, it's easy to turn pressing deadlines into a life lesson: *had you started the process earlier,* I would tell them, *this would have been a better paper. Learn from your mistakes and don't wait until the last minute next time.* But with attorneys, client requests and court mandates are out of their control and can come at any time. It has nothing to do with procrastination. Instead, it's about writing under intense external pressure.

Another difference between legal writing and college writing is authorship. Legal documents usually have multiple authors. The finished product submitted to the court is a collaborative effort. A handful of associates will each work on a section of a brief, then submit their respective sections to the partner. This partner will make revisions then hand the sections back to the associates, who will then revise and resubmit. Then, the partner pulls the sections together into a formal brief, and this piece of writing is often reviewed by one or more senior partners. It is indeed a very fluid and dynamic process, with ongoing revisions throughout. Briefs are often completed amidst a flurry of emails and meetings. From a coaching perspective, this presents a challenge: when I meet with associates late in this dynamic process, we might be reviewing text that has been revised or rewritten by several authors. As a result, the writing I see in the coaching process may not belong entirely to the associate, thus limiting our effectiveness. This effectiveness is further blunted when we address awkward style, incorrect usage, or poor punctuation that the partner contributed. Associates are often reluctant to revise writing—however much it needs to be revised—from a superior. "I can change it," they tell me, "But the partner will just change it right back." To ensure that my message is delivered firmwide, I offer writing seminars exclusively to the partners on the elements of clear and concise writing in the hopes that my points will trickle down to the associates.

Lastly, the difference between writing for the courts and writing for the professor is purpose: lawyers write to persuade and to convey information, whereas students write to impress and to seek validation for the quality of their writing. Lawyers write because their job depends on it.

When people ask what I do, their first question is, "How can you *read* stuff like that? It's impenetrable." But what these people don't realize is that they are answering their own question. Legal writing is not supposed to be impenetrable. It's my job to ensure that all of these groups find it not only readable, but—dare I say—engaging.

I was once asked by an attorney, rather incredulously, "So do you really *like* this job?" She seemed surprised that I would actually enjoy working with attorneys all day (and remember, she *is* one). My answer, unequivocally, is yes. I travel all over Europe twice a year, working with associates whose native language is not English. My job is rewarding because I work with people who value my efforts at the firm. Undergraduates are sometimes more concerned with getting the A than with learning the material presented. They take the class for the grade, not the knowledge (I will readily admit to having been one of these students). Students in a professional setting, however, recognize that to be successful in their jobs, they must be good writers. As a result, they are eager and enthusiastic learners in the classroom and the coaching setting. To an educator, there is no better place to be.

Notes

1. I wrote in-depth about my decision to leave academia in my article "From Global Lit(erature) to Global Lit(igation) in the *Chronicle of Higher Education*.

2. There are sixteen core competencies at Howrey that attorneys must master to be successful at the firm (that is, to be promoted). Associates who demonstrate weaknesses in one of these areas could be put on review. For example, an associate could be put on six-month review for poor writing skills. If the writing is not improved in six months (the time of the next review), the attorney can be exited from the firm.

Works Cited

Castel, P. Kevin. "Practice Meets Pedagogy." St. Johns University (NY). December 5, 2008.

Dickens, Charles. *Bleak House.* London: Chapman and Hall, 1868. http://bit.ly/d1W42H. Web. 30 March 2010.

Haussamen, Brock. *Revising the Rules: Traditional Grammar and Modern Linguistics.* Dubuque: Kendall Hunt, 2000. Print

Jefferson, Thomas. *The Writings of Thomas Jefferson.* Vol. 9. Washington DC: Taylor and Maury (1854). Web. 30 March 2010.

Opipari, Benjamin. "From Global Lit(erature) to Global Lit(igation)." *The Chronicle of Higher Education.* 16 June 2008. Web. 30 March 2010.

Swift, Jonathan. *Gulliver's Travels.* London: Oxford UP, 1919. http://bit.ly/9oG0Hr. Web. 30 March 2010.

9 My Unexpected Success as a Technical Editor

Shannon Wisdom

Many people in the workplace today cannot write well, and business leaders know this. They recognize the importance and difficulty of workplace writing, but still, little priority is placed on it (Davies and Birbili 439). Systematic training is typically prioritized over writing training, and for this reason, technical communicators—editors and writers—play crucial roles in the modern corporation. There is even a growing body of research on professional writing and entire journals devoted to technical communicators (e.g., *Technical Communication Quarterly* and *Technical Communication* published by the Society for Technical Communication). Individuals with PhDs in rhetoric and composition are well-suited to fulfill the roles of technical communicators, if a position in academia is not available or desirable, and they will likely find such careers rewarding. In this article, I focus specifically on technical editors, more and more common in the modern corporation, respected for their language skills, management skills, and people skills. As a technical editor, I often get to act as teacher, a role I love and long desired. I will describe how my graduate training in rhetoric and composition prepared me for a career in technical editing, even though that was certainly not my initial intention. I will also discuss the areas in which I was ill-prepared, voids that graduate programs must address so that their graduating students have employment options outside the academy.

How It All Began

I graduated with my master's degree in English in the spring of 1992 and luckily got a job as a full-time instructor at Macon College in

Macon, Georgia that fall. I say "luckily" because I had sent in my curriculum vitae in the spring and was told that there were no full-time openings, only adjunct positions. Three weeks before fall semester was scheduled to begin, one full-time instructor gave her notice. Because I lived in the area, the dean called me immediately and asked me to come in and interview. I was given the job.

I was hired to teach first-year composition and first-year English literature courses, and I loved every minute of it. Macon College was a two-year college at the time (it is now a four-year college), offering both day and evening courses, therefore drawing both traditional and nontraditional students. I found satisfaction teaching both types of students, and I discovered that my true love was the composition course, not the literature course. I enjoyed teaching the writing process and everything that came with it—brainstorming, drafting, writing for the audience, revising, and collaborative writing.

I knew that the only way to receive a permanent position or become tenured at Macon College or at any other college or university was to go back to school for my PhD. So, after three years of teaching I applied for admission to the rhetoric and composition program at Georgia State University and was accepted. I began taking classes full-time that fall.

During the program, I prepared myself for a career in academia, enrolling in all the courses that would fulfill that plan—composition theory and pedagogy, history of rhetoric, writing and research methodology, linguistics, American English, grammar, and technical writing. Many rhetoric and composition programs across the country require similar courses, unless students are enrolled in a technical communication graduate program. Then students are offered courses specific to technical communication as well, such as teaching technical and professional writing, technical reports, technical manuals, and technical editing. Many programs also offer courses to prepare students for a career in the university, such as grant and proposal writing and writing for academic publication. I found myself interested in professional writing courses, but I enrolled in them primarily because I thought I might *teach* such courses one day.

After I completed my coursework in 1997, I moved to Vermont with my husband and was hired as an adjunct English professor at Norwich University. The pay was terrible. No full-time positions were available at any colleges or universities in the area, and I hadn't completed my PhD yet, which lowered my chances of attaining a full-time position. I intended to study for my exams and then write my dissertation while looking for my dream position.

While teaching at Norwich, my career path shifted. As my husband was self-employed with no benefits, I needed a full-time position with a good salary and benefits. I started attending meetings of the Vermont chapter of the Society for Technical Communication (STC)—a national organization I had heard of when taking a technical writing course in graduate school. At one of the meetings, I met the publishing group manager for a small telecommunications training company called Hill Associates located in Colchester, Vermont. She was looking for someone to edit training material written by the company's subject matter experts (SME). She liked my rhetoric and composition background and my teaching background, and she believed that both would translate well to editing technical material. The flexibility of the Hill Associates working environment and the salary and benefits package were enticing. Within one month I was working as a copyeditor for the company, and within six months, I was promoted to technical editor; I have received other promotions since. I have been with the company for over twelve years, through the ups and downs of the telecom sector and the economy in general. The company has gotten smaller, but our business has remained the same. We still write and teach our own material, and I edit all of it.

There are likely many graduate students of rhetoric and composition in similar situations. What are they to do if there are no jobs available when they graduate? There are many options for the graduate who writes well, thinks critically, works well with others, and considers whom he/she is writing for. I chose a career in the field of technical editing when there were no full-time teaching jobs available. I did not have the luxury of moving anywhere in the country to get a job, as my husband had just opened a business. I have worked as a technical editor for over twelve years now and have loved every minute of it. Working as a technical editor gives me the opportunity to teach useful, practical writing; my "students" are writing to real audiences, whom they interact with in the classroom—as instructors—shortly after they have "published" their writing. My students get to see how their writing is used and if their writing reaches their intended audience. Finally, my students are not only learning how to write better through their instruction from me, their editor, but also—and more importantly—

through their own experience of writing. From a teacher's perspective, what could be more rewarding? Will I go back to teaching one day? Possibly . . . probably. I do miss it. But for now, this career uses my training well and satisfies the teacher in me.

Corporate Profile and Writing/Editing Process

I work at an organization called Hill Associates, which writes and teaches its own course material on data and telecommunications topics. Founded in 1981, the company markets itself as a premier provider of such training. One of our main competitors, TRA (Telecommunications Research Associates), also writes its own course material, but only in PowerPoint format. What separates Hill Associates from TRA and other competitors is the text that accompanies each visual.

Hill Associates' client list primarily includes major telephone service providers (wired and wireless) and cable companies across the country. We teach a variety of individuals in various positions in their companies—managers, corporate executives, and entry-level or experienced engineers and sales personnel. (Individuals are grouped into courses according to experience level.) When a client purchases a new course, or Hill Associates determines a certain topic needs to be developed, a subject matter expert (SME)—at Hill Associates called a Member of Technical Staff (MTS)—is assigned the task. There are five MTSs in the organization, down from eleven just a few years ago, because of the economy (all male, identified solely for purposes of pronoun use). The MTSs are also our authors and instructors; there are no technical writers on staff. Currently, I am the only technical editor; we have had as many as four.

Typically, an MTS creates an outline for the course, which includes several chapters, and after at least one other MTS/reviewer has approved it, the MTS/author begins work. When the draft is complete, the draft is reviewed by another MTS. After the author reconciles the comments, he submits the draft to the technical editor. The technical editor is responsible for editing content, style, organization, and grammar. The editor is free to rewrite material, but the editor and MTS work very closely together to ensure that the editor does not alter the meaning of the work. During this phase, I meet with the MTS face-to-face or speak over the phone, and I assume the role of teacher, there to help, instruct, and answer questions. I avoid email at this phase, unless I use it to arrange a meeting. This personal interaction helps me gauge the individual's reactions to constructive criticism more accurately and avoid hurting his feelings.

After the editor and MTS have agreed on all the changes, our publishing department compiles the text and visual pages into chapters, and the chapters into volumes. Though each volume is like a book, expanding on a single topic (e.g., Internet Applications), each text and visual pair can be used anywhere else in our course material and in other volumes as appropriate. All of our material must read like a single author wrote it, which makes the author's and editor's jobs even more challenging. In addition, any of our MTSs must be able to teach all of our material. So, the text/visual content and volume organization must be clear and thorough enough to make it usable to all the MTSs.

The Role of the Technical Editor in the Corporation

I started at Hill Associates as a copyeditor. Typically, copyeditors are not required to have any knowledge of the content they are editing. They are responsible for style, grammar, and language use in a text. The copyeditor's task is to make the document correct, consistent, accurate, and complete, to ensure the document's readability. The copyeditor also gives instructions about "how to prepare the text for its final form" (Rude 107). Copyediting tasks and responsibilities do not require as much interaction with authors, and changes made in this phase are often more objective (e.g., grammar, punctuation, format). Copyeditors are also not as likely to be required to possess project management skills—to oversee a project from its conception to its completion.

Individuals with graduate training in rhetoric and composition would certainly be qualified to perform copyediting, but they should not pursue this as a long-term career. Instead, they could copyedit to gain editing skills and work toward finding a position as a technical editor. Such graduates have extensive experience writing, organizing, reading critically, and considering the audience, and their talents and training would be better used in a technical editing position. I was a copyeditor for six months and then participated in six weeks of training in telecommunications (the content I was to be editing), after which I was promoted to technical editor. As a result of the training, I was expected to have a baseline knowledge that would allow me to perform substantive editing: in other words, I could understand the content well enough so that I could identify mistakes in the content and improve the organization and grammar, if necessary.

Graduate training in rhetoric and composition qualifies its graduates to seek an alternate career as a technical editor because they are highly skilled in writing for different rhetorical situations and for different audiences. They are always writing for their readers. Technical editors are in a unique situation, between the author and reader, and they must be able to understand both perspectives. A good technical editor needs to take a *rhetorical* approach to editing (my emphasis)—one that considers the rhetorical situation: the speaker or writer, the message to be communicated, the purpose of the message, and the intended audience (Buehler 459). Students with advanced rhetoric and composition training are able to take such an approach to editing: I do, every day. It is my job to make sure the material written by our telecommunications members of technical staff (MTS) is usable to a variety of audiences—from network engineers with a great deal of subject knowledge and experience to inexperienced new hires of a national telephone company. The audience dictates the language the MTS uses, the level of detail the MTS uses, and the assumptions he makes when explaining different concepts. Without a technical editor to review the MTS's work, the SME might unintentionally write for his peers. I constantly shift between the role of author and reader to ensure the material achieves its purpose and is useful to its audience.

Technical editing can be very challenging work, work well-suited to an individual with advanced academic training. Technical editing involves more than verifying language use, grammar, punctuation, and style—more than verifying the presentation of a finished piece of work. Judith Tarutz defines technical editing as editing material of "any specialized subject that addresses a specific audience, has its own jargon, and whose approach is objective" (4). Some of the skills technical editing involves are reading critically and objectively, reading from the audience's point of view, questioning what you read and reacting to it, and evaluating usability (Tarutz 4). As a technical editor, I edit a variety of materials with technical content, including PowerPoint visuals, text that explains the visuals, business proposals, sales sheets, and website content.

If I wanted to edit material in a different technical field, I could. According to Carolyn Rude in *Technical Editing,*

> Technical editors work on documents with technical subjects. Technical connotes technology, and typical subjects are computer science and engineering . . . but technical editors also edit in medicine, science, government and agriculture, education, and business. A technical editor may be employed in any field for which the documents aim to help readers solve problems or gain information. Because of the specialized subject matter, editors ideally have technical (subject matter) knowledge as well as language expertise (15).

Technical also refers to the "method of working with the subject matter—to analyze, explain, interpret, inform, or instruct. . . . The art and skill of editing require specialized knowledge of the use and methods of making sense of information" (Rude 16). My organization has always hired language experts as technical editors and then provided them subject matter training. This way, the editors are able to make sense of the highly technical subject matter of our training materials and revise our texts so that readers can understand them.

Expectations of the Technical Editor

Collaboration and project management are other key skills required by technical editors. Collaboration is taught to some degree in academia, but it needs even more emphasis there. Thrush and Hooper's study of collaboration between industry and academia found similar results: "The lack of skills for working with clients and colleagues was the most severe handicap . . . and perhaps the biggest gap in preparation of our graduates for the workplace" (312). The two skills I rely upon most, and the two I constantly strive to improve are described below: collaborates well with others and resolves conflicts productively.

Collaborates Well with Others

In 2001, Hill Associates hired a consulting firm to benchmark our job descriptions and salaries, based on national data. The successful Technical Editor must exhibit other skills besides editing, skills, which fall under the larger category of collaboration:

- Manage product through the publishing process
- Interface with authors or other technical staff to provide or assist with rewrites of technical material
- Work with developers and publishing on project organization and procedures
- Possess excellent team work abilities

Moreover, the successful Senior Technical Editor is often responsible for managing the document life cycle, from inception to shipping.

Eaton, Brewer, Portewig, and Davidson found that authors "appreciated editing relationships that were based on a dialog during which both author and editor listened with open minds: they also appreciated relationships that enabled them to ask questions comfortably" (122). Carolyn Rude agrees: "People who enjoy editing collaborate well with people and respect the contributions of people in different jobs" (Rude 17). Finally, Rainey, Turner, and Dayton interviewed 67 technical communication managers regarding the core competencies for technical communicators (of which technical editors are one type) and found that skills in collaborating with both subject matter experts and coworkers ranked top on the list (1).

The person the Technical Editor collaborates with most is the subject matter expert (SME) who writes the material being edited. In my first year at Hill Associates, I had a confrontation with one of the veteran MTSs. When he discovered I had reorganized a page of a document he had written, he was upset, and he forcefully told me not to change something he had written. Graduate school certainly hadn't prepared me for this! I remained calm, kept the focus on the writing, stood my ground, and explained why I made the change. He then calmed down, set his ego aside, read my suggestions and reflected upon them, and ultimately agreed with me. From that point on, he never questioned me again. Until he left the company a few years ago, we collaborated almost weekly, with no problems. I took away from that conflict a valuable lesson. A writer's writing is very personal. I as editor must tread carefully when I make changes, and make sure they're important, purposeful changes. If they are, and I am confident that they will make the document better, then I will be able to explain their worth to the writers. In turn, the writers/MTSs will have more confidence in me.

I have also found it helpful to assume the role of teacher during conferences with MTSs, after I have completed my edit of their writing. They are often vulnerable, insecure about their writing (regardless of their educational background, B.S. or PhD), and they are looking to me for help. I am careful to be kind, noting the positives first and then easing into the negatives. I take the approach that I cannot correct all the writing problems at once; that will take time. And I have definitely seen progress in the writing of the MTSs I edit. For example, I used to spend six hours editing our monthly newsletter, and now I spend only about three hours. The MTS in charge of the newsletter has learned from my comments over time. Eaton et al. also found that writers often view their editors as teachers, appreciating the opportunity to learn from them and improve their overall writing skills.

Resolves Conflicts Productively

Perfecting the skill of collaboration includes perfecting the ability to resolve conflict. Technical editors often act as project leaders, overseeing the project from beginning to end. The team might include one or more writers, illustrators, publishing specialists, and copyeditors. Because technical editors are often managing several people on a project, they will need to know how to manage conflict—that which arises between team members and that which arises between the editor and the writer(s). Although some graduate programs give students opportunities for teamwork, that experience is not yet typical. Most graduate students research and write alone.

The editor/writer relationship can be an adversarial one. Most of the time effective editing prevents negative conflicts, because effective editing helps editors win the trust and cooperation of the writer (as it did in my case). However, editors will often have to defend their editing and engage in a form of conflict to do it. Successful technical editors know how to manage and even encourage substantive conflict among project teams and between the editor and SME. Successful technical editors defer consensus about the project and purposely engage teams in cooperative—not confrontational—substantive conflict, which Rebecca Burnett defines as voicing explicit disagreements and considering alternatives. Burnett (1993), Bernhardt and McCulley (2000), and Palmeri (2004) have all studied substantive conflict among teams in the workplace, noting that while encouraging conflict can slow down the writing process, ultimately it led to higher quality documents.

Are graduate students trained in rhetoric and composition prepared to engage team members in substantive conflict? There is often little collaborative writing in graduate school, aside from the dissertation, and then the power relationship assumes students will follow the direction of their advisor and committee. If graduate students have engaged in peer review in graduate school, I believe they are *somewhat* prepared. The peer review process invites readers to take a critical look at the author's work—asking provocative questions, asking for elaboration, clarification, and support for arguments made. Readers (acting as editors in the peer review process) are invited to express their disagreement with points the author makes and play devil's advocate when appropriate. I rely on my peer review experience and my graduate training to read texts critically when I am editing. I will often go back to the author and ask detailed questions about the author's intention in the material and whether or not I believe the material matches that intention. I am always asking the question, "So what?" of all material I read, meaning, what is the point of the material and is that point clear to the audience? This skill is one honed in graduate school, as we are asked continuously to read texts critically for the points they are trying to make.

Still, experience with the peer review process did not completely prepare me, perhaps because it was not emphasized in all my courses or because I was not instructed to take on the role of an employee during the process. I still viewed myself as a student, part of the academy, reading another student's writing. Neither was I prepared for the defensiveness or insecurity of the authors concerning their writing, even if they are specialists in their fields. I was not prepared for resolving conflict between myself and the MTS or for just how closely I would work with another individual whose project goal was similar, yet so different (he, the writer, I, the editor, but we both have the goal of producing high quality documentation). Finally, I was not prepared for the importance of establishing a good relationship with all authors *first,* so that the editing would progress more smoothly. And then, I did not realize how hard I must continually work to nurture the relationship, encouraging it to grow and develop. Collaboration is a complex process and needs much more focus in graduate programs in rhetoric and composition.

Graduate Training in Rhetoric and Composition and Workplace Collaboration

Given my experience, graduate programs in rhetoric and composition are providing students many fundamental skills for a career in technical editing. I have been able to apply my training in writing, critical analysis, and rhetoric to my career. However, one area needs significantly more emphasis: workplace collaboration.

Yes, often the primary goal of PhD programs is to prepare students for a career in academia, but why not also prepare them for other careers as well, to provide them more options upon graduation and make them more marketable? Perhaps an entire course on collaboration should exist, one that focuses on teamwork, project management skills, building a sense of community in the corporation, and managing conflict. These are crucial skills for technical communicators, specifically the technical editor, who typically manages project teams. One of the managers interviewed by Rainey, Turner, and Dayton would agree, saying that if "she were devising a curriculum for technical communicators, besides covering basic writing and editing skills, information design, and usability, she would require courses in organizational psychology and business to demonstrate to students the fit between technical communication and business goals" (10).

Such courses will certainly emphasize collaboration and teamwork and better prepare students for on-the-job collaboration. Students could work in teams for the entire semester on assigned projects that cover other important topics such as document design, usability testing, and audience analysis. But they learn about these topics by working collaboratively, by writing a document beginning to end together, by engaging in peer review, and by negotiating conflict throughout the process. Part of the final project could include a description of the issues that arose and how the team members navigated through each one. Or, teachers could require a few short projects so that all team members get a chance to act as manager, writer, editor, and peer reviewer; such an approach teaches students how to assume all roles on the writing team. Students might also look for ways to collaborate with each other on research and publication, even if that kind of work isn't encouraged by the program, because it has more transferability than the kind of isolated writing that many graduate students assume they must do. There are many other pedagogical possibilities, too many to mention here—such as workplace/industry collaborations—and the focus of a great deal of ongoing research.

I simply cannot emphasize enough the importance of teamwork and being able to negotiate conflict in the workplace. Remember my story about my confrontation with a veteran MTS at my organization? He still stops by the office twice a year and he always comes in to visit with me. A month ago, he contacted me about editing a course he's writing for his current company, a nationwide technical training company. (His company contracts out editing of course material.) I firmly believe that he contacted me not only because of my editing background but also because of the collaborative relationship we created during our time together at Hill Associates. However, I had to learn on the job to engage in substantive conflict with him, where he and I voiced our disagreements in our author/editor conferences, and I had to learn how to work with him as a team. My graduate school experience did not adequately prepare me for such collaboration.

More time to work on collaborative skills must find its way into graduate level courses in rhetoric and composition programs if we want to prepare students for as many career options as possible. A career in technical editing does not mean an individual is abandoning his/her rhetoric and composition training. In fact, such a career actually puts it to very good use. Ultimately, rhetoric and composition training should not only prepare students for a career in academia but also for a career outside of it—the success of workplace writing depends on the very individuals trained in these areas. Individuals trained in rhetoric and composition will make the whole process of workplace writing that much more effective.

WORKS CITED

Bernhardt, Stephen A., and George F. McCulley. "Knowledge Management and Pharmaceutical Development Teams: Using Writing to Guide Science." *Technical Communication* 47.1 (2000): 22–34. Print.

Buehler, Mary Fran. "Situational Editing: A Rhetorical Approach for the Technical Editor." *Technical Communication* 50.4 (2003): 458–64. Print.

Burnett, Rebecca E. "Conflict in Collaborative Decision-Making." Ed. Nancy Roundy Blyler and Charlotte Thralls. *Professional Communication: The Social Perspective*. Newbury Park: Sage, 1993. Print.

—. *Technical Communication*. 6th ed. Boston: Thomson Wadsworth, 2005. Print.

Davies, Chris, and Maria Birbili. "What Do People Need to Know about Writing in Order to Write in Their Jobs?" *British Journal of Educational Studies* 48.4 (December 2000): 429–45. Print.

Eaton, Angela, Pamela Estes Brewer, Tiffany Craft Portewig, and Cynthia R. Davidson. "Examining Editing in the Workplace from the Author's Point of View: Results of an Online Survey." *Technical Communication* 55.2 (May 2008): 111–39. Print.

Palmeri, Jason. "When Discourses Collide: A Case Study of Interprofessional Collaborative Writing in a Medically Oriented Law Firm." *Journal of Business Communication* 41.1 (January 2004): 37–65. Print.

Rainey, Kenneth T., Roy K. Turner, and David Dayton. "Core Competencies for Technical Communicators. *Technical Communication* 52.3 (August 2005): 323–42. From *General OneFile*. Web.

Rude, Carolyn D. *Technical Editing.* 4th ed. New York: Pearson Education, 2006. Print.

Tarutz, Judith A. *Technical Editing: The Practical Guide for Editors and Writers.* Reading: Addison-Wesley, 1992. Print.

Thrush, Emily A., and Linda Hooper. "Industry and the Academy: How Team Teaching Brings Two Worlds Together." *Technical Communication* 53.4 (August 2006): 308–16. Print

10 Conversing with the Same Field: Same Questions, Different Road

Nick Carbone

As I draft this essay, it has been nearly a decade since I left my life as a full-time, tenure-track academic to work for Bedford/St. Martin's, a leading textbook publisher in college composition, where I now serve as Director of New Media, a role that is one part research, one part pedagogical consulting, and one part developing technology for teaching and learning. What I find, however, is that while my location in the field of composition and rhetoric has changed, much of the work I do, the questions I think about, the people I talk to, remains as it was when I was working as full-time faculty and full-time graduate student, where my work was also divided between research, pedagogical consulting, and developing digital teaching and learning. My current career, then, runs parallel to and often still intersects with friends and colleagues who remain full-time faculty.

To explore those parallels, this essay has three parts: a narrative which describes how I came to be where I am; a description of what I do in my work; and some thoughts on what others can do to carve their own alternative path.

WHERE I AM NOW AND HOW I GOT HERE

I began working full-time with Bedford/St. Martin's in June of 2000, a few weeks after ending my academic career at Colorado State University; in 2002 I became the Director of New Media, a title I still hold. I had joined CSU in the fall of 1998, in a tenure-track role as the writing center director and writing across the curriculum coordinator. Prior to CSU, from fall of 1995 to spring of 1998, I was full-time faculty and chair or co-chair of the English committee at Marlboro College in Marlboro, Vermont. I came to Marlboro while still a graduate teaching associate in the University of Massachusetts, Amherst's English PhD program, which I entered in 1991 after three years of trying to live an adjunct's life at Lyndon State College in Vermont. My teaching career, however, began in 1986 at Boston College, where I worked as a graduate teaching assistant while getting my MA, the last degree I completed.

When I started graduate school for my MA in 1986, conventional wisdom about the future need for PhDs was that assistant professor openings in the humanities would grow. That optimism was given imprimatur in 1989 when William G. Bowen and Julie Ann Sosa published *Prospects for Faculty in the Arts and Sciences: A Study of Factors Affecting Demand and Supply, 1987 to 2012*. My ambition in 1986 was to get a master's degree and then to go back to Lyndon State College to become a full-time faculty member. The year I completed by BA there, all but one of the professors in the English Department had only an MA. But upon completing my MA, I learned that the college was now demanding a PhD, one of the factors that Bowen and Sosa mentioned as a reason more PhDs would be needed. With only an MA, the best I could do was teach as an adjunct, a perilous way to make a living because a promise to be assigned three courses could be undone by enrollment shifts and turn into a semester teaching only one course. I entered a doctoral program, then, because at Lyndon I discovered I really did like to teach, but I didn't like letting myself be exploited to do it.[1]

As it happened, while in the doctoral program at UMass, Amherst, I learned that the thing I liked most about the field of composition and rhetoric was its scholarship, which looked at the classroom to see what teachers were doing and how what they did worked or did not work, often relating classroom observations and studies back to particular theories of writing and learning. For me, teaching is the most fun thing about being a college professor. And teaching writing, to me, is the most fascinating thing one can teach. It's also very important work. As a graduate student and then a faculty member, I liked reading about teaching, researching it, understanding and experimenting with best practices informed by useful theory. I liked talking to other teachers about teaching. And so while at UMass, I got better at working with colleagues; I learned how to give teaching workshops and how to consult with teachers on their writing pedagogies and assignments.

Another part of my life is teaching with technology. I gravitated to that early on, taking students to the computer lab at Boston College's library to teach them how to use the footnote function on the word processor (even though I had to learn how to do it the day before I showed them). When I got to UMass, I asked for a teaching assignment in a networked computer classroom. I hit that classroom at the same time I was learning about composition theory, reading the work of, and talking to, Charlie Moran and Marcia Curtis (who led the teachers in the computer labs) as well as Peter Elbow and Anne Herrington. I found a voice in the subfield of computers and composition through Charlie's mentoring, most explicitly through joining an email list discussion he'd heard about at a conference—Megabyte University. As soon as I joined MBU-L, I found myself conversing with the scholars I was reading in Charlie's course on computers and composition as well as with fellow graduate students. Now those graduate students run writing programs, mentor their own graduate students, and help lead our national professional organizations. When I went to graduate school, the place and timing were perfect in so many ways. I found the right program, with the right people for me, and began teaching deeply with technology at the same time I was learning about composition and rhetoric theory and practice. This timing, this concurrence of theory, practice, technology and fun at applying them all to teaching and thinking about teaching, gave me my voice.

And that voice, especially that online voice, helped me to meet college textbook publishers. One day, at a CCCCs conference in Washington, DC, an editor from Houghton Mifflin asked Eric Crump and me to do a book. To be honest, he mainly wanted Eric, who at the time was a graduate student at the University of Missouri and a very active participant on MBU-L and other lists, but more importantly, he was an indefatigable thinker and tinkerer with online learning, writing, and playing. Eric and I wrote a small guide, *English Online: A Student's Guide to Writing on the Internet*. When the book went into a second edition, Eric moved on to more interesting digital-only projects, and I solo authored.

Working on that project taught me one of the purposes of a textbook: to take what Eric and I knew as techno-rhetoricians and teachers and to make that knowing and doing available to other teachers and students. Extending good techno-pedagogy mattered to me, and so I saw textbooks as a natural and good extension of the things I cared about. The Houghton Mifflin project introduced me to publishers. And publishers introduced me to other scholars in our field. After a conference presentation during which I touched on what I learned about teaching online from writing *English Online*, Marilyn Moller, at that time an editor for St. Martin's College Press, asked me to review some content for Andrea A. Lunsford's and Bob Connor's *St. Martin's Handbook*. I had read a lot of Connors and Lunsford in graduate school, so the request was heady. I wrote what turned out to be useful comments on the manuscript. So Marilyn, who liked my work, introduced me to Andrea Lunsford and Lisa Ede at breakfast during a CCCCs Conference. And Bob later introduced himself to me at the same conference. We talked about textbooks. And teaching. And theory. And writing. And what teachers would need to know about technology. The editor took part in that discussion; she cited articles in our field. She talked about sessions she had been to and how what she heard applied to what Andrea or Lisa were working on in their scholarship and their next textbooks. That was the second major revelation to me: textbook editors know about the field, are informed by it, and sometimes play a mentoring role via introductions and bringing people together.

Meanwhile, I was still a graduate student at UMass, Amherst, working on my doctorate. I passed some early exams, but wasn't moving quite at the pace necessary, and my TA allowance time was running down. However, a nearby liberal arts college, Marlboro College, needed a full-time instructor for one year to co-chair the English committee and to teach writing courses. I got the job, and one year became two, then three. My time at Marlboro coincided with many fellow UMass graduate student friends going on the job market, a market that was not turning out as bright as Bowen and Sosa had predicted in 1989. In fact it was a market that turned out to be dismally the opposite of what they had predicted, but it wasn't until 1994 that their research was questioned (Magner).

Had my doctoral studies been on pace, 1994 would have been my dissertation drafting year, and I would have gone on the market in 1995. It was about this time that the issue of the academic job market and the PhD glut pierced into public discussion, perhaps best marked when two cultural mainstays addressed the issue within a week and a day. On September 22, 1996, Louis Menand wrote "How to Make a Ph.D. Matter," in the *New York Times Magazine* which questioned the inhumaneness of producing so many humanities PhDs in an oversaturated hiring market. That piece appeared after a Doonesbury comic strip cycle on adjunct hiring that ran from September 9 to 14. The strip of September 10 opens outside the gates of Walden College, where the dean stands with a bull horn yelling out adjunct slots, like a farmer rounding up harvesters to do piece work at an unemployment agency. Faculty are assembled, with hiring going to those who will work for the least amount. Thus a Cornell PhD who wanted a two-year contract, medical benefits and severance is turned down for someone who shouts, "Over here! I'll work for food."

At the time, I was aware of the looming job crisis but still confident of finding work when I did decide to hit the market. After all, I was working as a full-time faculty WPA, getting paid as well as I ever had. I had a textbook published and a few articles. I was not confident, necessarily, that I would find a tenure-track job, but believed that if I didn't, things would be okay. I didn't feel that I needed a tenure-track job to be happy and believed that my time in graduate school and in teaching and in learning technology design had given me plenty of other options should the need arise. So I decided to stay in the PhD program while also teaching full-time at Marlboro.

But three years of full-time teaching and running or co-running a small writing program made it even harder to work on the dissertation. Still, UMass and Charlie kept with me, and at me, and I finally got to the point of having a plan for the dissertation and saw an end in sight when, ABD, I took a tenure-track job at Colorado State University as writing center director and WAC coordinator. Looking back, I can see now that my approach to the job search in 1998 was fatalistic. I applied to only three jobs, even though, with my background in composition and rhetoric and technology, I was in one of the few hot fields. Hiring was extremely rough for PhDs with traditional literature degrees, but there was a healthy crop of openings for people in composition and rhetoric studies, with many ads asking for technology experience. In 1998 my family and I moved to Fort Collins, Colorado. But despite being in a good program with supportive colleagues, I began to grow dissatisfied with the non-teaching aspects of faculty life: the committee work; the pressure to publish certain kinds of articles; the scramble for resources; and other necessary—but what were for me—ennui-inducing endeavors that took my focus and time away from the things I cared most about. And let me be clear: I went into the position knowing the requirements, knowing something about the other aspects of faculty work beyond teaching, and knowing too that CSU was supportive in helping faculty to succeed. Further, at CSU, I worked with people who knew technology: Kate Kiefer, a founding editor of *Computers and Composition,* and Mike Palmquist had lead the way in building one of the best online writing resource websites in the field.

Despite those riches, I realized simply that being a full-time academic wasn't a good fit. As the tenure-track job and full-time faculty life became less appealing, I lost interest in revising my dissertation, and finally my dissertation focus dissipated. I didn't finish, leaving the Colorado State English department chair with no option but to not renew my contract.

I still loved the field of composition and rhetoric and the values and commitment of the people in it, the issues it engages, the writers we teach. As I was mulling what to do, I began talking more and more with people from Bedford/St. Martin's. At first the discussions were about what other projects I could help with to have some income while I found a new full-time gig. Then one thing lead to another, and after a few months of conversation back and forth, I flew to Boston to interview for a full-time job with Chuck Christensen and Joan Feinberg, then the president and vice president of the company.

I remember that visit as a third key moment in my understanding of what a publisher does because it was there that Chuck said something I'd never heard before, but that I (and others at Bedford/St. Martin's) repeat often. We were talking about technology and how technology wasn't about books per se, and certainly not just putting a book online. I forget the exact context, but Chuck said, "Well, you know, we're not in the book business. We're in the pedagogical tools business." That made infinite sense: that way of thinking confirmed what I had learned writing the book with Eric for Houghton Mifflin, and it extended my understanding because it recognized that work I cared about—online teaching and learning—had a place in textbook publishing. I found a place where I could continue to think, talk, workshop, write, conference, design, and dream about writing and the teaching of writing in increasingly digital ways.

WHAT I DO NOW

My work now fits into three broad and often overlapping categories: teaching development and support; research in the field; and figuring out where our print and digital pedagogical tools might need to go. When people ask me what I do at Bedford/St. Martin's, the easiest way to explain it is to draw a comparison. When I was at Colorado State and Marlboro College, doing writing and WAC work, I spent a lot of time visiting teachers in their classrooms and offices, talking about writing and the teaching of writing and technology's role in that. That's what I still do, pretty much: I visit teachers and talk to them about the teaching of writing. Only instead of one campus, I travel around the country.

So I see teaching more broadly than I ever had seen it as an academic; I have a deeper and richer sense of the field on a material level. As an academic, my view was limited to my campus and to people I read or talked to at conferences, and to the occasional campus I visited for a workshop or presentation. But now I visit fifteen to twenty campuses a year and work closely with teachers. I see their working conditions; the age of their technology; the colors, dialects, ages, and variety of their students; and how those teachers and students access and use computers. I also see things that go beyond the material and physical: the assumptions about curriculum; the pressures teachers face to meet administrative demands; how decisions get made about technology, about course content and design; what role assessment plays and when and how; and so much more that shapes the life of the faculty with whom I visit.

My travel often takes me to a geographical area, where a single trip over a few days might include visits to more than one campus. So for example, drawing from some notes on a recent trip, I visited a four-year college in one state and then crossed the border to an adjacent state to visit a community college. At the four-year college, I talked to the writing center director about tools for tutoring online and tutor training; with members of the writing curriculum committee about ways to use hybrid teaching to free up face-to-face classroom space and to shift the curriculum to something where more TA participation would be possible (MA students could not be instructors of record until they had enough graduate courses completed); I visited the center for teaching with technology to lead a workshop for writing faculty on doing more with peer review; and I met with a dean about a WAC idea and what that might mean for support of the program.

My visit to a college is often in association with business the program has with Bedford/St. Martin's—one of our handbooks is used in all their first year courses—or that Bedford/St. Martin's would like to get down the road. But sometimes a visit is just a visit, a trip to a campus where we don't have business and where the department has made it clear they're happy with the books and media they have. On those trips, even though there's no direct benefit to the bottom line, the chance to see, to talk, to learn, to understand, to advise and maybe to be of help is worth the visit.

Sometimes I visit a campus not to do something for anyone specific, not to lead a workshop or to consult or to back up a writing program administrator in a meeting with her dean, but simply to learn. It's one thing to do as I used to do—listen to a good conference panel and then chat with a speaker from it, maybe get a handout and a website to visit. It's another altogether to go to that speaker's campus, to see him or her teach.

I see a lot of good teaching with technology, the kind of thing that happens all the time but never gets published or studied because the person doing it publishes on other things or doesn't publish much at all. And even if they did publish on their teaching, or posted to an email discussion list about a classroom practice, my seeing that teacher in action in class with students is the difference between reading about music and hearing music. It's very possible to understand music in the abstract, but you cannot really know it until you hear it. All of us can understand an argument for a pedagogy, but being there and seeing the teaching, observing the students, feeling the vibe of the class and getting a tangible sense of how writers and their instructor engage the technology more powerfully conveys the challenges and promises that the field at large considers and that my colleagues at Bedford/St. Martin's need to know as we evolve the pedagogical tools we hope to offer.

And so the conversations I have in the office with my colleagues, on campuses with teachers, and in conferences, discussions, and as I read the literature of the field, always begin by talking about writing and the teaching of writing. That conversation is the one that has always mattered, the one present in the field's books and textbooks, its journals and collections, its conferences and workshops, and its computer networks and classrooms. It's a conversation I've never left, but because of where I've been able to have it, I know it better now, I think, than I would had my career gone the traditional way.

FINDING YOUR WAY TO YOUR OWN ALTERNATIVE

I have been lucky, blessed really, to have the career I have. I work every day I am in the office with extremely smart and genuinely kind people, many like me who have been teachers, many who continue to teach college writing part-time or who volunteer their time to tutor writers. My colleagues write poetry, fiction, and essays for enjoyment. Many of them have their MAs in the fields they edit (Bedford/St. Martin's publishes in communication, history, and music as well as English), several have their PhDs. I work, then, with people who are very much like you.

And while it might seem obvious, it's worth stating: there are lots of places where you can work with smart people who care about ideas in places other than the academy. These places are not better or worse, just different.

After my final review at CSU, when it was clear I could not stay even if I wanted to, I had a year to think about what to do next, and looked at many alternatives: technical writing, work with educational materials companies, research positions, and other work that involved thinking, working with words, managing programs, teaching, and/or technology. I remember at the time—though the numbers escape me—that there were more offerings in non-academic jobs that I felt qualified for than there were academic jobs I would have applied for had I decided to stay in the academy.

I was diligent. I prepared variations of my CV for different jobs, converting the academic vita into many different kinds of resumes. I wrote letters, practiced how to present myself, and had lined up several interviews outside the academy. I was lucky that in addition to my academic writing, I had done other kinds of writing along the way: worked at a newspaper, wrote some speeches, did some technical writing. I also built on my academic training in other settings: taught in nonacademic venues, worked on political campaigns as an organizer, managed restaurants, freelanced as a researcher. Ultimately, I landed in publishing because I had been working with publishers and came to appreciate the role they play in the field. If you want to expand your academic experience in a way that naturally builds on your expertise, it's a great first step to seek and accept opportunities from textbook publishers to review project ideas, to consult, to attend focus groups, and to propose projects.

And it's necessary for the life of the field's teaching for textbooks and learning technologies to support best theory and practices and to have good scholars and teachers participate in the publishing process. As Libby Miles, a scholar who left publishing to become a tenured professor and whose early work studied the intersection of the field with publishing, notes:

> Reviews are perhaps the most important step in the developmental process of textbook creation—and as professionals in composition studies we can theoretically applaud the mechanism that allows for ample committed, focused, formative peer reviewing. It is both good pedagogy and good practice in writing theory. Unfortunately, too many reviewers do not make most of the opportunity when it presents itself. (39)

Publishers value good reviews. Even fully critical reviews, if they are articulate and reasoned, matter. As Miles notes, very often reviews are not done as well as could be and because they are not, much is lost: a moment of agency for the reviewer is lost, and the chance to do more reviewing, to have more agency down the road is also lost.

The relationship between textbook publishing and the field of composition and rhetoric is deeply symbiotic and complex. As you know from my narrative, my understanding of the relationship is at heart optimistic, downright simplistically rose-colored even. Yet Miles's argument, echoed most recently by Barclay Barrios (2010) remains true: it is essential for composition scholars and teachers to engage the work of textbook publishing when and where they can. Which is to say, not only is doing reviews and other work for publishers a good opportunity to build alternate career pathways and experiences, it is critical, over time, to improving the teaching and learning the field cares so much about.

As for alternative careers, there are, of course, options beyond college textbook publishing. There was always a side of me, even when I was full-tilt intending a career as a tenured professor, that kept an eye and ear open for other opportunities while in graduate school. It was this side of me that led me to apply for only three tenure-track jobs when I went on the market[2]. I also tried to find projects that advanced my professional interests, projects that would open career doors I wouldn't mind pursuing: technical writing freelance work, report writing, workshops for local business on how to write better documents, some speech writing, some copy writing, press release writing, research projects, and other projects that would open non-academic paths.

This variety of work led to my meeting more people in the field, which led to opportunities to publish, do online work and projects, present at conferences, and to participate in the then emerging discussion-list life of the field. That engagement in and with the field, and especially in my case, my work online, helped me to meet others, including those folks who work in publishing. From doing workshops at the CCCCs and other conferences came invitations while still a graduate student to do workshops on other campuses. A lot of the doors that opened for me did so because someone opened a first door: Charlie Moran introduced me to MBU-L and encouraged me to send an article to *Computers and Composition*. I went to my first academic conference—Computers and Writing—and met people face to face whom I had been talking to online for over a year. I talked to publishers there confidently about their products and ideas, and they asked me to look at other things.

And so it goes: networking matters. I was mainly able to slide over into publishing because I had met and worked with publishers. I found myself drawn to the folk at Bedford/St. Martin's because they most often talked about teaching and writing and technology in the ways that I was used to talking about those issues with people in the field. They talked a lot like me, like us.

And writing matters: the writing done on email lists, Twitter, Facebook, blogs, and other places where one's intellectual life and academic thinking are there to be read matter. People read what you write and come to know you before they meet you because of what you write. What you present at a conference and how you present matters. Reviews that you might do—whether for a journal, a scholarly press, or a textbook publisher matter. The insights that you share with the authors of the pieces you review matter. It all matters, it all makes a difference in many ways, and it all contributes to your getting noticed, heard, known, and trusted.

I know part of my success came from being heard in nontraditional as well as traditional spaces. This is truer now than it was twenty years ago when I began. When we're considering whom to invite to a focus group, whom to visit on campus, whom to ask to do a review, we ask people in the field whom we already know, but we pay attention, too, to discussion list postings, to conference presentations, and to blogs and social networks.

The online professional presence matters. It's an accumulative presence, made up of the work and participation you might do in many online places. It's a powerful tool because it gives you the freedom to be who you are beyond the walls of your local program. These online tools can accelerate entry into the national conversation. You still need to participate in the traditional paths of the field—conference papers, journal articles, the dissertation and defense, perhaps a book—as you go, of course, to keep open the most options. Your work and presence online, however, is unique in that whatever path you choose—a traditional academic path or an alternative path—your online work will be explored by those whom you meet professionally or apply to meet in an interview.

Use all this to your advantage. Construct a professional voice and presence online that you will be happy to stand by, that present you as someone another person will want in their professional lives: as collegial, kind, rigorous, caring, curious, patient, and smart. In other words: be yourself.

Notes

1. What counts as exploitation has changed for me. When I began adjunct teaching with an MA in the hopes that magically the college would make me full-time, I was letting my deep wish for full-time work cloud my choices. I snapped out of that quickly when I went in one fall to see what three courses I would have—three was the max because four would have been full-time and benefits would have kicked in—only to discover I had one course. The next day I was filling out paper work for food stamps, and the day after that, the application for a PhD program. But now that my livelihood doesn't depend upon monies from adjunct teaching, I enjoy doing it from time to time. The pay is probably less, in terms of buying power, than what I earned in 1987–90. But the pay isn't absolutely essential and my ambition is no longer to be a full-time teacher. Thus the same job that felt exploitative to me once, no longer does because I do it for different reasons: choice not desperation.

2. Sending so few applications was a risky approach but I took it because I was prepared to walk away if it didn't work and was prepared to find other

work where writing, teaching, and research skills mattered. I believe that this attitude—the readiness to look elsewhere and the expectation that one might have to—is increasingly essential for the mental health of PhD candidates because things have only gotten more dire since 1997. Tenure lines have continued to be eliminated overall, and the reliance on adjuncts has grown, while the number of PhDs has continued to outpace the demand as tenure-track jobs in English decreased forty percent from 2008 to 2010 (Lu).

WORKS CITED

Barrios, Barclay. "On Custom: Revisiting the Relationship between Publishers and WPAs." *WPA: Writing Program Administration.* 33:3 (Spring 2010): 10-33. Web. 29 July 2011.

Bowen, William G., and Julie Ann Sosa. *Prospects for Faculty in the Arts and Sciences: A Study of Factors Affecting Demand and Supply, 1987 to 2012.* Princeton: Princeton UP. 1989. Print.

Lu, Emily. "Job Seekers Face Historically Weak Academic Job Market." *The Association of Writers & Writing Programs Job List.* November 2010. Web. 12 August 2011.

Magner, Denise. "Junk Analysis." Blog Post. "On Hiring Blog." *The Chronicle of Higher Education.* 15 May 2009. Web. 14 August 2011.

Menand, Louis. "How To Make a Ph.D. Matter," *New York Times Magazine,* 22 September 1996. Web. 12 August 2011.

Miles, Libby. "Constructing Composition: Reproduction and WPA Agency In Textbook Publishing." *WPA: Writing Program Administration.* 24.1–2 (Fall/Winter 2000): 27-51. Web. 10 August 2011.

Trudeau, Gary. *Doonesbury.* Comic Strip. 9 September 1996. Web. 12 August 2006.

11 Mentoring for Change

Cindy Moore

As previous chapters demonstrate, our notions of what it means to achieve professional success must change to reflect both the shifting landscape of the academic job market and the complex realities of our varied lives. The tenure-line research university positions promoted in the past as a kind of academic gold standard are not only diminishing but the prospect of a life guided by a "publish or perish" mantra has lost its luster—especially among people who pursued (or are pursuing) graduate degrees with the primary desire to serve others through teaching and/or administration. Additionally, more and more holders of advanced degrees in English are finding fulfilling, well-paid work outside academe, often within their local communities. In the face of these new realities, we cannot continue to define success in traditional terms.

Successful Mentoring as More than Good Relationship

Of course, redefining success means rethinking how we support students as they work to achieve fulfilling lives during and after graduate school. Groundwork for this kind of rethinking was laid in the 1990s by scholars across the disciplines who were concerned that traditional mentoring relationships did not fully accommodate the values and perspectives of an increasingly diverse population of graduate students. Such scholars, many of whom had experienced (either first- or second-hand) no mentoring or poor mentoring of females, returning adults, students of color, and/or of working-class backgrounds, called for moves away from dyadic, hierarchical and unequal relationships toward more reciprocal, collaborative relationships (see, for example, Brand, Cain, Enos, Ervin). This work was enhanced by other articles that outlined the benefits of pairing students from nontraditional backgrounds with faculty mentors from similar backgrounds—and the difficulties of making these arrangements in disciplines where potential mentors (of like gender, race, ethnicity) were scarce (Cullen and Luna; Turner and Thompson).

While this work prompted many professors to think carefully about the composition and power dynamics of the mentoring relationship itself, it did not inspire much public examination of mentoring content, i.e., the messages about professional development and success conveyed to students. Much like the tension felt in a "student-centered" writing class in which participants are encouraged to write formulaic texts, the typical mentoring relationship—no matter how friendly—has been compromised by a growing mismatch between the desire to empower students, on the one hand, and the desire for a standardized professional product or "text," on the other. In fact, throughout the literature, while there appears to be a conscious effort to change the dynamics of mentoring, the imagined product of mentoring has remained amazingly consistent: a full-time, tenure-track job at a research university. Indeed, the push to prepare students for research-university positions by, for example, emphasizing conference presentations and publications, has been palpable enough for scholars like Janice Lauer to worry about the potential negative "side effects" (including premature subject-area specialization, superficial scholarship, and delayed completion of the dissertation) of conflating work required for graduate school with that required for tenure and promotion (231–32).

As a result, narratives of even the best mentoring *relationships* (i.e., relationships "based in mutuality—of learning, trust, risk, care, and challenge" [Cain 113]), told from the student perspective, too often seem unresolved, ambivalent, and even bitter. For several years, I helped organize an annual mentoring panel for the CCCC Committee on the Status of Women, through which graduate students and new assistant professors shared stories about the professional mentoring they received (or didn't). Aside from the expected stories about disagreements over dissertation topics or forms, I heard many heart-wrenching narratives about advisors who conveyed dismay or disappointment when advisees expressed an interest in "just teaching" or finding alternative work close to home. Some participants even reported that advisors withdrew wholesale from mentoring relationships if they sensed that students were uninterested in pursuing a traditional career path. Indeed, the title of the sessions, taken as a group, easily could have been something like "They want me to be like them and are disappointed that I'm not."

Such a perspective on the final outcome of mentoring seems especially problematic for a field that has been at the forefront of promoting student-focused teaching, self-critique and reflection, and alternatives to traditional views of writing, research, teaching, and the tenure/promotion guidelines they might inform. It also raises an important question about what we really mean when we say, through our scholarship on mentoring, that we support relationships based on "respect, candor, trust, intimacy, even love" (Brand 64). According to the past decade of MLA job-placement statistics, we continue to admit forty to sixty percent more students into our programs than can reasonably expect to obtain and keep traditional academic jobs (MLA 10). If our perception of student need is limited only to desires associated with a single career path, how compassionate are we really being? More pointedly, if a mentoring relationship works only to prepare someone for a job that is nonexistent, how respectful is it, really?

Questions like these force us to confront the uncomfortable possibility highlighted by Marc Bousquet and other cultural critics: that maintaining hundreds of graduate programs and enrolling thousands of students against the backdrop of an ever-shrinking academic job market allows universities (and, by implication, all of us who enjoy well-paid, secure university employment) to offer instruction as "cheaply" as possible (Bousquet 222). Graduate-degree-granting universities appreciate the savings realized when graduate assistants teach the introductory courses that might otherwise be taught by tenure-line faculty, and the larger "academic labor system increasingly prefers" hiring the most minimally qualified instructors for the lowest possible salaries and with the least amount of institutional commitment (222–23). Additionally, most professors enjoy graduate teaching, as well as the status it confers, and would resist giving it up in the interest of shrinking the "supply" of students whose expertise and experience are no longer in "demand." It is also true that there is steady demand for graduate education, despite the poor prospect of full-time academic employment.

Given that universities and faculty will not readily abandon the privileges and status that graduate programs help ensure (and, thus, will continue to start new programs and fill-up existing ones), and in light of the fact that students will continue to seek specialized training for jobs that don't exist, the least we can do is ensure that our students understand what the real opportunities are for them, what the pros and cons are for various options, and how to develop the skills they will need to secure the positions they seek. That is, the least we can do is provide informed, thoughtful, *useful* mentoring for all of the students we admit.

Mentoring for All

A mentoring program that is responsive to the needs of all students must extend the concept of an openness to "other" threaded through much mentoring literature beyond obvious differences in gender, age, race, and class to incorporate differences in goals and expectations. Further, responsibility to students must extend beyond emotional support to an intellectual recognition of current employment realities and the willingness to accept and communicate these. While many of us who work with teaching assistants admonish them to accept the fact that "your students aren't you," we are not very good at applying this idea to our more general professional mentoring of graduate students. Our students are not us, and the career prospects they have are not necessarily what they were for us.

While larger academic systems may chug along as if neither students nor universities have changed in the past fifty years, individual professors interested in mentoring that is both responsive and responsible to all students would do well to acknowledge—and help their students understand—"what's (truly) what." Since earning my PhD in 1998, I have tried hard to do just that: to develop an approach to mentoring that is supportive of students, but also realistic about what they can expect to do with the degree(s) they earn. My inclination in this direction had something to do with my early relationships with peers who felt misled, under-informed, or uninformed about career options and prospects. It also reflects my own experience as a graduate student, working with many faculty members who encouraged me to pursue my own objectives without, at the same time, discouraging me from aspiring to goals they once had. This approach, which I helped facilitate in various ways at three MA-granting universities, is based on three principles, outlined in a professional-development guide I recently co-authored with Hildy Miller: 1) help students determine what they want to do with a graduate degree and why, 2) guide them in determining whether their goals are realistic and, if so, what they need to do to successfully reach these goals, and 3) educate them about alternatives to the traditional academic career path (without minimizing attention to—or appreciation of—that path). Though my own mentoring efforts have been focused largely on master's-level students, these same principles can be applied to work with PhD students.

Determining—and Honoring—Students' Goals

Graduate professors often assume that the application to graduate school follows a thoughtful assessment of career goals on the part of the student. After all, students typically say in their application letters that they want to pursue research on this or that, work with this or the other scholar, and teach "at the college level." The problem is that while most students who perceive themselves as capable of graduate-level study would naturally be adept at writing a persuasive application letter, they may not actually have a good sense of what their stated goals truly mean—and what the attainment of these goals really will require. In their recent study of student perceptions of life after graduate school, Jeffery Bieber and Linda Worley found, for example, that undergraduates tend to "cobble together" an image of a university faculty member as someone "who, primarily, teaches and mentors" (1018) and enjoys a lifestyle of "flexibility" and "personal autonomy" (1020). In my own work with upper-level undergraduates and new MA students, the lack of real knowledge about academic life is well-illustrated by these common scenarios:

- the student who wishes to "teach at the college level," but doesn't understand that, unless one continues on for a PhD (yes, even in creative writing), this goal typically translates into teaching part-time, with no job security, low pay, and no benefits (and, of course, these days even a PhD is no guarantee of anything);
- the student who wants to teach Shakespeare, without an awareness that relatively few faculty members teach only Shakespeare, let alone only literature;

- the student, unfamiliar with typical teaching and service demands, who wants to be a professor, so she will have plenty of time to work on her own writing;
- the student who cannot move, has no intention of moving, but wants to "teach at the college level" in a city (or state) that has only a handful of universities.

Without some type of early intervention, Bieber and Worley suggest, students' "ideal scripts" of academic life will have "extraordinary resilience and staying power" (1024).

Helping Students Explore Goals

The first phase of a responsive—and responsible—mentoring program is to help students articulate (or refine) their goals and understand what these goals mean. Ideally, such mentoring would occur during the undergraduate program, and it does, to some extent, at many universities. It is not uncommon these days for an English department to offer a workshop on "what to do with an English degree" that includes some attention to the pros and cons of graduate school. Another approach is to require or strongly recommend an on-campus interview, as part of the graduate-school application process. During the interview, a graduate advisor can make clear the realities of academic life, including graduate school, as well as the job market in students' areas of interest. Of course, many students cannot appreciate even the best advice, even the most hard-nosed narrative of scholarly rigor or the most dismal job-market account, until they experience it for themselves—until they get their first B or C on a scholarly paper, until they spend fifty to sixty hours per week on their course work and teaching, until, as TAs, they share offices with part-time instructors who have MFAs and PhDs, and even good publications, but have not been able to find well-paid, permanent employment. For this reason, professional mentoring must occur in a sensitive, systematic way throughout a graduate program.

Helping graduate students examine and understand their career goals can be done informally, through classroom discussions directed by a single faculty member, and/or more formally, through a series of program-sponsored workshops. Depending on the particular context (e.g., level of students, size and kind of program), students can be surveyed informally in class, with a question like "So, what are your plans after you finish your degree?" or more formally with a printed questionnaire that lists possibilities, including, for instance, full-time university teaching, community college teaching, secondary-school teaching, editing, writing, or program administration. Discussions and/or workshops are then designed around the most popular topics, with the dual purpose of exploring what (in terms of aptitude, experience, expertise) attaining the goals will require and considering the likelihood of meeting presumed requirements.

As suggested above, a crucial part of the surveying is providing students with the most comprehensive sense of career possibilities. Beginning MA students, for example, need to know that there are many career options within the academy—not just "teaching at the college level." In addition to teaching, program-level administrative jobs are a promising option for graduate students who have experience as, for example, administrative assistants in writing centers, composition programs, or ESL programs. Further, there are opportunities for students with good writing and editing skills at university-run presses and PR offices. Outside of the academy, possibilities for people with teaching experience and strong communication skills abound. Graduate students I've known or mentored have gone on to become teachers in public and private high schools (in America and abroad); writers for nonprofit agencies; textbook editors; and freelance writers.

The most comprehensive (and, arguably, best) approach to helping students fully explore career options is a professional-development series, sponsored by a department's graduate program. The series is titled something like "What to Do with Your Degree" and includes three to five sessions focused on different career paths, within and outside of academe. Ideally, the sessions are organized collaboratively by a faculty member from each sub-field represented in a department. Depending on the particular composition of the department, representatives might include specialists in literature, creative writing, composition and rhetoric, TESOL/ESL, and/or English education. Individual sessions are then planned according to student interest, but also according to the calendar. For example, if a number of MA students indicate an interest in applying for PhD programs, it is helpful to offer a PhD-focused session in early fall (well in advance of winter deadlines). A community-college teaching workshop might best be placed early in the spring semester, as job ads begin to be posted.

Because these workshops are meant to inform students not only about the options themselves but about the reality of the job market and experience required for various jobs, organizers should plan on ninety minutes to two hours for each session. Most workshops I've conducted began with a general introduction to the topic, followed by a presentation of both anecdotes and facts by various faculty members, and then a discussion of how to prepare for the particular career focus. It is even better if the last part (preparation) includes a hands-on activity of some type (e.g., drafting a resume or teaching-portfolio contents page). A good illustration is the "Community College Teaching" workshop I've helped facilitate several times. Typically, it begins with an overview of what a community-college teaching position usually involves (e.g., the kind and level of instruction, service expectations, scholarship requirements)—and how such a position may differ from other types of academic roles. Copies of job ads from a variety of community and two-year colleges can be of great help here. Working inductively, a workshop facilitator can ask students to study the ads and make a list of common requirements. This list, then, guides discussion focused on how students might prepare themselves for community college positions. Faculty and students observe, together, that such positions typically require experience teaching both standard and developmental composition to a diverse population of students, as well as introductory courses in literature and creative writing. In many cases, expertise in ESL or technology is a definite plus. If students who are inclined toward community-college teaching understand these requirements early on, they can choose elective courses that will provide them with such expertise (e.g., courses in ESL pedagogy or Web writing); apply to work in the writing center or other tutoring program; and ask to assist with or guest-teach classes in areas where they may not normally get teaching experience.

In the interest of responsibility to students, such a session should also involve frank discussion about job prospects. With respect to community-college teaching, this sometimes means disillusioning students of the notion that they can easily get a community-college teaching position in their hometown. I have often referred to current rosters of community-college faculty to show that many faculty not only hold PhDs these days but earned their degrees out-of-state. Such a discussion naturally dovetails with a professional-development session on pursuing the PhD because, as many of us know, community colleges have become a viable option for PhDs in glutted sub-fields, thus narrowing opportunities a bit for MA-credentialed applicants. Another current reality is that, much like comprehensive and research universities, community colleges are now relying more than ever on contingent (semester or yearly contract) faculty (both full- and part-time). For sessions like these, it can prove very helpful to invite guests from outside the university to participate in the workshop. The last community-college teaching workshop I co-facilitated featured the Humanities chair of a local community college, who talked about job possibilities in her department, what her department looks for in a potential colleague, and the kinds of experiences that are valuable for applicants. (Two students who attended and took her business card were hired by her the following year.)

Supporting Students as They Refine—or Change—Their Goals

While the ostensible goal of mentoring workshops like these is to help students explore and refine their goals, one common result is that students change their goals, sometimes drastically, based on the information and advice provided. Students whose initial goal was pursuing a PhD may opt for community-college teaching, for example, after they learn through thoughtful, thorough, honest mentoring the realities of post-graduate job markets, program-application requirements, and the diminishing prospects of even the best students being accepted into top programs. Those who had assumed that they could pursue graduate work and obtain well-paid employment in their home state—or even hometown—turn their attention to public-school teaching after realizing that in all but the largest metropolitan areas, well-paid university teaching positions are relatively scarce and that universities typically do not hire their own former students. Sometimes, students who are pegged early on as academic stars, easily capable of getting into the best programs and enjoying the best selection of professorial positions, decide to pursue a career in editing, after researching and writing their tenth seminar paper on Lawrence's later poetry—and discovering that their work on Lawrence's later poetry probably would need to sustain them through tenure.

One of my former graduate students, Karen, offers a good example of how important it is to help students articulate their goals early on in their programs, support them as they refine those goals, and affirm decisions that we may not have made ourselves. Like many new MA students, Karen started graduate school thinking that she would go on to get a PhD "in some area of English," as she put it. Now, three years later, she is enjoying her first year of public high-school teaching in her hometown. As she explained in a recent letter to me (which I've abridged below with her permission), her decision to forego a PhD (and, later, an MFA in creative writing) was made based on discussions with various faculty, from diverse subfields within English.

> ... after all the comments I'd heard during the last couple of years from you [and others], about the prospects of getting accepted into a [PhD] program and the even dimmer prospects of landing a full-time teaching position afterward, I began to think better of it. This is not to mention the fact that I wouldn't really consider moving somewhere else while my kids are still here in college.
>
> After getting to know [Professor A], I really thought about getting an MFA and just teaching part-time at ___; I thought I'd have time to focus on my creative writing. [This professor], who I have a lot of respect for, asked me when I would have time to write if I were teaching two or three classes each semester on a part-time basis (with part-time pay, she pointed out). She said I should be realistic about the amount of time it would take to teach two or three classes a semester. Then, Professor B told me he had to get a PhD after he had his MFA because he couldn't get a full-time teaching position on the college level without it. I also knew that every time a position came open, around 200 people applied.
>
> I remember several times in class that you talked about the shortage of teachers in high schools. ... I always felt that you encouraged us to be realistic about our prospects if we were to pursue a terminal degree. I think I always felt that while not discouraging us from applying, you were realistic and suggested we keep our options open—that we shouldn't depend on getting into an MFA or PhD program, that we should consider other positions both in and out of academia.
>
> You made a point of usually asking us during [our composition pedagogy] class how we would react to particular situations in the classroom if that classroom was in a high school.

> Every time you said that it made me consider how I would react in a high school classroom. Even though I never consciously considered teaching on the high school level. . . . I can see now that maybe I was preparing myself for it mentally for quite a while.
>
> Economics became a factor too. [My husband's] business is dwindling and he is nearing retirement. Working five minutes from home made sense for me. . . .

As Karen's experience suggests, rather than submit to the temptation to tell students to "stay the course," as we may have been told by our own mentors, it is probably more appropriate—and less presumptuous—to support them in pursuing their newfound path. Though some students will find that it's too late to take different kinds of classes, they may still have time to participate in extracurricular activities, such as program administration (e.g., helping with assessment); service initiatives (e.g., revising the department's Web site); campus-sponsored workshops; or exchange teaching with a community college. Students nearing the end of their studies also can be encouraged to pursue postgrad certificates in areas like technical writing or ESL teaching.

REQUIREMENTS, REWARDS, AND RISKS

As suggested above, a mentoring program that is sensitive to students' diverse goals and interests as well as changing job-market realities requires a shift in perspective on the end-result of our efforts. Such a shift requires, first and foremost, that we confront—and let go of—the feeling that what worked for us should work for all of our students. This shift is more difficult than we may think. Those of us who happily left home to attend graduate school and then happily moved again (or in my case, again and again and again) to take advantage of new opportunities have trouble understanding why anyone would want to stay in one place and, beyond that, sacrifice a better-paying position for a less-secure one close to home and family. Similarly, if we started our own careers as public school teachers, community-college teachers, or part-time instructors at universities (I did all three) and returned to graduate school to escape what we saw as unappreciated, untenable work, then it will be hard to see why our students seek such positions—and actually enjoy them when they get them.

Another former student, Kelli, is a good case in point. Though I was very supportive of her desire to apply for community-college teaching positions near her hometown, I also encouraged her to keep a PhD program in mind. As a TA, she loved teaching—and excelled at it—but she also showed great promise as a writer and scholar. Toward the end of her MA coursework, she began to apply for jobs at community colleges, thinking "maybe it would be okay [to] take a break from school before [getting a] doctorate." She was hired for a two-year temporary position which then turned into a full-time tenure-track position, not far from home.

When I contacted her recently for her insights about the topic of this chapter, I was expecting that, after nearly five years of teaching a five-five load of composition at a community college (which she translated for me as "500 papers per semester"), she would ask me about a reference for a PhD program in Comp/Rhet, so she could move on to greener grasses. Though, as her email to me made clear, her workload is "intense," she loves her job, and thoughts of a PhD have grown more and more remote. Given my commitment to supporting students' varied interests, I have to admit that I was surprised by my own surprise at how she described her devotion to her community-college teaching, despite the long hours:

> My primary motivation [to teach] was loving writing, but what sustains me is the love of the students, and the community college setting delivers an interesting variety of folks. It has also enhanced my teaching as it has forced me to be innovative to reach as many students as possible. I change assignments and lesson plans every semester to best meet the needs of the students. I can also say that the pay is comparable to a four-year college.

Letting go of narrow visions of success demands acknowledgment that times change and, with it, the willingness to keep up with current job-market trends in academia and elsewhere. If all faculty are involved in mentoring, representing the various sub-fields in English, then it should be enough for each area representative to follow the trends in his/her own subfield. Routine professional reading will need to expand to include periodicals that publish "state of the profession"-type articles and reports, periodicals like *The Chronicle of Higher Education*, MLA's *Profession* and *ADE Bulletin*, and AAUP's *Academe*. Yearly glances at graduate-program directories can help faculty at master's-degree institutions stay abreast of low-residency options for students, like Kelli, who might wish to keep their jobs while pursuing an MFA or PhD degree during winter and summer breaks. For possibilities outside of academia, faculty might do well to keep in touch with colleagues or alumni who have found fulfilling work in the private sector and can suggest relevant career guides and job lists for students interested in such work.

To be sure, there are challenges to a mentoring scheme that embraces change. First, students themselves may not be able to appreciate the reality of faculty lives or be willing to seriously contemplate alternative career paths. Despite exhaustive attempts on the part of faculty to dissuade students from outfitting their professorial offices before they have even finished their course work or taken their exams, a few will imagine themselves as the exceptions, the ones who will beat all odds. One way I've handled resistance to even considering other options is to ask students to sketch out a Plan B, "just in case" their Plan A doesn't pan out.

It also may be hard for some graduate programs to encourage students to take advantage of opportunities that will support alternative careers (e.g., tutoring assignments, editing internships, administrative assistantships), if these opportunities don't exist. Some departments solve this problem by teaming-up with other schools or programs in their local vicinity. A good model for this type of professional exchange is the Preparing Future Faculty program, whose institutional members often arrange for teaching exchanges with other members. (See http://www.preparing-faculty.org.)

If the mentoring program is a required component of graduate study, some faculty members (especially those in PhD programs) will worry that professional development workshops not directly related to the traditional academic path may take up time that students with traditional goals should be spending on scholarship. This concern can be alleviated through an approach that emphasizes how research and writing is valued in all pursuits, whether a student imagines himself as a tenure-line literature specialist or wishes to start a freelance writing business. Sessions devoted to writing for publication might include attention to both scholarly publication and nonscholarly publishing, writing within the university and writing outside it.

Ironically, students who show scholarly promise may, *because* of responsive, responsible mentoring, opt for a teaching- or service-oriented career. In fact, it is possible, that a good mentoring program will actually inspire students to leave graduate school altogether and take a position that does not require academic credentials. If a university, program, or faculty gauges its success by the number of students who pursue advanced study or find full-time academic work, then statistical failure is certain, as these students will not be accounted for. However, if program success is evaluated in terms of students' own feelings of career satisfaction three, five, or ten years later, then the results will be different and, I would argue, both quantitatively and qualitatively better.

In addition to being responsible and respectful, the best mentoring programs are collaborative, involving as many graduate faculty as possible (preferably, all graduate faculty) as well as alumni and local community members, when appropriate. On a practical level, an emphasis on collaboration helps programs address two of the most common problems noted by faculty advisors: lack of time and lack of attention to mentoring in faculty-reward systems. If the primary mentoring vehicle is a professional-development series comprised of four or five ninety-minute sessions per year, individual faculty should feel less burdened than they would if they were solely responsible for five to ten students, all with varying career interests. Additionally, if all faculty members are sharing the mentoring load, they will be more likely to speak with a single voice about the importance of mentoring to the well-being of students, the department, and the university.

Another practical benefit of collaborative mentoring is that it brings together professors who may only rarely have reason to talk with each other. In my experience, one form of collaboration has often led to other types, including more readily working across sub-fields on curricula, new-teacher orientation and training, and TA office-space allocation. If approached in the right spirit, formal collaborations will not only promote a sense of common cause across a faculty but set a good example for students who too-often perceive their professors as isolated from each other, if not downright hostile.

With more participants, come more—and more-diverse—perspectives, which can help students more fully understand and appreciate various career prospects. Practically speaking, students will believe what they hear more readily if others are affirming the point. It is one thing for me, as a composition and rhetoric specialist, to say that it's difficult for students to get into literature PhD programs or to get jobs in creative writing; it's another thing for a newly hired literature specialist to talk about her experience applying to fifteen PhD programs and getting accepted by two or for a creative writer to talk about his experience applying for fifty full-time teaching positions and landing one campus interview. When faculty don't agree, as may be the case with the benefits and drawbacks of nontraditional career paths (e.g., high-school teaching), if differences are framed as potentially productive, they can prompt students to consider a topic or, in this case, a career area more thoroughly and deliberately.

Theoretically, a community-mentoring model makes sense as well. Our social-constructivist theory tells us, for example, that we develop a sense of ourselves or, in the case of graduate school, a *new* sense of ourselves through engaging multiple discourses and the diverse perspectives they reflect. Such a multivocal approach is supported by research and theory on graduate TA preparation offered by scholars such as Wendy Bishop, Nancy Welch, and Catherine Latterell, who contend that "WPA-centric" practices (Latterell) and "conversion models" (Bishop and Welch) of scholarly exchange may alienate both TAs and other writing faculty and give the (false) impression that there is one way to teach writing and that this "way" can be successfully articulated by a single person or small group of people. A deliberately dialogic design is further supported by Elizabeth Rankin and Judith Goleman, who suggest that the "dissonance" that can result from perceived conflicts among theories or between the developing theoretical perspectives of new teachers and the more established viewpoints of their professors or supervisors can stimulate professional growth or, in constructivist terms, the negotiation of a teaching "subjectivity" (Rankin 40-42, 80-81, 119; Goleman 88-91). The fact that more recent scholarship on mentoring relationships has not only been informed by this theorizing, but has been collaboratively produced by (teaching, research, and/or administrative) mentors and their students also highlights the productive possibilities of community mentoring. (For a good example of such scholarship in composition and rhetoric, see Eble and Gaillet).

Perhaps even more importantly, given the broad implications of mentoring, such an approach is supported by the same theories of intellectual development and identity formation that underlie our most effective teaching methods (e.g., dialogic journals, peer-response groups, class discussion, and collaborative writing projects). Constructivist perspectives offered not only by Mikhail Bakhtin (who is invoked by Goleman) but by Lev Vygotsky and Kenneth Bruffee seem applicable here, as do the views forwarded by feminist theorists concerned with development of a sense of identity, or "voice" (e.g., Belenky, et al; Gilligan; hooks). For all of these theorists, self-actualization is a highly social process, dependent upon connection, conversation, and negotiation. In Gilligan's words, "it is an intensely relational act" (xvi).

A Final Note: Mentoring and the Transient Life

Though I have discussed the need for a new mentoring model within the context of academia, it can be helpful to consider our advising efforts within larger discussions of contemporary career trajectories. If it is true that the average American changes career paths several times during adulthood, then maybe we should feel less anxious about encouraging openness to alternative professional options. Our tenured positions protect many of us from forced career change; indeed, even those of us who could leave tenured positions, who want to leave tenured positions, often stay put. What this implies depends upon the individual, of course, but we should at least consider the possibility that openness to change, if not a basic evolutionary necessity, can be a useful quality to have.

Works Cited

Belenky, Mary Field, Blythe McVicker Clinchy, Nancy Rule Goldberger, and Jill Mattuck Tarule. *Women's Ways of Knowing: The Development of Self, Voice, and Mind.* New York: Basic Books, 1986. Print.

Bieber, Jeffery P., and Linda K. Worley. "Conceptualizing the Academic Life: Graduate Students' Perspectives." *Journal of Higher Education* 77.6 (2006): 1009–35. Print.

Bishop, Wendy. *Something Old, Something New: College Writing Teachers and Classroom Change.* Carbondale: Southern Illinois UP, 1990. Print.

Bousquet, Marc. "The Rhetoric of 'Job Market' and the Reality of the American Labor System." *College English* 66.2 (Nov. 2003): 207–28. Print.

Brand, Alice G. "MisMentoring: What We Learn." *Issues in Writing* 10.1 (1999): 58–65.

Bruffee, Kenneth A. "Collaborative Learning and the 'Conversation of Mankind.'" *College English* 46.7 (1984): 635–52. Print.

Cain, Mary Ann. "Mentoring as Identity Exchange: Conflicts and Connections." *Feminist Teacher* 8.3 (1994): 112–18. Print.

Cullen, Deborah L., and Gaye Luna. "Women Mentoring in Academe: Addressing the Gender Gap in Higher Education." *Gender and Education* 5.2 (1993): 125–37. Print.

Eble, Michelle F., and Lynée Lewis Gaillet, eds. *Stories of Mentoring: Theory and Praxis.* West Lafayette, IN: Parlor Press, 2008. Print.

Enos, Theresa. "Mentoring—and (Wo)mentoring—in Composition Studies. *Academic Advancement in Composition Studies: Scholarship, Publication, Promotion, Tenure.* Ed. Richard C. Gebhardt and Barbara Genelle Smith Gebhardt. Mahway, NJ: Laurence Erlbaum, 1997. 137–45. Print.

Ervin, Elizabeth. "Power, Frustration, and 'Fierce Negotiation' in Mentoring Relationships: Four Women Tell Their Stories." *Women's Studies* 24 (1995): 447–81. Print.

Gilligan, Carol. *In a Different Voice: Psychological Theory and Women's Development.* Cambridge, MA, and London: Harvard UP, 1982. Print.

Goleman, Judith. "Educating Literacy Instructors: Practice versus Expression." *Preparing College Teachers of Writing: Histories, Theories, Programs, Practices.* Ed. Betty P. Pytlik and Sarah Liggett. New York and Oxford: Oxford UP, 2002. Print.

hooks, bell. *Talking Back: Thinking Feminist, Thinking Black.* Boston: South End P, 1989. Print.

Latterell, Catherine. "Training the Workforce: An Overview of GTA Education Curricula." *WPA: Writing Program Administration* 19.3 (1996): 7–23. Print.

Lauer, Janice M. "Graduate Students as Active Members of the Profession: Some Questions for Mentoring." *Publishing in Rhetoric and Composition.* Ed. Gary A. Olsen and Todd W. Taylor. SUNY P, 1997. 229–35. Print.

Modern Language Association. "Report of the MLA Task Force on Evaluating Scholarship for Tenure and Promotion." *Profession 2007.* 9–71. Print.

Moore, Cindy, and Hildy Miller. *A Guide to Professional Development for Graduate Students in English.* Urbana, IL: NCTE, 2006. Print.

Rankin, Elizabeth. *Seeing Yourself as a Teacher.* Urbana, IL: NCTE, 1994. Print.

Turner, Caroline Sotello Viernes, and Judith Rann Thompson. "Socializing Women Doctoral Students: Minority and Majority Experiences." *The Review of Higher Education* 16.3 (1993): 355–70. Print.

Vygotsky, Lev. *Thought and Language.* Ed. and trans. Alex Kozulin. Cambridge, MA: MIT P, 1986. Print.

Welch, Nancy. "Conversion, Resistance, and the Training of Teachers." *College English* 55.4 (April 1993): 387–401. Print.

12 Composing a Life: Negotiating Personal, Professional, and Activist Commitments within the Academy

Jennifer Ahern-Dodson

As a graduate student in composition and rhetoric at a Research 1 institution, I was part of a creative community of first-year writing teachers, studied with a supportive and engaged faculty, and I gained an appreciation for the diverse applications of the composition and rhetoric PhD.[1] My hope was to land (eventually) a tenure-track position in an English department and to direct a writing program, my definition of a "dream job" in composition and rhetoric given my training, interests, and (sometimes competitive) conversations with graduate student peers.

Nine years later I am teaching in a non-tenure track position, advising faculty from a range of disciplines on how to incorporate writing as a mode of inquiry in community-based pedagogies, and developing a research agenda that I am excited about and that is in line with my social values and commitments. In this essay, I discuss the circuitous path I've taken and how I came to make active, creative choices about my work in the academy. A termed instructor position (postdoctoral teaching fellowship) in an interdisciplinary writing program provided me the opportunity to explore what I really wanted to do with my work. This non-tenured position enhanced my career options in ways I had not expected.

The Post-Doc and New Possibilities

As I entered the job market in Fall 1999, I identified jobs that would allow me to combine teaching and research, so I could continue to teach writing as well as consider how to expand my dissertation research on the ways universities support (or not) underprepared readers and writers through literacy centers. I also realized, however, that with few publications, and a degree of uncertainty about my life in the academy (two mentors had recently been denied tenure; graduate school colleagues were unsuccessful on the job market; English department politics were unsettling and unprofessional; I didn't know how to adapt my dissertation into publications), I would welcome a short-term position. I wanted time to figure out the kind of teacher, scholar, and writer I wanted to be.

I accepted a postdoctoral teaching fellowship at a private Research 1 institution. This fixed-termed appointment (three to five years) came with a small teaching load (five sections of academic writing per year), courses capped at twelve students, and a strong commitment by the program to support the professional development of faculty (see Hillard and Harris; Harris). Along with faculty in disciplines ranging from history to English, musicology, anthropology, epidemiology, and biology, I designed and taught first-year writing courses in support of the core curriculum. This course, Academic Writing 20, was the only required writing course for all undergraduates.

Time off the tenure clock was one of the most valuable assets of this position, and I took advantage of it, predominantly by reflecting on whether I wanted to continue in the workplace of the academy and, if so, how I could make a contribution. Given my ambivalence toward my dissertation research and lack of a new research agenda, a tenure-track position not only would have been difficult to secure but also potentially disastrous without a clear sense of scholarly direction. Like many of my colleagues in the program, I was excited by the opportunity to focus predominantly on my teaching (it was a teaching fellowship, after all) and to have some breathing room for publishing. The small class size and teaching load opened up many opportunities for career exploration and for (optional) committee work within the program, including the job search committee, and service within the university, such as advising for premajor students. These types of opportunities provided insight into the world of academia that I had little training for in graduate school.

Most of us designed writing courses around themes relevant to our dissertation research. For my research, I used ethnographic techniques to study the ways that a land-grant university supports its under-prepared writers through the writing center, the multicultural student support center, and the athletic academic student support center. More specifically, I examined the pedagogy of "help" practiced at each of these centers and how center participants' attitudes toward writing and writing courses affected students' academic writing development and the type of support provided (skills based versus writing as craft). Given this research, I had a particular interest in academic literacy narratives and so designed a writing course focused on academic literacy.

My interest in learning more about the literacy issues in the local public school system and a personal interest in connecting university students to real-world applications for their writing prompted me to design a service-learning course in which students not only studied literacy narratives within the classroom (their own and published accounts), but also worked with fourth-grade writers each week on creative writing projects. The *No Child Left Behind Act* became palpable when writers in my classes considered the impact end-of-grade testing could have on a particular child, a different set of stakes for academic writing than they were facing. Teaching flexibility in the program allowed me to design or revise a course each semester, and I continually improved my teaching and my understanding of community literacy and service-learning by conducting course-based research. I recognized that service-learning pedagogy not only helped me deepen students' understanding of academic literacy, but also enabled them to contribute to other writers in meaningful ways. Further, this work rekindled my passion for community engagement. Inspired by Ellen Cushman's call for rhetoricians to serve as public intellectuals (1996), I sought out other faculty at the university who were teaching community-engaged pedagogies. The flexibility of the postdoctoral position and the ability to work independently opened up a new field for me.

Still, I was developing professionally within the post-doc position. Teaching in an interdisciplinary program with no pressure to publish and many opportunities for cross-discipline dialogue added to my sense of collegiality. We formed writing groups and teaching collectives to share ideas about assignments and to discuss responding to student writing. We considered thoughtfully how to integrate our disciplinary knowledge into the first-year writing goals and practices documents we crafted (often disagreeing and deliberating!), and we had many conversations about what we had in common and where we differed in our beliefs about writing. Even disciplinary language became a site of critical reflection and hard work. At one of our fall retreats, a postdoctoral fellow with a science background interrupted a group discussion about a student essay to say, "I have no idea what you people are talking about!" Words like *intertextualization, writerly moves*, and *unpacking* the essay sounded completely foreign to her. Having interdisciplinary colleagues helped me envision what it might be like for people outside my own field and how I could find common ground and a common language if I wanted to invite them into it. As Rebecca Nowacek argues in "Why Is Being Interdisciplinary So Very Hard to Do?," "Interdisciplinary work—interdisciplinary teaching, learning, and thinking—is work on the boundaries and intersections of disciplines, work that does not transcend but rather transforms our understanding of disciplines" (494).

We all became more aware of the ways we had been shaped by our own disciplinary training and how to integrate our ways of seeing into our program and teaching. How did our disciplinary training help us to teach academic writing? How did our training help us to discuss *with students* what it means to write from our own disciplinary backgrounds? I learned what it meant to *be* a colleague and to listen authentically and seek to understand faculty from other disciplinary backgrounds. I began to envision what it would be like to be a part of the academy as a teacher and scholar.

Questions, Choices, and Another Nontraditional Academic Appointment

It was in this interdisciplinary space that I recognized I had a dissertation I did not want to revise and that did not seem to point toward a research program that I wanted to pursue. Although I was dedicated to studying university support for under-prepared readers and writers in the *process* of researching and writing about it, after I completed the dissertation I felt it was done (for me intellectually, at least), and I was not interested in revising any part of it into a book or articles. After two years of teaching in the post-doc, I knew I wanted my academic work to have a social angle and engagement with real issues as people live them, as it did in my dissertation. But what would that look like if I did not continue with my dissertation work? Didn't I need to get on with the work of publishing, so I would be a more attractive candidate on the job market after the fellowship ended? How could I continue to engage in substantive dialogue with faculty from different disciplines, and where might my scholarship fit in?

I knew I could not just keep teaching a different writing course each semester, which would likely lead down the path of becoming "invisible faculty" (Gappa and Leslie). Was I setting myself up for subordinate status within the academy? I had a decent salary, good colleagues, interesting teaching, but I felt adrift. What was the larger sense of purpose for my work? I recognized after teaching the writing course as service-learning that for any real difference to happen in community literacy work, we needed a collective, interdisciplinary effort to address literacy needs of the children we worked with—and long-term project planning informed by assessment and sustainable support from both community and university stakeholders. Helping fourth-grade students develop as writers also raised other questions that could not be answered within the scope of our writing class:

- What were the motives and barriers that affected their attitudes toward writing? (psychology)
- How did school and district policy issues impact their writing opportunities and assessment? (public policy)
- How might family or community literacy projects work in tandem to support students' literacy? (English or education)

Writers in my courses wanted to know what they could do to address the underlying reasons for their service. I began to see how a developmental and interdisciplinary approach to students' work as literacy volunteers could enhance their civic learning about literacy issues and their ability to contribute to their community in a variety of ways beyond direct service. I wanted to learn more about interdisciplinary approaches to community-based work and associated student learning outcomes.

At a state-wide faculty conference on service-learning, I learned that a position had opened up as the community partnership coordinator for a recently awarded Fund for the Improvement of Post-Secondary Education (FIPSE) grant, "Scholarship with a Civic Mission: Research Service-Learning at Duke." This project, a collaborative venture between the Hart Leadership Program in Public Policy, the Kenan Institute for Ethics, and the vice provost for undergraduate education, would expand the service-learning program and include *research* as service. The goal was to teach students to ask questions relevant to the research needs in their communities and to work with faculty and community partners to design and implement research projects to address these needs, a focus that directly responds to Ernest Boyer's call to make research relevant beyond the academy (*Scholarship Reconsidered*). The service opportunities would be linked to the themes of the course (e.g., emerging diseases, sustainable engineering, literacy development, or impacts of technology on society), and students would learn basic research skills, such as how to conduct literature reviews, identify research questions, take field notes, gather and analyze data, and interpret results. Students also would learn to reflect critically on the ethical, intellectual, personal, and civic aspects of their experiences while producing tangible research products (usually reports) for their community partners. This initiative employed a partnership model in which students, faculty, and community partners each play integral roles, and each received training, support, and grant funding. Perhaps even more importantly for me given my emerging interests in student and community partnership development, this program provided a structure and support for a staged approach to community-based learning: after taking a "gateway course" (Stage 1) with an introduction to basic research methods and direct service, students could choose to pursue a collaborative research project with a community partner (community-based research, CBR) that includes field research (Stage 2), and then to pursue an independent research project (like a senior thesis) that builds on the CBR project and collaboration with the community partner (Stage 3). I began to see connections to my own writing courses: students who might finish my course (a gateway) could go on to pursue a research project through another course, and deepen their understanding of community issues while also providing needed research. In each stage, I saw great possibilities for enhancing the teaching of writing, in individual reflection, in collaborative contexts, and in writing for multiple audiences.

Although I still had two years left on my termed appointment, I took a risk and accepted the coordinator position, which was a half-time staff position funded by the FIPSE grant for three years. With the help of one of the co-PIs for the grant, I also secured an adjunct teaching position within the Program in Education and taught two courses per year, both writing intensive service-learning courses, to make my position full-time.

Teaching Writing in Research Service-Learning Courses: Writing across the Curriculum

My responsibilities in this new position included identifying and supporting local community agencies connected to research service-learning courses, working with faculty to develop projects that both connected to course learning outcomes and contributed to the public good, and helping make visible community issues and the research needs of community-based organizations. The ethnographic and interviewing skills I acquired through my dissertation research allowed me to appreciate multiple perspectives and to translate those perspectives to multiple audiences who didn't always find common ground. My dissertation research about marginalized writers and the complexity of institutional politics surrounding literacy programs inspired me to make visible the needs of the local community and to translate those needs to a university audience.

Given my composition background, I was able to develop and recommend writing assignments that provided opportunities for critical self-reflection for students and systematic ways for getting students to think about their work in the community and the issues that work raised for them as students, researchers, and community members. Many faculty were assigning writing, but they were not all responding to what students wrote, and the assignments were not necessarily connected to the goals of the course. For students, the writing felt "tacked on"—they were asked to write about community issues to prove they had volunteered with their community agency that week (attendance checking), but due to workload the faculty often didn't respond to issues that emerged ("should I edit an eighth-grader's paper?"; "my child's family is being deported"; "the Hospice family said they're ready for the patient to go") nor gave credit for the writing beyond participation. This writing about community was not integral to the subject matter of the course, and students did not take it seriously.

Faculty felt overwhelmed by the extra work associated with teaching research service-learning courses (establishing partnerships, managing students and transportation, balancing course content with risk/liability/ethical issues associated with volunteering in the community), but they also needed some way to keep track of students' work in the community and to help them integrate that work into the classroom conversations. Writing seemed like a good fit. Some faculty wanted guidance on designing on-line journal assignments. Others wanted ideas for responding to students' writing in an efficient way or helping students to respond to each other's writing. And some faculty wanted suggestions for creating writing assignments that connected the course content with the community experiences of the students. My knowledge of writing groups (Brooke, Mirtz, Evans), responding styles (Straub and Lunsford), approaches to teaching writing (Young and Fulwiler; Bishop) and reflection (Yancey) enhanced my ability to cultivate student writing across a range of courses from Spanish to education, sociology, and biology and in a variety of contexts, from community-based research writing, to informal journaling about one's own attitudes toward service, to an essay that integrates course texts, personal experience, and community issues, to reporting on service through field notes. I returned again and again to Ellen Cushman's "The Public Intellectual," Bonnie Sunstein and Elizabeth Chiseri-Strater's *Fieldworking: Reading and Writing Research,* and Tom Deans' *Writing Partnerships* for ideas and inspiration. I used my composition background to inform the teaching of writing in research service-learning courses across the curriculum and to work with faculty on individualized plans that allowed for substantive assignments, course content specific learning outcomes, and reasonable assessment mechanisms.

In addition to the pedagogical parallels between service-learning program development and writing across the curriculum, there are interesting administrative parallels. On our campus, the service-learning program was relatively new, seven years old when I joined, although service-learning had been practiced in individual courses for many years before that. The director of service-learning was a combination of "peace corps volunteer" (110), developing a program as a part-time staff person, with few financial resources and minimal administrative support but lots of enthusiasm, and "missionary" (111) trying to "convert" others to this pedagogy. As Susan McLeod argues in "The Foreigner: WAC Directors as Agents of Change," the challenge with both these roles is the WAC director is cast in a service position (110) and so has few opportunities for substantive dialogue with faculty (111). As with service-learning, this situation often leads to little institutional buy-in, making sustainability unlikely, and enhances the potential for director and staff burnout. Because I was familiar with these issues, I worked actively to position myself in the role of "change agent" (112), to "move slowly and thoughtfully, with respect for the difference of others" and to use [my] own difference to bring about meaningful, lasting change" (115).

By working *alongside* faculty to change the practice of writing in service-learning courses, I recognized the value of time, commitment, and an "outsider" status as a community partner *and* writing specialist. As an adjunct faculty member in the Program in Education and a staff member on the FIPSE grant, I was in a unique position to advocate for change: I could work individually with faculty to teach them *how* to include writing in their particular course to meet their learning objectives. Rather than providing assignments as a template or just encouraging faculty to use writing to teach critical reflection ("missionary"), I worked individually with many faculty before, during, and after to develop writing approaches *with* them, just as I encouraged them to develop student service and research projects *with* community partners.

This particular approach yielded some interesting results: faculty had more engagement with the student writing in their course and students found the writing more meaningful. In "Writing and the Disciplines," Jonathan Monroe argues that "if faculty are truly to own writing, this ownership needs to be located and cultivated within the disciplinary investments of individual faculty—not as an add-on or a detour, but as integral to the kinds of research and teaching on which students' success in their respective disciplines necessarily depends" (5). One of the challenges for both WAC and WID programs is to avoid being perceived by faculty as top-down initiatives or the directors as administrator-centered. But whether WAC, WID, or writing enhanced research service-learning courses, if faculty see writing as enhancing their teaching and they have support, it's a win-win. Because these particular faculty members were part of a learning community with FIPSE funded courses, they also had opportunities to teach and to learn from each other. Although writing was not the only form of critical reflection in these courses, it became a core concept in some faculty workshops.

CHALLENGES

Negotiating a nontraditional path in the academy is not without its challenges, particularly in terms of personal and professional compromises. In *Rethinking Faculty Work,* Judith Gappa, Ann Austin, and Andrea Trice propose a framework "for rethinking the academic career to meet the needs of the twenty-first century" (128), a framework that helps recruit and retain outstanding faculty who are committed to institutional goals and who feel respected and valued, regardless of their rank or status. They argue that "employment equity," "academic freedom and autonomy," "flexibility," "professional growth," and "collegiality" are the essential elements, "the glue that holds the individual faculty member and the college or university in a mutually rewarding reciprocal relationship" (131). In both of my fixed-term appointment positions, I had the unique opportunity to design and teach courses that I was passionate about, with small class sizes (twelve to fifteen students), and few departmental or committee obligations. I enjoyed a strong sense of autonomy with my teaching and research and grew professionally as well by participating in projects or committees that interested me and through collaborative work with faculty on their courses and community partnerships. I often had access to professional development funds through my work as an academic advisor or by applying for course development or technology grants. These funds allowed me to participate in both composition and service-learning conferences on a regular basis, to purchase books, and to teach with new technology, including iPods and Flip cameras.

Employment equity, however, was a key concern and challenge. In each position, I knew I was in a liminal space and did not have long-term job security: the post doc was a three to five-year appointment; the staff/adjunct position was a three-year, grant-funded position. Although I had every expectation that my position would continue once the grant ended (which it inevitably did as part of a stand-alone program), I had no guarantees. It is difficult to harness creative and research energies when trying just to secure a position with health benefits, particularly since I started a family during this time and had no paid parental-leave. At times I had to rely on the goodwill of others, and I had to be pro-active in salary negotiations. I did not always get what I asked for. I never knew if I should look for another position, and my family was in a constant state of uncertainty in our own long-term planning: we never knew beyond a year or two what my income would be.

Additionally, evaluation processes were not always clear, and receiving awards and recognition for my work proved a challenge. At one graduation ceremony, the chair named several departmental faculty (non-adjuncts), asked them to stand, and then said, "If there's anyone else, please stand up, too." When students wanted to nominate me for a teaching award, they (and I) discovered that I did not qualify because I was not regular-rank faculty member.

Ambiguous collegiality was yet another challenge. Although I had a strong feeling of collegiality in my postdoctoral teaching position, it was also clear that we were not viewed as colleagues by the rest of the institution: we had little interaction with other programs and departments other than what we as individuals initiated. My staff/adjunct teaching position was particularly tricky. As a team member on the FIPSE grant, I was invited to participate in important conversations about curriculum development for Scholarship with a Civic Mission: Research Service-Learning at Duke and helped shape policy and planning for the future of the program. This was due to leadership goodwill and collaborative processes, not because it was part of my job description. For three years I was part of a visionary, high-powered group that valued my work and my perspective. After the grant ended, however, and the program transitioned to new leadership in a stand-alone office, I no longer had an active role in shaping program policy or university-wide curriculum discussions. I was excluded from committee work directly related to my areas of expertise because I no longer had an advocate, and the new hierarchical structure discouraged collaboration.

Because my work was not valued in the new iteration of the program, I actively sought colleagues in other programs and to build on those interdisciplinary relationships I had established as the community partnership coordinator. I began to realize that I did not have an intellectual "home" program, particularly since this university did not have a composition and rhetoric program. I had to advocate for myself and embrace ambiguity; however, as I continued to take advantage of course support funds and creative teaching opportunities, to identify like-minded colleagues interested in curricular civic engagement, and to reach across to colleagues in two other research universities in the area, I, like other colleagues, began to see the value of focusing my work to align with the university's mission and strategic plan: Making a Difference: Knowledge in the Service of Society. I reread the essay "Institutional Critique" (Porter, et al.), which had helped me "map" the university I studied for my dissertation and now helped me to identify ways to connect my work to my current institution's priorities and key issues. Although I had long worked to make my research relevant to the communities I was working with (in the spirit of Ernest Boyer's *Scholarship Reconsidered*), I had not considered ways to make that same research relevant to the *university*. In my current position as a faculty member and community outreach consultant in the Thompson Writing Program, my work includes grant development for a community writing center, teaching service-learning composition courses that integrate writing, civic engagement, and education research, and collaboration with two university programs and three community-based organizations. This work not only connects directly to one of the core aspects of the strategic plan, it also is made public because of multiple stakeholders. I learned to address the challenge of liminality by working across the university and forming strategic partnerships.

FINDING MEANINGFUL WORK IN THE ACADEMY: AN INTERDISCIPLINARY RESEARCH AGENDA

In each of these nontraditional academic positions, I sought ways to follow what I am passionate about and to pursue a research agenda over time through community activism, interdisciplinary collaboration, and faculty development. The postdoctoral fellowship and staff/adjunct teaching position both helped me to find common ground with faculty across the university, particularly with the intersections between writing and civic engagement, and this path may not have been possible had I landed right on the tenure track, with pressure to produce and publish in my specific discipline.

One of the key challenges with a tenure-track position is the need to publish single-authored texts (typically valued more highly than co-authored) in top-tier composition journals, on the tenure clock. What made the most sense for my research and teaching interests were co-authored, interdisciplinary publications, often in scientific journals. Because I had time to learn from faculty and to listen authentically to their ideas, disciplinary conventions, and assumptions and attitudes about writing and student learning, my research agenda (which took years to develop *as* an interdisciplinary agenda) also served as a site of professional development for me. Rather than negotiating some of the traditional challenges of the tenure track position—working to publish quickly and prolifically, serving on various committees that may or not be connected to my research and teaching agendas, and a heavy teaching load—I instead had the time to focus on my own individual and collaborative learning with other faculty. Joan Mullin's article "Interdisciplinary Work as Professional Development" has been particularly helpful with this critically reflective thinking. Further, I've found that my collaborative and interdisciplinary work with a range of faculty also has pushed me to ask research questions differently—considering how my language and my disciplinary background might blind me to other ways of seeing writing and civic development, potentially missing sites for writing across the curriculum engagement.

In one research project with a sociology faculty member, for example, we both wanted to investigate how to improve the quality of a group community-based research project, a project that was designed to meet a need within the community. In most instances, students created a research paper (which the community partner did not always find useful) and often one student ended up writing the majority of the paper. I thought we would be researching how to help students collaborate *as writers* with each other (what were their assumptions about "good writing"; how did they make decisions about the final product's form; how did they share ownership), yet she wanted to have practical mechanisms for assessing student contributions (in many forms) to the final written product.

Once we discovered our "double bind" (Nowacek) and negotiated our different disciplinary perspectives on writing and collaboration, we developed the following research project: *How does collaborative writing with peers in community-based research courses impact student ideas about authorship?* We are studying how students in her sophomore-level community-based research (CBR) class "Sexuality and Society" make decisions about writing and research in their work conducting qualitative research for a community-based organization. We are interested in how they negotiate authorship within these groups, how they negotiate "double binds" that may come from different writing or research experiences, and how this experience can help them learn what it means to write and research as a sociologist. One of our goals is to develop templates for students to use in making these conversations visible to the faculty. Because faculty teaching community-based pedagogies often have minimal training in the teaching of writing, particularly in a collaborative context, and so miss opportunities to connect the collaborative inquiry and writing processes to civic learning outcomes, I am also using this research project to develop a model for training faculty across the disciplines on the design, implementation, and assessment of writing assignments that enhance student civic learning outcomes.

In a second interdisciplinary research project, *How can writing foster civic responsibility within and across the curriculum*, I am working with an ecologist and a biologist to study how writing in discipline-specific community-based research courses or independent study projects prepares students for lives of civic responsibility, particularly when courses and projects are linked. We see these courses as offering opportunities for faculty and students to use writing to reflect critically on disciplinary approaches to civic engagement, including how disciplines can best contribute knowledge to local and global communities and create new knowledge *with* the community rather than *about* or *on* the community. From my experience teaching research service-learning courses with students from a variety of majors and supporting faculty through the FIPSE grant (including these two faculty), I recognized that students did not always connect what they were learning in one class to another—even if they continued to work with the same community partner or research question. These faculty also wondered about this disconnect and how we can help move students from *collectors* of experience and knowledge to *reflectors*. We hope to use this research to develop a grant proposal to study courses in the STEM disciplines.

Conclusion

I am a very different scholar now than when I came out of graduate school. As a teacher, community activist, and researcher, I now consider ways my training as a compositionist might contribute to on-going conversations about the nature, practice, and theory of community-university partnerships and the intersections between writing and civic engagement. By taking full advantage of the opportunities afforded through the two termed-positions, I ultimately realized how best to match my academic work with intellectual, activist, and personal interests. Further, I appreciate just what's so hard about interdisciplinarity, mainly the time and space for faculty and students to discuss and reflect critically on their assumptions and "double binds," to develop longitudinal writing and research projects, and to have those projects, and associated teaching and research outcomes, recognized on a university level (senior thesis, promotion and tenure, cross-departmental collaboration). As first a post-doctoral teaching fellow in an interdisciplinary writing program and then as an "outsider" faculty adjunct and grant staff member who was able to combine bottom-up faculty energies with top-down university-wide initiatives (Scholarship with a Civic Mission/ Knowledge in the Service of Society), I have been in the unique position of collaborating as a change-agent to foster writing across the curriculum in unexpected ways. I'd like to see more opportunities for non-regular rank faculty compositionists to collaborate across disciplines on mutually beneficial writing and civic engagement projects, and strong, visible support from universities to make interdisciplinarity a core teaching and learning value for faculty as well as for students. Combining writing across the curriculum and civic engagement initiatives is one avenue for doing just that.

Note

1.Title inspired by Mary Catherine Bateson's *Composing a Life*.

Works Cited

Bateson, Mary Catherine. *Composing a Life*. New York: Grove, 1989. Print.
Bishop, Wendy, ed. *The Subject Is Writing*. Portsmouth: Boynton/Cook Heinemann, 1999. Print.
Boyer, Ernest. *Scholarship Reconsidered: Priorities of the Professoriate*. Princeton: CarnegieFoundation, 1990. Print.
Brooke, Robert, Ruth Mirtz, and Rick Evans. *Small Groups in Writing Workshops: Invitations to a Writer's Life*. Urbana: NCTE, 1994. Print.
Cushman, Ellen. "The Public Intellectual, Service Learning, and Activist Research." *College English* 61.3 (1999): 328–36. Print.
---. The Rhetorician as Agent of Social Change." *College Composition and Communication*. 47.1 (1996): 7-28. Print.
Deans, Tom. *Writing Partnerships*. Urbana: NCTE, 2000. Print.
Gappa, Judith M., Ann E. Austin, and Andrea G. Trice. *Rethinking Faculty Work: Higher Education's Strategic Imperative*. San Francisco: John Wiley, 2007. Print.
Gappa, Judith M., and David W. Leslie. *The Invisible Faculty: Improving the Status of Part-Timers in Higher Education*. San Francisco: Jossey-Bass, 1993. Print.

Harris, Joseph. "Thinking Like a Program." *Pedagogy: Critical Approaches to Teaching Literature, Language, Composition, and Culture* 4.3 (2004): 357–63. Print.

Hillard, Van, and Joseph Harris. "Making Writing Visible at Duke University." *Writing and the New Academy.* Spec. issue of *Peer Review* 6.1 (2003): 15–17. Print.

McLeod, Susan. "The Foreigner: WAC Directors as Agents of Change," *Resituating Writing: Constructing and Administering Writing Programs.* Ed. Joseph Janangelo and Kristine Hansen. Portsmouth, NH: Heinemann-Boynton/Cook, 1995. 108–16. Print.

Monroe, Jonathan. "Writing and the Disciplines." *Writing and the New Academy.* Spec. issue of *Peer Review* 6.1 (2003): 4–7. Print.

Mullin, Joan. "Interdisciplinary Work as Professional Development." *Pedagogy* 8.3 (2008): 495–508. Print.

Nowacek, Rebecca S. "Why Is Being Interdisciplinary So Very Hard to Do?" *College Composition and Communication* 60.3 (2009): 493–516. Print.

Porter, James E., Patricia Sullivan, Stuart Blythe, Jeffrey Grabill, and Libby Miles. "Institutional Critique: A Rhetorical Methodology for Change." *College Composition and Communication* 51.4 (2000): 610–42. Print.

Scholarship with a Civic Mission: Research Service-Learning at Duke University. Fund for the Improvement of Postsecondary Education Grant #P116B020776 Final Report. December 2006. U.S. Department of Education. Web. 10 Feb 2010.

Straub, Richard, and Ronald Lunsford. *Twelve Readers Reading: Responding to College Student Writing.* Cresskill, NJ: Hampton, 1995. Print.

Sunstein, Bonnie Stone, and Elizabeth Chiseri-Strater. *Fieldworking: Reading and Writing Research.* 3rd ed. Boston: Bedford/St. Martin's, 2007. Print.

Yancey, Kathleen Blake. *Reflection in the Writing Classroom.* Logan, UT: Utah State UP, 1998. Print.

Young, Art, and Toby Fulwiler, eds. *Writing Across the Disciplines: Research into Practice.* Portsmouth: Boynton/Cook Heinemann, 1986. Print.

13 Researching to Professionalize, not Professionalizing to Research: Modular Professionalization and the WIDE Effect

Stacey Pigg, Kendall Leon, and Martine Courant Rife

> *If it is not removed from the practices that sustain it, reality is multiple.*
>
> —Annemarie Mol

Students who leave the Writing in Digital Environments (WIDE) Research Center at Michigan State University go on to do interesting things. As a research center that focuses on making knowledge about digital communication, WIDE brings together faculty members, community partners, and students to develop solutions to complex digital writing problems and to share digital communication knowledge in school, workplace, and community contexts. WIDE also serves as an important professionalizing institution for students who work within it. In fact, when the three of us first met in a Lansing coffeehouse to discuss how WIDE has impacted our professional development, we were only half joking when we remarked that we are the most boring of the bunch moving on from WIDE and heading out into the "real world." Our graduate student WIDE alumni/colleagues hold positions that allow them to coordinate the social media outreach strategy for a science museum, lead software development designed to innovate writing review practices, edit ebooks for a major publishing company, write professional proposal documents for corporations, and coordinate the web strategy for a small liberal arts college. Graduate students remaining in academia have traveled as far as Israel to work with local communities and have collaborated with academic colleagues who run the gamut of disciplinary and institutional affiliations. In terms of geographical, institutional, and disciplinary variety, former WIDE student researchers are spread widely.

In some ways this diversity is expected because students who work in the WIDE center often do not have typical work profiles when they finish graduate studies. For us, the path to becoming professionals has included experiences different from many of our colleagues (including, at least for two of us, having less teaching experience than many of our peers). It might seem that a research center environment with its obvious focus on funding and performing research and inquiry projects would push graduate students into what many have referenced as the typical (and often ill-fated) hunt for the rhetoric and composition "Research 1" job (see Leverenz and Goodburn 16). However, we have found something different to be true. While the three of us currently work inside institutions of higher education, placing the approaches to doing and sustaining research we learned at WIDE at the center of our professional outlooks has made us more likely to seek out and consider nontraditional opportunities, including alternative approaches to academic work.

In this chapter, we make what might seem to be a counterintuitive argument. Graduate students whose professional training is centered in the work of a functioning research center are well prepared to work outside of typical academic research models. Research center work helps graduate students respond to many of the current complexities of the academy, where situations and politics can change without warning, and where collaboration is often necessary to create change or solve problems. Graduate students who work in a research center acquire practical experience in collaboration and group dynamics, navigating institutional structures and working contextually across multiple rhetorical situations. These practices come as part of a modular model of participation and development, one in which graduate students are able to assemble different kinds of professionalizing activities into a trajectory of participation that is tailored to their own development goals. Different individuals have vastly different work experiences at WIDE, shaping their own diverse career paths and their learning for future work within or outside the university. Modular participation is not a magic formula to graduate student success; it means that people who are successful working in this way often have to be strongly individually motivated and willing to jump into a variety of tasks that may not always make sense to them on the front end. Furthermore, those who use their WIDE experience for professionalization often have to spend time reflecting on and synthesizing diverse experiences after they have completed them. However, we think that this way of approaching professional development has clear benefits in terms of the variety of career paths for which it can prepare graduate students, as well as the mentality and attitude that it can help graduate students develop. It is a professionalizing model that builds from and responds to an understanding that rhetoric and writing practice is essentially multiple and plays out in diverse locations and with diverse people.

We approach the topic of modular professionalization and research center work from the point of view of individuals who have experienced professional development through the WIDE center, not as those who designed it. Thus, while we do not reflect on the design of graduate experience at WIDE (we feel sure that our mentors and WIDE directors, Jeffrey Grabill and Bill Hart-Davidson, would be happy to chat with you the next time you run into them), we are situated to give insight into how we have perceived and employed research center work as professional training and to reflect on what it has prepared us to do. In this chapter, we first describe the WIDE Research Center, focusing on the ways graduate students participate within it and detailing a few of our own experiences. These experiences focus on collaborating with community and university stakeholders, working persuasively within and outside of the institutional structures of the academy, and learning to write grants and support our own research. We then step back to discuss some of the effects of modular professionalization on our own development. To do so, we discuss what we have begun to affectionately call "the WIDE effect" of working rhetorically with a focus on collaboration, audience and signification, and contextual learning and performance. Finally, we apply the WIDE effect and modular participation to our respective positions at the time we initiated the article—experiencing the "dissertation year" of graduate school, being on the job market, and maintaining a full-time faculty position in a two-year college setting—to discuss the ways in which we feel prepared to work outside of traditional career models in the humanities.

THE WIDE RESEARCH CENTER AND THE MULTIPLE ACTIVITIES OF RESEARCH CENTER WORK

As its website explains, "The WIDE Research Center creates new knowledge about digital communication and promotes the transfer of this knowledge to school, workplace, and community contexts to promote learning, knowledge work, and citizenship." In practice, this means that WIDE delves into digital writing as it is experienced in real life and often works with community, professional, and academic groups who have real problems to solve. This work typically focuses around a number of ongoing research and software development projects, some of which we initiate and lead, and others of which we work with through smaller consulting roles.

As part of the practical work of these multiple projects, the WIDE Research Center offers many different opportunities for graduate and undergraduate students. They can join projects already underway at the center as hourly research associates, often in addition to their other teaching assistant or writing center appointments. WIDE also fully supports graduate students who hold half-time or quarter-time appointments as research assistants (RAs) in the center. General RAs work on a number of projects and also carry out administrative duties like filing reports to account for the center's activity. Kendall and Martine both worked in this capacity during their time at WIDE. Project RAs are attached to grant-funded projects and often work as project managers to perform a range of organizational and research duties for a particular project. Stacey worked as a project RA for "Take Two: A Study of the Co-Creation of Knowledge on Museum Web 2.0 Sites" during her time at WIDE.

Both project-based and center-funded RAs attend weekly staff meetings at WIDE and participate in the ongoing administrative and research work of the center. These activities include discussing strategies for funding research, developing research plans, pitching ideas for new projects, and reviewing and contributing to the work of fellow undergraduate, graduate, and faculty colleagues at the center. RAs participate equally in these activities. RAs and hourly workers also work on individual projects at WIDE. The roles and kinds of activities that people perform related to these projects vary depending on the goals of the project and what it is designed to study or accomplish.

For example, in projects that the three of us have worked on, we have engaged in the following:

- organizing and writing the many parts of a federal research grant application;
- designing a survey instrument to assess the range of writing genres college students do in their daily lives;
- coding and analyzing data in a controlled experiment on the topic of differences between students writing on blogs versus students writing in private spaces;
- writing articles for different kinds of publications related to our research;
- researching how to leverage digital technologies to facilitate alumni donations and
- building a sustainable community organization's web-based portal including needs assessments, usability tests, and evaluation surveys.

While research activities are central, the work activities of WIDE graduate students extend beyond developing and carrying out research. Graduate students also learn to manage writing-intensive work, what it means to conduct research with human participants and IRB applications, and how to plan a conference call or weekend-long work excursion for researchers without burning them out or boring them to death. Some WIDE jobs also focus explicitly on teaching outside of typical classroom spaces and in situations populated by people who are not required to learn from us: community stakeholders who want to learn how to better leverage technologies, middle schoolers in an afterschool program for digital storytelling, and undergraduate students who are joining a WIDE project but who have never done research before. Other activities are more internally and institutionally focused: designing accountability measures for the center, implementing effective ways to promote the center, creating vision statements and plans, and implementing strategies for tracking funding opportunities. This multiple nature of what work means within a research center like WIDE is the defining backdrop for how it can provide a different kind of professionalizing experience for graduate students.

The WIDE Effect, Multiplicity, and Modular Professionalization

In *Situated Learning: Legitimate Peripheral Participation,* Jean Lave and Etienne Wenger describe a process through which individuals' embodied actions and participation in activities constitute their process of ongoing development and learning. According to Lave and Wenger, "A person's intentions to learn are engaged and the meaning of learning is configured through the process of becoming a full participant in a sociocultural practice. This social process includes, indeed it subsumes, the learning of knowledgeable skills" (29). From this point of view, learning and development can be seen as "an aspect of all activity" that one performs in a given context. In this model of development, it is through activity that "learners inevitably participate in communities of practitioners and that the mastery of knowledge and skill requires newcomers to move toward full participation in the sociocultural practices of a community" (37–38, 29).

From our perspectives, Lave and Wenger's model of development maps very well onto the way we have perceived working at WIDE as professional training. Our learning and development results from direct participation and socialization into particular skills and attitudes associated with becoming members of the unique world of the research center (Lave and Wenger might call us "legitimate peripheral participants"). In other ways, however, the process of development that we have experienced differs from Lave and Wenger's model because becoming a "full participant" in the research center community is not our ultimate goal. Instead, we are asked to leverage our experiences at WIDE to prepare ourselves to participate in multiple communities we could eventually join. The locale of rhetoric and writing specialists and the communities to which they belong are not static or singular. Even across the breadth of academic institutions that employ people in our field, commitments, concerns, and activities vary greatly from English departments to freestanding rhetoric and writing programs to writing programs housed in other disciplinary locations, and from large, to medium-sized, to small institutions. Rhetoric and writing scholars also find themselves in a range of corporate, organizational, and institutional places. Much of the literature on graduate student training and professionalization is linked explicitly to classroom performance and writing (Berkenkotter, Huckin, and Ackerman) or to the problems and potential of teacher-training, WPA work, and graduate students' status as TAs and future teachers (Burnham and Jackson; Long, Holberg, and Taylor; Marshall). However, the reality is that graduate student opportunities in rhetoric and writing extend beyond those to which these activities are specifically linked.

If the ultimate end point or goal of graduate work in rhetoric and writing is singular, then it makes sense to think of professionalization in terms of a linear line from novice to expert with one particular end point in sight. However, if we begin to think that success for someone with a rhetoric and writing graduate degree means any number of positions in any number of locations, a linear process of professionalization makes less sense. Thus, one current programmatic challenge in terms of professional development is a problem of multiplicity. It is challenging for programs to provide a range of professional experiences that fit a range of student interests and needs. As Karen P. Peirce and Theresa Jarnagin Enos have explained, the problem of matching graduate training to potential professional responsibilities is one that extends throughout curricula and course offerings (205), as well as professional opportunities that extend beyond coursework (209-10).

A research center like WIDE is able to respond to the problem of multiplicity at a couple of distinct levels. The concept of "modular professionalization" describes how graduate students can take advantage of participating in research center activity as professional development. First, because WIDE offers a number of different jobs working with a number of different kinds of partners, it can offer different kinds of engagement to professionalizing graduate students. Because WIDE collaborates with partners across different academic institutions and disciplines, community organizations, and business institutions, its activities and the relationships that accompany them unfold in different ways based on the project at hand. As a result of this multiplicity, graduate students' engagement can vary in terms of the individuals and groups with whom they collaborate, the time commitment required, and the tasks planned and completed. Graduate students can choose to participate in projects that will provide engagement opportunities with particular kinds of research methods, community or disciplinary partners, and material spaces (e.g., museums, libraries) depending on their own research and teaching interests and what kinds of experiences will most benefit them.

However, the fact that WIDE is able to offer multiple experiences alone does not add up to a changed model of professional development. Graduate students have to seek out and involve themselves in the kinds of work that ultimately will be beneficial to them, reflect on the purpose of this work within their own career plans, and create their own narratives to describe how the often vastly different kinds of work they have done adds up to something valuable. That is not to say that graduate students must do this work alone; mentors within and outside the center are a central component in helping graduate students learn what work they should be doing and why. However, thinking of the process of graduate development in this way shifts the understanding of professionalization. Instead of an experience in which graduate students perform expected kinds of work in the times and places that are expected of them, graduate students have much responsibility for deciding which professionalizing activities to participate in, when, and to what end.

Multiplicitous work can be daunting, and feeling individually responsible for "putting together" the materials of one's own professionalization can be a lot of pressure. Graduate students working at WIDE are often thrown into positions of doing things they have not done before, and for which they have to explore and develop strategies for problems with no easy answers. In short, this kind of work experience is not and could not be for everyone. Some graduate students simply are not interested in the work of a research center. Furthermore, because of the limited capacity of the center, not everyone in a graduate program can work with WIDE to the extent that the three of us have. Additionally, multi-year RAs have very real challenges when it comes to describing and justifying their experiences. For example, many of us who have worked in research instead of teaching positions have had the experience of having colleagues insinuate that teaching is not important to us. From our perspective, teaching just unfolds differently and in spaces not normally recognized as domains for this kind of rhetorical work; however, conflicting with traditional beliefs in rhetoric and writing about how, where, and when professional development happens can be challenging for graduate students.

Despite these challenges, WIDE experiences position graduate students to work effectively in contemporary workplaces where tasks change suddenly, work is multilayered, and relationships and politics are complex. The effect of WIDE for those of us who have done many different kinds of work over several years is a change in attitude or outlook. Rather than focusing on practices or skills tied to a single domain, working with WIDE teaches graduate students to think contextually across a number of different project areas and rhetorical situations and to plan intervention and research in response to questions and problems raised by each rhetorical situation. The practicalities of this work often involve complex negotiations of personal relationships, institutional politics, and ideologies. Thus, working with WIDE teaches a model of professional being that we understand as deeply rhetorical: it involves inventing solutions, interventions, and ways of acting that are contextually relevant and responsive. The "WIDE effect" is a model of action that puts collaboration; audience and signification; and ongoing, contextualized, and adaptive learning and inquiry at the center of academic engagement.

- *Collaboration:* Most projects that WIDE sponsors are projects that could not get done by one person. Thus, every project at WIDE is made up of a diverse group with different expertise and backgrounds. Putting collaboration at the center of a professional outlook means learning to choose colleagues carefully, while genuinely valuing others' time, resources, and abilities.
- *Audience and Signification:* Because our projects are sponsored and collaborative, WIDE researchers devote careful time and consideration to demonstrating the value and insight writing researchers bring to projects. These discussions have to be crafted to appeal to potential collaborators, as well as grant funding agencies and internal entities that provide monetary and material support.[1]
- *Contextualized and Adaptive Learning and Inquiry:* WIDE graduate students learn how to learn in the moment. We learn how to produce scholarship for others outside our field, how to develop arguments that are persuasive to people with very different perspectives from our own, and how to perform research and teaching activities adapted to the situation at hand.

THE WIDE EFFECT AT WORK IN PROFESSIONAL LIVES

It is this combination of collaboration, a focus on audience and signification, and contextualized and adaptive learning and inquiry that creates an outlook through which we see work in the humanities differently and approach our current academic positions with different attitudes. With this in mind, we share the way the WIDE effect plays out in our lives in a few key moments of professional development: in the dissertation phase, job market year, and in becoming a full time faculty member at a local community college.

Stacey: Taking the WIDE Effect into the Dissertation Year

Working at WIDE has made me more likely to seek out and participate in diverse research collectives. My desire to research with others came as a result of working on two projects with different kinds of research teams, while seeing other similar collective research unfold under WIDE's umbrella. Here I focus briefly on the two projects and teams I worked with and reflect on what I gained from those experiences. I conclude by describing how this work has positioned me (at times strangely) and discuss future work for which it has prepared me.

First, as a half-time RA for the *Take Two* project, I worked with a team comprised of many researchers who are from different disciplines or not affiliated with universities. Our team, which studied how writers use Web 2.0 technologies on a science museum site, was made up of graduate students and faculty researchers from two universities, as well as administrators, educators, and designers from two large science museums. Interacting as a part of the research meetings for this project required a set of skills that I realize in hindsight are not always a part of academic professionalization. I learned, first, that group dynamics are delicate: they need to be planned and negotiated carefully. Playing a productive individual role in group research requires careful management of one's own identity in relation to others. Within this setting, I became better at explaining myself, arguing for ideas, and negotiating with audiences of people who did not share a disciplinary affiliation or were skeptical (for good reason) toward an academic point of view. I realized that to successfully work with diverse groups, I needed to listen—really listen—to different perspectives, which involved asking a lot of questions to draw them out.

I also had the opportunity to work with a different kind of research team: one comprised of rhetoric and composition scholars at different institutions and in different positions. As a member of the *Revisualizing Composition* project, I participated in a large collective that planned and is carrying out a multi-phased, multi-institutional study of student writing. Many of the lessons I learned were the same; the work of negotiating diverse perspectives and positions is still important even when a disciplinary identity is shared. However, I learned that good research often progresses more slowly than planned and takes unforeseen detours. I also gained experience in mentoring undergraduate researchers, which I learned requires flexibility, the ability to set achievable goals and schedules for others, and, again, good listening and relational skills.

Researching and writing in teams sometimes felt like a strange way to operate during the end of my graduate studies. When colleagues were focusing scholarly attention inward on very personal projects, I was often focused outward, contributing to shared goals and depending on others for the success of my work. Of course, my dissertation is still a single-authored document, and I am still conducting research on my own. However, I think what I've gained from conducting team research is invaluable. I am prepared for positions in which I will work with others, manage my own workflow and identity in group settings, organize the time and contribution of others, and create strong narratives and arguments to justify my ideas and actions. During a time when getting a job in any field is tough, I sense that I could work in a variety of locations with different kinds of people, especially when this work involves an institution that values relationship-building and working in teams to solve complex problems.

Kendall: Taking the WIDE Effect on the Job Market

As a PhD candidate, this has been my year on the market, which comes with all the moments of rapid remembering of everything I have accomplished (or not) these past few years, and the immediate need to define myself as a scholar and a teacher. While it is hard to reflect in the moment that it is happening—and yes, I am still in the midst of it—what I can do is reflect on the "WIDE effect" on my market experience. By the "WIDE effect" I mean both its effect on the ways that I appeared to be read as a teacher and scholar, but also its effects on the interactions I have had during this job seeking process.

Prior to the job search process, I had been told by several wise colleagues that I would feel most comfortable in similar institutions, namely research ones where teaching ability garnered less attention and weight in one's tenure review file. As someone with perhaps less experience teaching in a traditional college classroom than most PhD students, I also thought this would be the case. Interestingly, what felt most natural to me was not context specific. In other words, the fit was not based on the type of institution per se—as I interacted with a range of institutions—but rather on the way the institution understood the relationship between teaching, research and administrative work. I was able to make explicit connections between these three facets of academic work through my experiences at WIDE. For example, building research projects, such as determining research project goals and evaluation methods, became the basis from which my conversations on teaching and curriculum design would begin, especially in conversations with programs working toward goals of collaborative learning environments for teachers. Correlatively, managing research projects and negotiating the range of people and personalities that comes along with collaborative projects, was fodder for discussions of administrative philosophies and techniques. My experience turning community-based initiative projects into material for teaching and research (and by association, publications) was at the center of conversations for folks in different institutional settings who cared about "service" but struggled with ways to make it "count."

What is also interesting is the range of readings I received in terms of specialization and abilities because of my experience at WIDE. In fact, it was this range of readings that led to the dubbing of the WIDE effect. When you work at WIDE, you are often asked to do and write things in areas you may have little, if any, background. A lot of this occurs when writing grant proposals—a moment I learned to appreciate for its inventional multiplicity. Many of the conversations I had while on the market about this multiplicity centered on the level of practice, applying my WIDE training to work collaboratively and to design measurable research projects to my teaching. I learned to articulate my practices explicitly through working at WIDE on the development of a community based media center, which entailed seeking external funding and creating and maintaining a community media workshop series and web resource. Both of these required that I be explicit about what we were doing and how. To the funders, for example, I had to explain why health disparity should be addressed through a community media project. And, in regards to community partners, organizations and government officials, I cannot count the number of meetings I went to or documents produced in which we discussed why Lansing needed a community media center and how our practices were different than other types of community media (i.e., public radio) or on-campus entities (i.e., a writing center).

Some of this ability to be articulate about practices stems from being in the position of learner at WIDE, as I struggled in the new situations that I faced as part of my assistantship. When I first was hired, Jeffrey Grabill sent me a request to update an organization's website. This organization was a pretty big deal in the area, but we did not work with them specifically on any project. We also maintained their website on a volunteer basis. I first wondered why we were doing the updates in the first place (I later figured out that it was part of a complex practice of relationship building), and then I next thought, "Why should I be updating a website when I know nothing about websites!" That was my entry into learning how to be adaptable, and also to be thrust back into being a learner. From this position, I was able to hone my own teaching practices because I was acutely aware of the learning process, what it felt like and what strategies learners can use when faced with an unwieldy task. I think (but cannot be certain) that this experience improved my teaching, and my ability to talk about teaching from the perspective of learning.

I am not going to profess that all of this was one-hundred percent beneficial—I mean who knows which schools chucked my vita because I seemingly had too little classroom teaching experience or not enough research in one particular content area. And, I am not exactly sure where I will end up. What I can say is that the WIDE effect afforded me the range and the ability to feel comfortable in these multiple contexts.

Martine: Taking the WIDE Effect into an Institutional Context

During my work at WIDE, I finished my master's degree in digital rhetoric and professional writing and was accepted to the PhD program. During my tenure in graduate school, and before, I had worked as an adjunct instructor of writing in the communication department (as opposed to the humanities department) at Lansing Community College (LCC), just three miles down the road from Michigan State

University. Just as I was accepted to the PhD program, I also was offered a full-time position at LCC, which I accepted. To that end, my time at WIDE ended as I chose to give up my assistantship since I'd be teaching full time and conducting my dissertation research. My two years at WIDE imparted two worldviews which will remain with me throughout my career: 1) Institutional change is possible, but that change is not without setbacks and resistance; and 2) No matter the setting, whether that of an institution of higher education or that of a "corporate" business setting, the bottom line counts.

Going from a research university to a full-time faculty position at a community college, where I was finally able to see the "back-end" of faculty work was, to say the least, a complete culture shock. I can say that I thought things should be one way (pedagogy, curriculum, faculty governance, emphasis on research-based decisions, assessment), but the community college seemed to be operating in a totally different realm. Here is where I did, and continue to, draw upon my experiences at WIDE. My perception of the center's work at the time—a center conducting empirical research and working collaboratively with multiple stakeholders both in and outside of the institution—was that it was completely revolutionary, especially since the center was both implicitly, and in some cases explicitly, tied to the humanities at the university. The center's emphasis on collaboration certainly bumps up against the humanities-based ideal of the lone author working in his garret, cranking out one piece of genius after another. Whether WIDE meant to do it or not, it positioned itself to fundamentally and forever change the culture at the institution with respect to how one perceives the "humanities." Likewise, my hiring at a community college where less than twenty percent of all full-time faculty (closer to ten percent) have doctoral degrees, was a move—intentionally or not—that would facilitate changing the culture in my writing program. I saw change was needed at my institution regarding first-year writing curriculum and student assessment. I thought decisions impacting first-year writing could be more astutely informed by data (the gathering and analysis of which I learned about at WIDE). Thus, since I began my full-time employment at a community college over five years ago, I have become involved in many committees and initiatives where my research background could be put to use to effect changes that will benefit students. I am still actively working on these changes in the area of writing curriculum and student assessment. This past summer I was invited by our dean to organize a college-wide writing summit and I was able to invite a guest speaker, so, of course, I invited Jeffrey Grabill (who created a following at my college during his keynote). As I introduced Jeffrey this past summer during the writing summit, I referred to the fact that I am still drawing upon the experiences at WIDE—and as I informed the writing summit audience, I still say "WWJD," "What would Jeff do?" At WIDE, I learned the importance of developing and sustaining connections and allies, and of understanding that with any proposed institutional change, there will be resistance. During my time at WIDE I saw the building of human (and non-human networks) through the co-directors' and research assistants' active presentations across the college and indeed across Michigan (their outreach). Simultaneously I saw what I interpreted as a kind of resistance to the idea of a "research center" founded on researching writing—resistance in the form of arguments over space and over funding. But ultimately I saw the center become increasingly successful and self-sustaining and because of that my time at WIDE continuously provides me with a vision of what can occur if the right moves are made at the right time.

The second world view that I learned from WIDE is that "deliverables" matter—someone somewhere has provided dollars to pay the salaries and benefits of those around you, whether you are a scholar of Shakespeare or a software inventor. Sometimes the connections between the generators of those dollars and the work you do become buried and difficult to see. But by completing administrative reports documenting WIDE's productivity, by seeking funding opportunities to sustain the center and the students involved in the center's work, by bringing into view the entities across campus where grant seeking was a normal part of daily activities, I became deeply aware of the importance of being accountable for the resources that are drawn upon to sustain one's institutional work. And now at my work at LCC, I see this in complex ways that, I believe, give me a certain advantage. I know that approximately $27 million of federal financial aid was distributed to students at my college. This is public knowledge. But this matters to me, because it means that I have a certain accountability that might not always be visible—not just to those individuals in my classroom, but also to the citizens who have funded their education and my employment. When I recently applied for a $500.00 teaching circle grant at LCC, I understood that to receive these funds, I should provide a clear list of "deliverables." After all, the institution was being asked to provide dollars for a group of teachers to meet six times. Why shouldn't that institution receive something of value for the funds it was investing, even if the dollar amount was small? This kind of thinking has helped me even at the community college to seek out the resources available to assist students and teachers and to see accountability in my actions that I might otherwise take for granted.

Preparing for Multiplicity Through Multiplicity: Modularity as a New Participatory Goal

It seems especially important in the current economy for graduate students to balance the work of creating a stable narrative to describe their career plans with the problem of being prepared to work in complex situations that require adaptability and collaboration. Now is a time when some of our historical understandings about specialization are particularly at odds with the potential for finding ourselves confronting unexpected yet important tasks. As questions of breadth and multiplicity versus depth are central right now, professionalizing work in a research center provides opportunities that can allow graduate students to experience both: they can participate deeply in multifaceted research projects with partners and organizations they might not have the opportunity to work with otherwise, and they can maintain their own research, teaching, and service agendas outside the center.

In some ways, we are the outliers of the group of graduate students who have worked in WIDE because, at least at the moment, we are in academia. And yet we find that WIDE has prepared us well for nontraditional academic paths, as well as for bringing nontraditional attitudes to more traditional academic positions. Stacey's narrative focuses on how skills of relationship building and group dynamics can emerge from working in team research settings. Kendall's narrative shows how similar practices and skills can help graduate students develop the ability to relate to potential colleagues in a number of different institutional settings. Finally, Martine's narrative shows how the WIDE effect can play out, as some of the central practices and understandings of research center work have been beneficial in helping her work toward institutional change in her current position.

We feel that we have gained much professionally from learning to work collaboratively, to value the multiple colleagues we work with and the viewpoints of the multiple audiences we write for, and to learn contextually as we encounter new opportunities and problems to solve.

We know that work in a research center is not for everyone, and not every institution of higher learning in rhetoric and writing can maintain a research center. In spite of this, we see the concept of a modular model of professionalization as potentially adaptable beyond our individual experience at Michigan State and at WIDE. A modular model of professionalization values diverse graduate student experiences with activities and material spaces that extend beyond the terrain of the university or the norms of the humanities. In turn, it places a premium on helping graduate students learn how to create narratives that assemble those diverse activities in a way that helps others understand why they are meaningful and valuable—even if they might seem out of the ordinary. As people who have made use of this kind of work experience in forming our professional identities, we see it as a viable option that can stand alongside some of the more traditional avenues of professional development in rhetoric and writing.

Note

1. We know that our work is read as falling within the humanities, which are not generally considered to be research-oriented from the perspective of grant-funding agencies. This is likewise the case when we argue for space and materials within the institution to carry out our projects. This is also the case when we discuss what we can bring to community-based endeavors as a university-based research center. What we have learned, then, is how to articulate our worth to a range of audiences.

Works Cited

Berkenkotter, Carol, Thomas N. Huckin, and John Ackerman. "Social Context and Socially Constructed Texts: The Initiation of Graduate Students into a Writing Research Community." *Textual Dynamics of the Professions: Historical and Contemporary Studies of Writing in Professional Communities.* Ed. Charles Bazerman and James Paradis. Madison: U of Wisconsin P, 2001. Print.

Burnham, Chris, and Rebecca Jackson. "Experience and Reflection in Multiple Contexts: Preparing TAs for the Artistry of Professional Practice." *Preparing College Teachers of Writing: Histories, Theories, Practices, and Programs.* Ed. Betty Pytlik and Sarah Liggett. Oxford UP, 2002. 159–70. Print.

Lave, Jean, and Etienne Wenger. *Situated Learning: Legitimate Peripheral Participation.* Cambridge: Cambridge UP, 1991. Print.

Leverenz, Carrie Shively, and Amy Goodburn. "Professionalizing TA Training: Commitment to Teaching or Rhetorical Response to Market Crisis? *WPA: Writing Program Administration* 22.1–2 (Fall/Winter 1998): 9–32. Print.

Long, Mark C., Jennifer H. Holberg, and Marcy M. Taylor. "Beyond Apprenticeship: Graduate Students, Professional Development Programs and the Future(s) of English Studies." *WPA: Writing Program Administration* 20.1–2 (Fall/Winter 1996): 66–78. Print.

Marshall, Margaret J. *Response to Reform: Composition and the Professionalization of Teaching.* Carbondale: Southern Illinois UP, 2004. Print.

Mol, Annemarie. *The Body Multiple: Ontology in Medical Practice.* Durham and London: Duke UP, 2002. Print.

Peirce, Karen P., and Theresa Jarnagin Enos. "How Seriously Are We Taking Professionalization? A Report on Graduate Curricula in Rhetoric and Composition." *Rhetoric Review* 25.2 (2006): 204–10. Print.

Willard-Traub, Margaret K. "Professionalization and the Politics of Subjectivity." *Rhetoric Review* 21.1 (2002): 61–69. Print.

WIDE: Writing in Digital Environments. *Writing in Digital Environments Research Center,* 2010. Web. 11 March 2010.

14 Bridging Town and Gown through Academic Internships

Lara Smith-Sitton and Lynée Lewis Gaillet

> *Internships can empower students by moving them out of student roles and into roles of active participation as they put into practice the theories they learn in course work, implementing their own ideas in academic real-world settings. Internships can also offer students a safe environment in which to discover, at an early stage of their careers, whether they want to do such work.*
>
> —Daphne Desser and Darin Payne

The nationwide economic crisis in education has led to ubiquitous furloughs and layoffs, increasing reliance on contingent faculty to flesh out departmental hiring needs, and university hiring freezes. The job market for PhD students is certainly in a state of flux. The Modern Language Association (MLA) reported in September, 2010, that analysis of the 2009–2010 *Job Information List* revealed a 39.8 percent decline in advertisements from 2008–2009 to 2009–2010; in addition, the advertisements for English tenure-track and assistant professor positions dropped 53 percent between 2007–2008 and 2009–2010 (Laurence 1–2). Rhetoric and composition graduates are perhaps in a slightly better hiring position than their literature counterparts, in part because of the predictable increase in college admissions that occurs during a recession. The un- and underemployed often decide to retrain themselves for shifting markets, resulting in burgeoning first-year class sizes across the country. Since most of these new students are required to take first-year writing courses, the demand for composition classes and administrators to run writing programs is high. Of course, as we all know, increasing enrollments are no guarantee that adequately trained new graduates will be hired to fill this need, and many rhetoric and composition students are not interested in teaching first-year writing. Reflecting the state of the economy and general trends for "retooling" or retraining that happens broadly within the workforce during a recession, *Rewriting Success* addresses ways in which curricular and pedagogical reform might better prepare rhetoric and composition students for both traditional and alternative careers. Our contribution to this discussion concerns internships—a fairly common component within rhetoric and composition education, but one that is often underutilized. Our expanded conception of internships combines traditional facets of the student work-study model (including research assistantships) with key features of service-learning. The result? A trained work force that is uniquely poised for a much wider range of academic careers and non-academic employment as well. Furthermore, our plan is easily adopted by traditional university departments, particularly those where friendly relationships exist among the different factions often housed in an English department or across the university, as we will explain.

Beginning in 2005, the South Atlantic Modern Language Association (SAMLA) and the English department at Georgia State University (GSU) initiated a different kind of service-learning experience for students. Through the establishment of an internship program with SAMLA—an eighty-five-year-old, 501(c)(3) nonprofit corporation, housed in the English department—students are given "real world" writing opportunities and work experience in a structured setting that provides substantial supervision and direction. What makes this program unique is that the internship operates like a class: students register for the course, report for work/class according to an established schedule, select a track within the organization that is in line with their professional interests, complete assignments during the semester, and receive ongoing feedback as they work on their projects in a safe setting, where errors due to inexperience will not cost them their jobs.

The work assignments are not just routine tasks, but rather substantive projects that require the interns to research, write, collaborate, and communicate with their colleagues, the leadership of SAMLA, and their professors. At the end of the internship, students leave with a portfolio of work, a professionally developed resumé, and experience in the completion of large projects that were developed for a "real" company. The program has a distinctive goal: to build a service-learning and internship program that prepares students for a range of academic and mainstream employment. We are looking to do more than just build an internship or service-learning initiative; instead, we operate as an alternative classroom. In the five years since the launching of this program, the number of students serving as interns continues to grow. Students who have completed the program report that the experience was invaluable, helping them to consider and find jobs outside the academic norm of teaching and tutoring, in a variety of different environments of which they were likely not aware, prepared or looking for.

Background: Considering the Need for a Different Kind of Internship

Service-learning and internships have a successful and established history in American higher education, particularly within English departments and rhetoric and composition programs. From Vita Dutton Scudder's work as a literature and writing professor at Wellesley College in the early twentieth century to the more recent expansion of service-learning curricula and research by scholars and professors (see works by Bruce Herzberg, Linda Adler-Kassner, Ellen Cushman, Thomas Deans, and Julia Garbus), the initiatives taking students beyond the walls of a classroom present a multitude of opportunities not only to expand their social conscience and connect writing to the community but also to demonstrate how the research, writing, and communication skills garnered through rhetoric and composition courses fit the needs of many nonprofit and business organizations. These experiences direct students to alternative employment possibilities outside traditional academic departments, the ivory tower, and the university itself.

In the same vein of preparing our students for careers, we also know that employers seek employees with strong writing and communication skills—a predictable skills set among rhetoric and composition graduates. Although most rhetoric and composition students at GSU enter the graduate program to become university professors, as hiring situations shift, these students are considering alternative (nonacademic) career paths, particularly in technical communication, journal editing, and new media. Our students often enter advanced programs of study expecting to exit as carbon copies of their professors, employed by prestigious colleges and universities, and engaged in the holy triumvirate of academic employment: research, teaching, and service. Even within academia, students are often unaware of the wide range of academic work that occurs in support of the ivory tower: conference planning, journal and monograph publishing, and administration of programs.

While the successes of service-learning and internship initiatives are often touted in the pages of our journals, the pitfalls and challenges of sending students into internships where their own lack of experience, the lack of supervision by the on-site manager, or even the assignment of menial jobs keeps the intern from developing better job qualifications is well documented (see Linda Adler-Kassner, Ellen Cushman, and Robert W. McEachern's work). Recognizing these problems, we saw an opportunity at our university to develop a service-learning and internship program that could become a different kind of pedagogical experience. Through a formal program with SAMLA, students (both undergraduate and graduate) work in a "real world" environment, but they also are still students—learning how to take their research, close reading, and writing abilities and put them to work on significant projects. As the recruiter and supervisor of SAMLA interns, we recognize that the intern should engage in large tasks (journal production, conference planning, web and database management, etc.), not just clerical work. We provide significant supervision and support so that interns become better writers, better communicators, and better prepared for varying job markets. Students are charged with multi-faceted assignments such as redesigning a section of the website (which includes not only the finished page but also research to understand the history of the need for the project), creating a budget, drafting a proposal, outlining a project plan with deadlines, writing actual pages, and formally presenting the page to the organization's managerial leadership. This type of approach requires interns to show they understand how to critically think and communicate within a specific organization, as well as do the actual work.

The SAMLA interns are not in a classroom with desks and white boards; they work in an office with files, computers, and other employees. Their assignments are not just graded, but presented to and approved by the supervisor before dissemination to an audience that includes professors and the general public. The interns' primary instructor is not a professor, but an individual with a twenty-year corporate background in management, administration, and professional writing, who works closely with rhetoric and composition faculty to ensure that the students are exposed to opportunities and projects beyond what they learned while sitting in a traditional classroom. And while most students do receive three course credit hours and a grade (others who can't fit the class into their academic plan or don't need additional hours often volunteer as interns or audit the course of instruction), the assessment comes from on the job work; ultimately, it is the letters of recommendation, the challenge of complex assignments, and the deliverables listed on their CVs that the interns primarily seek. The students also prepare narratives summarizing their internship experiences. This final element unites the internship and alternative classroom experience with the values of service-learning initiatives. As Thomas Deans tells us, "Service-learning is not volunteerism or community service; nor is it simply an academic internship or field placement . . . it is at heart a pedagogy of action and reflection, one that centers on a dialectic between community outreach and academic inquiry (2).

How the Internship Appointment Begins

Upon taking over the role of SAMLA Executive Director in 2004, Lynée initiated the internship program and recruited the early interns from both her graduate and undergraduate rhetoric and composition classes. Gradually, the net widened, and now students come to SAMLA by recommendation from a broader range of faculty members. Lara serves as the associate director of SAMLA and the managing editor of our literary journal, *South Atlantic Review* (*SAR*). Upon receiving an internship referral, she and the student meet to discuss the opportunities at SAMLA, the student's professional aspirations and experience, and to outline the requirements and goals of their course (or internship program). The student is then assigned to one of four focus areas: editing and research, event planning, technical and professional writing, or general nonprofit sector administration. Interns are also informed that regardless of their area of focus, they must complete a technical writing assignment (often a section of the policy and procedural manual or instructional document related to an assigned project), write a series of short reflective pieces regarding their internships, and prepare a resumé and professional writing portfolio that reflects the work completed during the internship program. Upon agreement to these terms, the student completes the registration process with Lynée or their graduate advisor.

In the first days of the internship, students review a packet of materials to familiarize themselves with the operations and mission of SAMLA, the oldest regional arm of MLA. SAMLA is a nonprofit humanities organization dedicated to the advancement of teaching and literary and linguistic scholarship in the modern languages—an organization firmly rooted in a spirit of working within our community of graduate students, professors, and scholars to serve the ideals of higher education and the humanities. The background and mission of SAMLA makes it an environment strongly supported by the leadership at the administrative and executive levels. After becoming familiar with the organization, students then attend small group meetings where they meet the salaried employees and other interns. Because they are considered a part of the staff, students receive computer passwords, copier codes, equipment operation instructions, personnel directories, and an inbox where notes and materials will be left for them. During these meetings, we also confirm the goals and work assignments in the semester ahead (journal publication, printing of convention program, preparation of the newsletter, drafting of a grant application, etc.) and confirm the work schedules of each intern. Students begin their internships by reflecting on what they hope to gain from this experience and then receive their initial assignments based on a selected focus.

Editing and Research: An Internship Focused on the Publication of an Academic Journal

Many of our students in the rhetoric and composition program have an interest in editorial work. Some interns report they wish to work as editors employed by a publishing house. Others have professional aspirations to work in public print media—magazines, newspapers, or Internet sources. We also hire creative writing students who desire a career path that will provide them a salary so that they can pursue their interests in fiction, creative non-fiction, or poetry writing on the side. Students are often quick to register for editing and electronic publishing classes, but soon realize that to be considered for competitive editorial positions, they need demonstrated work experience and documented, written, workplace deliverables. The SAMLA internship offers skills for employment not only in traditional publishing houses or as journal editors, but also in academic publishing, university administration, and corporate positions. Our internship program provides a way for students not only to *tell* a future employer what they think they can do, but *show* them what they have done through work on *SAR*.

SAR is a seventy-five year old, peer-reviewed, literary journal, published quarterly. While the content is primarily focused on literature and language topics and book reviews, on occasion, creative writing, rhetoric, composition, and other disciplinary divisions are featured. While this journal does not primarily serve rhetoric and composition scholars, it provides an abundance of opportunities for editorial and publishing work that may easily translate into qualifications for jobs outside the internship. In addition, we often team with the creative writing journal housed within GSU, *Five Points,* and refer students with good editorial abilities to its executive director, Megan Sexton. Students who cut their teeth on academic publishing as an editorial assistant reviewing submissions and copy editing essays can then expand their professional experience to include editorial work on more than one journal. With the *Five Points* experience, interns have an opportunity to work with different content and audience considerations.

Damien Schlarb, a student who moved from an unpaid internship to a paid graduate research position as our layout and design editor says:

> Working as an intern in an academic environment provided the time and support to apply what I'd learned about visual rhetoric and writing to a job. When I started, I had a few skills in layout and I found the whole process of the publishing world intimidating because there seemed to be so many parts. Through my time with SAMLA, I worked on a redesign of the journal's layout, created ads, and covers. I have such a better understanding of how to work with others through this process because I saw how the individual steps of production come together to make a whole. I am more confident as a writer and know I have a substantive amount of experience that would allow me to move into layout, design or editorial positions within academia or in a company outside of a university.

Incidentally, when Schlarb began his internship, he was an MA student. He is now a PhD student, and though he intends to pursue a research and teaching career, he fully anticipates serving as an editor or working in the field of academic publishing in some capacity. Schlarb also commented that because of the experience he now has, he would have no hesitation in pursuing a publication or editorial position inside or outside of a college environment. He has accepted graphic design freelance projects as a result of his experience with the journal. The skills he first learned in the classroom were expanded during his internship. He now fully understands the printing process from selection of a press to the selection of content to the production of a final product.

As we evaluate the appropriateness of a project for the student, we carefully ascertain the abilities of the intern. In simple terms, we educate students about the processes of academic journal publishing and allow them to pursue assignments in line with their aptitudes and interests. The goal of this internship track is to provide knowledge of the complex considerations senior and managing editors face when publishing a periodical. Experience in the administrative details of publishing, line and copy editing, compilation of a mailing list, negotiation of postage contracts, layout, etc., expand the intern's understanding of what is involved in the publication of any work. At the end of the internship, the student not only understands the many facets of publishing and editing, but also can show prospective employers final products that they edited and helped create. Critical thinking, editing, writing, and communication skills are crucial for completion of the assigned tasks, which often incorporate rhetorical analyses, visual rhetoric, technical writing, and research skills. Students learn appropriate correspondence tone and format through the email and business correspondence they draft. Some of the items added to end-of-semester portfolios include business letters, evaluation forms, a journal, an advertisement, a journal cover, or proposals for changes to the operations related to *SAR*. Interns perfect editorial skills, learn a range of citation styles, and improve communication abilities on this track.

Convention Planning: An Internship Focused on Managing Large Projects

SAMLA's annual conference brings approximately 800 individuals together for a two-day conference in the southeast region of the U.S.

While the associate director and a part-time administrative assistant oversee the planning of the convention and communication with the program and executive committees, student interns are the hands that do the bulk of the work in preparation for the annual event. Rhetoric and composition students are particularly well suited for these tasks, as they typically possess necessary strong written and oral communication skills. Typical assignments include drafting a speaker's biographical sketch or writing letters to exhibitors or creating sections of the convention program—components of large event planning. Interns learn how to break a large project into smaller pieces while collaborating to achieve a common goal. While not all of our interns will move on to plan other academic conventions, former students have found themselves in other positions that use these skills.

Kay Ware, a rhetoric and composition student, sought the SAMLA internship because of her interest in grant writing, but found that through the months she worked for SAMLA, she had a real interest in convention and special event planning and saw ways this work incorporated much of what she garnered from her coursework:

> Though I came to SAMLA to help research and write possible grants for the organization, I jumped at the opportunity to work on the production of the convention program. I kept seeing how the foundation of rhetoric prepared me so well to draft sections of the program or correspondence to exhibitors and presenters because I understood how important it is to consider audience. I wanted to write, edit, and communicate with others and convention planning gave me all of these opportunities. Through this project, I expanded my understanding of Internet and electronic research methods, technical writing, and working with others.

Upon graduation, Ware applied for and obtained a permanent position with SAMLA because she had the experience the organization needed. In this role, she coordinates the creation of the convention program and relies heavily on editing and writing skills to prepare business communication, calls for papers, and various materials for the convention. She commented further, "The SAMLA internship and my subsequent employment have utilized each item in the rhetorical canon. I learned the canon in a classroom, and then applied it in SAMLA's classroom environment. Here, I was taught how we can employ positive rhetorical devices to communicate effectively with those we work with and those outside of our offices."

Individuals working on the SAMLA Convention receive a myriad of assigned tasks. They use layout and design skills for preparing the program or publicity posters. Assigned tasks often call into play technical, business, and creative writing skills. We have students learning how to address and format formal letters and emails to professors, speakers, and vendors. Professional writing opportunities include lengthy sections in the convention program or "scripts" for special events during the conference. Interns develop their technical writing skills by creating mailings, posters, website pages, and sections of our policy and procedural manual related to the convention. Additionally, interns work with local arrangement volunteers to staff the registration desk, address concerns of those in attendance, and troubleshoot onsite. Some interns have the opportunity to learn how to read and negotiate contracts required for large events, while others plan the receptions and learn how to create a budget. By working on the convention, our students practice the writing and communication skills learned in their academic programs and see how the success of a large project affords an opportunity to put into play so much of what is covered in individual classes. They learn much more than how an academic conference comes together: they see how the success of large events and projects are rooted in communication and rhetorical skills.

Former intern Sheila Ameri thought she would likely teach with her rhetoric and composition degree, but that's not really what she wanted to do. Through her internship, Ameri connected her rhetoric and composition background to other employment opportunities and saw how she was qualified to compete with students who obtained hotel management degrees for event planning positions. Ameri explains:

> Through my experience with SAMLA, I learned how to communicate professionally with anyone, whether they were the chair of a college English department, an editor at an academic press, or a writer from Spain. The hands-on experience preparing for the conference and attending to the details while I was there enabled me to see how a convention comes together for both sides. I learned how to roll up my sleeves and do whatever it takes to make an event happen—I made nametags, wrote business letters, worked on the menus, and created PowerPoint programs. I now have a position in a hotel

where my communication and organization skills are utilized every day. SAMLA not only showed me career options, but also refined my writing and communication skills. I have a much better understanding of the 'big picture' when it comes to event planning, and this got me a job.

The planning of the convention is a year-round event. We negotiate hotel contracts two and three years in advance; speakers are invited months before their names are announced; special topics and sessions are organized a year or more ahead of time. While one intern may work on the session schedule for the convention in one calendar year, another may prepare a publicity plan and materials for a convention two years out. During the convention, students see the demands of a large-scale event, are exposed to the complexities of customer service, and learn how to problem solve under pressure. Some interns are photographers, others design PowerPoint programs, and still others simply confirm all is in order for each day of sessions. Although most professors and many graduate students regularly attend and present their work at conferences, few academics understand the complexities of conference planning—much in the same way researchers don't know much about the work of archivists. Alice Myatt, a PhD candidate currently writing her dissertation in our rhetoric and composition program recently secured an academic position at the University of Mississippi. Given her work with SAMLA, Myatt is now very comfortable in her new position, which includes administration of a program and perhaps organizing a conference in the future. In her words:

> Through the convention, I now very much appreciate and see the role conference attendance can provide for professional development. I understand the function and how to write calls for papers. I also believe it is important for graduate students and scholars to attend conferences to hear what is occurring in our profession now—rather than waiting for the often-slow print cycle to communicate it. I would like to see there be more funding available. I met so many scholars and students from a variety of English study backgrounds. I anticipate my administrative skills and internship with SAMLA will be a part of my career.

Conference planning takes a large team of individuals willing to work together to reach a common goal.

TECHNICAL AND PROFESSIONAL WRITING IN THE WORKPLACE

Writing careers, of course, are not limited to prestigious editorial positions or exciting journalism assignments. Some of the most critical writing takes places in small formats in corporate, educational, and nonprofit environments. Interns following this track of our program focus primarily on writing and editing projects that support the efforts of the journal, the convention, and the organization as a whole, and create a portfolio of technical and professional writing pieces that include correspondence, newsletter articles, website pages, membership materials, and policy and procedural manual sections. Interns write both collaboratively and independently to produce deliverables for the organization. This focus is different than the other internship tracts as we truly place the emphasis on short writing projects with very little attention given to administrative responsibilities. Brian Dormit, a graduate of GSU's rhetoric and composition program, describes the impact of the internship on his career:

> The opportunity to intern with SAMLA provided me with valuable experience. My portfolio included web pages, program pieces, and a newsletter. SAMLA's trust in me to redesign the newsletter template, plus develop the plan to move the distribution from regular mail to email was invaluable. I was able to explain that I have the ability to handle large projects that call upon many different skills, and I can think through a situation and come up with ways to improve a project. I got the job as a technical writer, and I believe without the internship, I would not have had this opportunity.

This facet of SAMLA's internship program can be particularly challenging. As we need high quality, strong writing for the tasks, we often find our interns may have mastered the dictates of academic writing but have not fully evolved into proficient professional writers. In response to this problem, we often break projects into small parts and have students work in pairs to complete a writing project. We take the practices of peer review and put them into place in a work environment by pairing interns to work as editors of each other's work before submitting it for editorial review. Often, interns work collaboratively initially, and then present the work independently, in the process developing strong interpersonal skills that are transferable beyond the internship. Svenja Schall, an intern whose first language is German, realized after receiving an assignment to correspond with the convention session chairs that her writing skills in English, particularly for an American audience, might not be up to the task:

> When I got the assignment, I first thought it would be easy and then realized I had never written a formal letter in English. A co-worker first read the letter and gave me some advice before I turned it in. Through this experience I learned not only how to write a letter, but the correct American format and tone to use. Understanding the considerations of letter writing has been so helpful to me in my job after graduation. I communicate with individuals in many different countries and usually in writing, not orally. The internship not only gave the confidence to do this work, but also the importance of knowing the expected form and tone of individuals in other countries.

Our interns often covet a position working on the organization's newsletter. For nearly seventy-five years the newsletter was printed annually, but as a result of the increasing number of outstanding emerging writers and editors interning each year, we now publish biannually. Jocelyn Crawley, a published fiction writer and student in our department was charged with the task of attending each of the speaker sessions at the convention and writing a lengthy "report" article. Her creative and composition writing skills are excellent; however, this project showed her that there is a distinctive difference between writing a piece of fiction or an essay and creating a news article. She reflects:

> I am so grateful for the time given to me at SAMLA. I was surprised by the edits and changes made, but understood them. This internship connected my classroom understanding of "audience" and "arrangement" to real world writing. I now have a published article in my portfolio that demonstrates my ability to write a journalistic piece. I am now pursuing additional technical writing opportunities on the website and through the policies and procedural manual so that I can show future employers that I am a versatile writer, able to adapt to any environment, and game for any writing or editing assignment offered to me.

DEVELOPING LEADERSHIP AND ADMINISTRATIVE SKILLS

The developing leadership and administrative skills focus is for interns with a desire for leadership roles in nonprofit or business settings. While they may primarily enlist writing and communication skills, these students seek positions where administrative and management abilities are required. This track provides the opportunity to not only write, but also to understand legal and business operations that undergird the organization. Interns serve as the recording secretaries at committee meetings and prepare the minutes. We currently have two students researching and drafting grant proposals and the contract with the university to maintain our sponsored program status at GSU. These students write memoranda, meeting agendas, policies, membership procedures; develop forms needed internally; and communicate with the organization's leadership regarding the nuts and bolts related to keeping a nonprofit operating. One intern wrote the materials for a convention travel grant program established in memory of one of our past presidents. These students complete real-world work assignments and learn what it takes to run a nonprofit company.

Gina Prescott, one of our first interns to work in this focus area describes what she gained from the experience:

> My business writing skills improved, definitely. I learned how to write concise, professional emails and letters. I saw how I could find the facts I needed for a project in the same way I did research for an essay. I also learned how to turn a project around quickly and why this is important. More than anything else, however, I developed confidence in my abilities as a professional woman, writer, and communicator. When I accepted my first position after graduation, I knew how to prepare for a meeting; I knew my input in a meeting needed to be on-point and concise; I knew how to select my tone in a way that was adding to the discussion, not trying to argue my point as the "right" point; I knew I could handle any writing task given to me. The internship took so much of what I learned in my rhetoric and composition courses that had greatly improved my writing and connected it directly to a work environment.

After receiving her MA in rhetoric and composition, Prescott decided to attend law school. She attributed her successes serving on the law review editorial board, organizing events for the ACLU, and communicating with her professors, fellow students, and law firms to her concentration in rhetoric studies and experiences gained from her internship. Prescott may pursue a position as an attorney in a law firm, but she has a strong interest in returning to the nonprofit sector to utilize her legal skills as well.

Pedagogy and Research

The establishment of the SAMLA internship program has been invaluable not only to our students but also to Lara as the administrator of the program and in her work as a rhetoric and composition PhD student. Before SAMLA, Lara enjoyed a career in the private sector as a technical and professional writer and business consultant. In the field, she discovered substantial writing problems within the ranks of upper management and among the eager young professionals who held MBAs. She was also discouraged that some of the most capable editors and writers were relegated to administrative support roles because their humanities degrees were not considered sufficiently specialized for other corporate positions. Those "other" jobs were often held by individuals with weaker oral and written communication skills, but who possessed advertising, public relations, and business degrees. The responsibility was twofold: employers presumed a specialized degree from a business school would best prepare a new employee for the rigors of the corporate world, and individuals with English degrees failed to recognize and articulate how the research, writing, and communication skills garnered through their coursework qualified them for a range of positions.

SAMLA is not a classroom, but it is an environment where Lara teaches—often one-on-one or in small groups—and can address the writing problems she witnessed in business settings. This alternative classroom provides her an opportunity to hone her instructional practices. Teaching in this environment requires a great deal of patience; interns naturally often make mistakes, and the fast-paced environment of an understaffed nonprofit business doesn't always accommodate this learning curve. As we mentor interns and help them connect their formal classroom studies to "real world" settings, we empower them to help others make the same connections. In turn, studying our students' progress and performance not only validates our assumptions about the value of service-learning and formal internship programs, but also provides data for our own research in these areas. It is also important to comment on one additional facet of SAMLA that Lara and other graduate students who intend to stay in higher education find through this program. In many ways, these interns function like stage hands in a play. As they review and edit submissions for the journal, rewrite calls for papers, develop an academic conference program, and work with faculty and college administrators in universities around the country, these students learn about the twenty-first century university and academia in a way that those sitting as audience members in a classroom may not. Over the past four years, Lara has reviewed and edited over one hundred full-length scholarly essays for the journal. She and her fellow graduate interns know citation styles backwards and forwards. They see the trends for research through the session topics at the conference. They observe seasoned scholars present their work alongside emerging academics still finding their voices. These experiences are priceless for a graduate student shaping a career in the field of rhetoric and composition.

Conclusion and Implications

We have an advantageous venue for internships given the partnership between SAMLA and GSU. Our funding comes from the regional organization, the local English department, and the dean's office. Our success is due in large part to institutional (financial) support, collaboration among faculty from different divisions and departments within the region, and mutual respect for the endeavor (often from faculty members and administrators not directly involved in SAMLA). Although we realize not all institutions have access to this sort of non-profit arrangement, our situation is not unique. Students in English departments and stand-alone writing programs across the country serve as research assistants and editors, provide tutoring and administrative assistance, teach in programs engaged in interesting work based on local exigencies, and enroll in internship and service-learning courses. In addition, most institutions of higher education support and staff numerous funded centers across campus; these centers already provide a multitude of hiring and volunteer opportunities for graduate students. We are suggesting that directors of existing academic centers and programs, leaders of national/regional/local organizations housed at their institutions, and editors of journals, newsletters, and websites examine ways in which they might not only prepare students for the kinds of traditional work academics do, but also expand their notions of graduate student training to include alternative positions within the university and preparation for careers outside academia.

On a final note, yes, the SAMLA internship program is invaluable for students, but in reality, we established our program not just as an ethical and practical training ground for students but because the organization was in trouble: too much work, too little funding, too few hands. In the last twenty years, the needs of the organization and technical demands quickly outpaced traditional staffing: an executive director, journal editor, business manager/managing editor, (very) part time accountant, and one or two departmentally-assigned graduate assistants. In particular, burnout and rapid turnover in the business manager position led to a lack of transparency in daily operations and a vast backlog of work. The addition of an internship program has created no less than a sea change in the operations of SAMLA—in part because management (not the department) brought on board staff and interns with prior experience and those who had a true interest in working for a nonprofit organization. The friction that for years characterized relationships between the operational staff and the organization's executive committee has disappeared. Because there is now a clear plan of business and qualified hands to carry out that work, the organization has revised its procedure and policy guidelines, revisited its publication practices, and expanded member services. As a result, conference attendance has grown; journal publication and dissemination is cheaper and now on schedule; and the organization is attracting new members from a variety of disciplines.

To be successful, an internship program must be collaborative and of benefit both to students and the organization. Top heavy, didactic academic programs engaged only in "benevolent" assistance to students neither prepare interns for real-world experiences nor offer opportunities for students to add to the value of the organization. In our case, we needed—in addition to the English students typically interested in journal production—interns with media and layout experience, membership and financial backgrounds, and an interest in event planning. Our wildly successful internship program (one that should have been created years ago in an organization of this size and profile) has literally breathed new life into SAMLA and—with the addition of a qualified workforce—offers financial sustainability. Most importantly for the goals of this collection, our specific program is easily replicable at other institutions in a variety of nonprofit centers and academic programs already in place.

Works Cited

Adler-Kassner, Linda. "Digging a Groundwork for Writing: Underprepared Students and Community Service Courses." *College Composition and Communication* 46.4 (1995): 552–55. Print.

Ameri, Sheila. Personal Interview. 19 November 2009.

Brooks, Katharine. *You Majored in What? Mapping Your Path from Chaos to Career.* New York: Viking, 2009. Print.

Crawley, Joycelyn. Personal Interview. 21 January 2010.

Cushman, Ellen. "Sustainable Service Learning Programs." *College Composition and Communication* 54.1 (2002): 40–65. Print.

Deans, Thomas. *Writing Partnerships: Service-Learning in Composition.* Urbana: NCTE, 2000. Print.

Desser, Daphne, and Darin Payne. "Writing Program Administration Internships." *The Writing Program Administrator's Resource: A Guide to Reflective Institutional Practice.* Ed. Stuart C. Brown and Theresa Enos. Wahwah, NJ: Lawrence Erlbaum, 2002. Print.

Dormit, Brian. Personal Interview. 10 February 2010.

Garbus, Julia. "Service-Learning, 1902." *College English* 64.5 (2002): 547–65. Print.

Hart Research Associates. "Raising the Bar: Employers' Views of College Learning in the Wake of the Economic Downturn. A Survey Conducted on Behalf of The American College and University Association." Washington, D.C., January 10, 2010. Web.

Herzberg, Bruce. "Community Service and Critical Teaching." *College Composition and Communication* 45.3 (1994), 307–19. Print.

Laurence, David. "MLA *Job Information List,* 2009–10." *Report on the MLA Job Information List, 2009–10. MLA.* September 2010. Web. 28 July 2011.

McEachern, Robert W. "Problems in Service Learning and Technical/Professional Writing: Incorporating the Perspective of Nonprofit Management." *Technical Communication Quarterly* 10.2 (2002): 211–24. Print.

Menand, Louis. *The Marketplace of Ideas: Reform and Resistance in the American University.* New York: Norton, 2010. Print.

Myatt, Alice. Telephone Interview. 1 March 2010.

Prescott, Gina. Telephone Interview. 8 February 2010.

Schlarb, Damien. Personal Interview. 26 January 2010.

Zernicke, Kate. "Making College 'Relevant.'" *The New York Times* 3 Jan. 2010. *NYTimes.com.* Web. 7 January 2010.

Index

Abraham, Matthew, xiii, xxii
Academe, 68, 169, 174
academic capital, xvi
academic discourse, ix, 36
Ackerman, John, 6, 7, 16, 196, 207
activist, 85, 92, 102, 175, 186, 188–189
ADE Bulletin, 169
adjunct, xv, xviii, 3, 5, 12, 14–16, 36, 38–39, 45–46, 64–65, 77, 133, 146, 149, 156, 180, 183–186, 189, 203
Adler-Kassner, Linda, 211–212, 226
advocacy, xix, 20, 56, 60, 66, 83–84, 90, 98–99, 102
advocate, community, 83
advocate, professional, 84–85
Ahern-Dodson, Jennifer, xxi, 175
Amado-McCoy, Moira K., xix, 83
Ameri, Sheila, 218, 226
American Association of University Professors (AAUP), 16, 57, 67–68, 169
American Civil Liberties Union (ACLU), 223
American Federation of Teachers, x, xxii
American Indian College Fund—Mellon Research Fellowship, 48
Amherst College, 20, 26, 31, 146, 148
Anderson, Virginia, xii–xiii, xxii

Aristotle, 40, 48, 112; *Rhetoric*, vii, xii–xiv, xvii, xix, xxii–xxiii, 1, 16, 30, 32–33, 35, 40, 47–50, 64, 66–67, 72–74, 89, 111, 142, 173–174, 196, 208–209, 217
assessment, 26–27, 37, 39, 43, 53, 56, 151, 162, 168, 179, 182, 188, 204, 213
Atlantic, The, 123
Austin, Ann, 184, 189

BAI Community Action Alliance, 93, 96, 100–103
Bakhtin, Mikhail, 173
Baldwin, Roger, 61, 67
Ballif, Michelle, vii, xxii, 32–35, 38, 48
Barrios, Barclay, 154, 157
Bartholomae, David, 24, 28, 30
basic writing, vii, 24, 142
Bedford/St. Martin's Press, xx, 31, 116, 145, 150–153, 155, 190
Berkenkotter, Carol, 6–7, 16, 196, 207
Berlin, James, 20, 30
Bieber, Jeffrey, 162–163, 173
biomedical engineering, 3, 5, 8–9, 11, 13
Bishop, Wendy, 172–173, 182, 189
Bornstein, Kate, 90, 103
Boston College, 31, 116, 143, 146–147, 150, 174, 190

227

228 *Index*

Bousquet, Marc, 36–38, 47–48, 160, 173
Bowen, William G., 146, 148, 157
Boyer, Ernest J., 20, 27, 30, 180, 186, 189
Brereton, John, 20, 24, 31
British English, 124
Broadview Press, 75
Bruffee, Kenneth, 173–174
Burke, Kenneth, 107, 116
Burnett, Rebecca, 140, 143
business writing, 222

Campbell, Joseph, 106, 116
Carbone, Nick, xx, 145
Carr, Jean Ferguson, 20
Carr, Stephen, 20
Castel, Judge P. Kevin, 120, 130
Catholic Church, 50, 99–100, 102–103
Catholic University of America, The, 118
CCCC Committee on the Status of Women, 159
Chin, Dianne, 46
Chiseri-Strater, Elizabeth, 182, 190
Choseed, Malkiel, xi, xvii–xviii, 18
Christensen, Chuck, 150
Chronicle of Higher Education, The, xii, 20, 48, 50, 117, 130–131, 157, 169
Chronister, Jay, 61, 67
civil rights, 92, 95, 102
Clark, Irene, 40, 47
Clark, Kim, 48
Cloud, Dana, 60, 67
Coalition on the Academic Workforce, x, xxii
Colgate University, 117–118
collaboration, xx, 9, 13–14, 66, 89, 91, 103, 138, 140, 142–143, 171, 180, 185–187, 189, 192–193, 199–200, 204, 206, 224

college: four-year, 19, 33, 133, 151, 169; two-year, xvii, 18–19, 21, 29–30, 33, 40, 81, 133, 165, 193
College Composition and Communication (CCC), 16, 31, 43, 49–50, 189–190, 226
colleges: community college, ix, xi, xvi–xvii, 19–20, 22, 26–30, 32–33, 38–39, 43, 45–46, 53, 151, 164–165, 166, 168–169, 200, 204, 206; tribal colleges, xvi
Colorado State University (CSU), 145, 149–151, 153
commodified, xv–xvi
community centers, xvi
community college, ix, xi, xvi–xvii, 19–20, 22, 26–30, 32–33, 38–39, 43, 45–46, 53, 151, 164–166, 168–169, 200, 204, 206
community literacy theory, 65, 177, 179
community-based: learning, 180; pedagogies, 175, 187; research (CBR), 180, 182, 187–188
composition: compositionist, 25, 188; composition studies, 20, 25, 37, 42, 154; first-year, xiv, 18, 21, 29, 41, 47, 133; theory, 19, 133, 147
Composition Studies, vii, 16, 31, 50, 174
Computers and Composition, 150, 155
Computers and Writing, 155
Conference on College Composition and Communication, vii, xi, 3, 16, 49, 159
Connors, Robert, 39, 41, 49, 148
contingent faculty, 3, 29, 35, 51–56, 58–67, 209
copyeditor, 134, 136

Cornell, 16, 149
corporatization, xv, xviii, 38–39
correspondence, 216–217, 220
Council of Writing Program Administrators (CWPA), 20, 27
Crawley, Jocelyn, 221, 226
creative writing, xix, 37, 105, 107–108, 113, 162, 164–165, 167, 172, 177, 214–215, 218
Crump, Eric, 147
culture shock, xiii, 204
current-traditional rhetoric, 88
curriculum, xiii, 9, 15, 21, 26, 38–39, 45–46, 52–53, 61–64, 66, 86, 97, 118, 121–123, 133, 142, 151, 171, 176, 182, 185, 188–189, 197, 202, 204, 211; development of, 21, 62, 185; writing, 74, 117–119, 121, 151, 204
curriculum vita, 78, 153, 203
Curtis, John, 65, 67, 147
Curtis, Marcia, 65, 67, 147
Cushman, Ellen, 177, 182, 189, 211–212, 226
customer journey map, 107

data, xi, 5, 6, 8, 10–12, 14, 38, 41, 47, 72–73, 79–80, 109–110, 115, 135, 138, 180, 195, 204, 224
Davis, Diane, vii, xxii, 32–35, 38, 48
De Botton, Alain, 34, 49
Dead Poets Society, 44, 49, 104
Deans, Tom, 182, 189, 211, 213, 226
Desser, Daphne, 209, 226
Dickens, Charles, 119, 131
disciplinarity, x, xvi
discourse: discourse communities, 108; academic, ix, 36
Doe, Sue, xviii, 51

Doonesbury, 149, 157
Dormit, Brian, 220, 226
downsizing, 36–37
Doyle, Terry, 47, 49
Dragga, Sam, 106, 116
Draper, Stephen, 114, 116
Duke University, xxi, 190, 208

Eagen, Kevin, 65
Economist, The, 123
Ede, Lisa, 148
editor: technical, xix, 132, 134–140, 142; textbook, 148, 164
Elbow, Peter, 28, 31, 147
English as a Second Language (ESL), 36, 39, 124, 164–165, 168
English department, xiii, xix, 23, 33, 37, 54, 83–87, 89, 91, 97, 104, 106, 111, 113, 116, 150, 163, 175–176, 196, 210–211, 218, 224
English education, 164
English Online, 147–148
English Only movement, 77
English Studies, xiii, xxii–xxiii, 23, 89, 91, 104–106, 111–113, 115–116, 208
Enos, Theresa Jarnagin, xxiii, 33, 49, 56, 67, 158, 174, 197, 208, 226
epistemology, 35, 39–40, 43, 72
exchange value, xv–xvi

Facebook, 99, 155
faculty: adjunct, xv, xviii, 3, 5, 12, 14–16, 36, 38–39, 45–46, 64–65, 77, 133, 146, 149, 156, 180, 183–186, 189, 203; contingent, 3, 29, 35, 51–56, 58–67, 209; junior, xiii, 72; non-tenure track, ix, xvii–xxi, 29, 33, 38, 67, 70, 175; tenure track, vii, ix–x, xviii,

230 *Index*

xx, 29, 32, 35, 37–39, 44–45, 48, 51–53, 55–57, 59, 61–67, 70, 75, 77–78, 81, 91, 117, 121, 132–134, 145–146, 148–150, 156, 158–160, 164, 167, 169, 170–172, 180, 186, 193, 204
faculty governance, 51–52, 58–60, 62–67, 86, 204
Faigley, Lester, 76; *Brief Penguin Handbook, The*, 76–77
Feinberg, Joan, 150
Finkelstein, Martin, x, xxiii
first-year composition (FYC), xiv, 18, 21, 23–24, 26–27, 29–30, 41, 47, 133
Five Points, 215
five-paragraph essay, 46
Foucault, Michel, viii, xxiii
four-year college, 19, 33, 133, 151, 169
Freeman, Denny, 9–10
Freytag, Gustav, 106, 116
Fulkerson, Richard, 40, 49–50
Fund for the Improvement of Post-Secondary Education (FIPSE), 179–180, 183, 185, 188

Gaillet, Lynée, xxi, 172, 174, 209
Gappa, Judith, 179, 184, 189
Garbus, Julia, 211, 226
gender studies, 86, 88, 91
genre, 10, 13, 45, 87, 117, 119, 121–122, 124
Georgia State University, xxii, 133, 210
Goleman, Judith, 172–174
Goodburn, Amy, vii, 192, 208
Grabill, Jeffrey, 190, 193, 203, 205
graduate training, x, xvi–xvii, xxi–xxii, 18–19, 114, 132, 136, 141, 197
Graff, Gerald, 46, 49

grant: proposal, 55, 78, 188, 202, 222; writing, 13, 98, 217
Graves, Heather Brodie, xviii, 69

Hart Leadership Program in Public Policy, 179
Hart-Davidson, Bill, 193
Harvard University, 16, 24, 41, 174
Haswell, Richard, 40, 41, 49
Haussamen, Brock, 128, 131
Hemingway, Ernest, 107, 128
Herrington, Anne, 7, 16–17, 147
Herzberg, Bruce, 116, 211, 226
Hill Associates, 134–136, 138–139, 143
Holberg, Jennifer, 36, 50, 197, 208
Hooper, Linda, 138, 144
Horner, Bruce, xv, xxiii, 20, 31, 36, 49
Houghton Mifflin, 147–148, 150
Howrey LLP, 117–118, 121–122, 124, 126, 130
Huckin, Thomas, 6–7, 16, 196, 207
Huot, Brian, 26, 31

identity politics, 39, 42, 84, 92
Inside Higher Ed, 16–17, 20, 49
interdisciplinarity, xix, 40, 86–92, 175, 177–179, 185–186, 188
internship, xxi–xxii, 85, 170, 209–225
iPods, 184

Jacobe, Monica, 65, 67
Jaeger, Audrey, 65, 67
Jefferson, Thomas, 119, 131
Jim Crow, 101
junior faculty, xiii, 72

KairosWiki, xi
Kenan Institute for Ethics, 179

Kezar, Adrianna, 62, 68
Kiefer, Kate, 150
Klausman, Jeffrey, 25, 31
knowledge: mobilization, 74; practitioner, xvi–xvii, 3–4; teaching, xvi, 74
Kopelson, Karen, 39, 42, 49
Krug, Stephen, 114, 116

labor, xv, xviii, 3, 14–15, 35, 63
land-grant university, 176
Lansing Community College (LCC), 203
Latterell, Catherine, 172, 174
Lauer, Janice, 159, 174
Lave, Jean, 196, 207
law, xvi, xx, 55, 88, 101, 117, 119, 121–122, 125, 127–128, 144, 223
law firm, xvi, xx, 119, 121, 125, 127–128, 223
lawyers, xx, 119–121, 130
learner-centered pedagogies, 47
LeCourt, Donna, vii, 4, 16
legal writing, xx, 117, 119–122, 124, 128–129
Legal Writing Institute, listserv, 122
Leon, Kendall, xxi, 191
Leverenz, Carrie, vii, 192, 208
LGBTQ, xix, 84, 91–95, 98–101
liberal arts college, 37, 45–46, 148, 191
linguistics, 37, 106, 133
literacy, xvi, 14, 32–33, 42, 45, 48, 65, 102, 176–177, 179–181
literary, 36, 85–86, 89
Little Penguin Handbook, The, 77
local conditions, xviii, 35
lore, xvi, 3, 20, 39
Ludwig, Jeff, xiii, xxii–xxiii
Lyndon State College, 146

Macon College, 132–133
Marlboro College, 146, 148, 151
Massachusetts Institute of Technology (MIT), xvii, 4, 8–9, 15, 174; Electrical Engineering and Computer Science, 9
Master of Fine Arts (MFA), 167, 170
McEachern, Robert W., 212, 226
McLeod, Sue, 17, 182, 190
Megabyte University (MBU-L), 147
Mejía, Jamie A., 36, 43, 49
Melis, Ildikó, xi, xviii, 32
Menand, Louis, 148, 157, 226
Michigan State University, xxi, 191, 203, 207
Microsoft PowerPoint, 75, 135, 137, 218–219
Mikva, Abner, 99
Miles, Libby, 154, 157, 190
Miller, Hildy, 162, 174
Miller, J. Hillis, vii
Miller, Susan, 20
Modern Language Association (MLA), xi, xxiii, 17, 38, 47, 49, 160, 169, 174, 209, 214, 226; Job Information List, xi, xxiii, 209, 226
modular professionalization, 193, 197
Moller, Marilyn, 148
Monroe, Jonathan, 7, 16, 183, 190
Moore, Cindy, xx, 158, 174
Moran, Charlie, 17, 147, 155
Mountford, Roxanne, vii, xxii, 32–35, 38, 48
Mullin, Joan, 187, 190
Myatt, Alice, 219, 226

National Council of Teachers of English (NCTE), 16–17, 24, 30–31, 43, 48–49, 174, 189, 226

National Science Foundation, 55
Neilsen, Jakob, 114
new media, 47, 96, 99, 113–114, 211
New York Times Magazine, 148, 157
New Yorker, The, 123–124
Newman Centers, 100
newsletter, 126, 140, 214, 220–221
No Child Left Behind Act, 177
nonprofit, xix, 84, 90, 92, 96–97, 102, 164, 210–211, 213–214, 220, 222–226
non-tenure track, ix, xvii–xviii, xxi, 3–4, 14–15, 25, 29, 33, 37–38, 48, 51–52, 55–56, 58–67, 70, 81, 153, 162–163, 166–168, 175, 182, 217
Norman, Donald, 114, 116
North, Stephen, xvi, xxiii, 20, 24, 31, 39–40, 49, 83, 85, 91
Norwich University, 133–134
Nowacek, Rebecca, 178, 187, 190
Nugent, Jim, xiii, xxii–xxiii

Obama, Barack, 99, 103
Olson, Gary, xxiii, 41, 49
Onondaga Community College, 18
open admissions, 19
Opipari, Benjamin, xix, 117, 131
Ostergaard, Lori, xiii, xxii–xxiii

Palmquist, Mike, 150
participant-observation, 52
Payne, Darin, 209, 226
Pearson, 76–77, 144
pedagogy, xxii, 4, 7, 16, 19, 21, 23–24, 26–27, 35, 42, 44, 76, 84, 86, 91–92, 95, 110, 130, 133, 142, 145, 147, 150–152, 154, 165, 167, 177, 182, 190, 204, 210, 212–213, 223; Freire-an, 95; learner-centered, 47; post-process, 42; service learning, 177; WAC, 4, 13; WID, 13, 15
peer response, 45
peer review, xiii, 9, 41, 46, 95, 141–142, 152, 154, 220
Peirce, Karen P., 197, 208
Petrosky, Anthony, 24, 30
Phipps, Allison, 88, 103
Pigg, Stacey, xxi, 191
placement, 23–24, 26, 39, 118, 160, 213
Poe, Mya, xvii–xviii, 3
postdoctoral teaching fellowship, 21, 175–178, 189
post-process pedagogy, 42
practitioner knowledge, xvi–xvii, 3–4
Preparing Future Faculty, 170
Prescott, Gina, 222–223, 226
Profession, xii–xiii, xxii, 16, 50, 68, 169, 174
professionalization, vii, xvii, xx–xxi, 34, 36, 83, 191–193, 195–198, 200, 206–208
project management, 136, 138, 142

queer, 90, 92, 101
Quid and the Whale, The, 44

Rankin, Elizabeth, 172, 174
research: empirical, xix, 24, 26, 115, 204; scientific, 10–11, 13; WID, 5–6, 9, 13
research assistants (RAs), 79, 194, 198, 205, 210, 224
Research I institutions, 16, 19, 52, 175–176, 192
Research Service-Learning at Duke, 179, 185, 190
resume, 119, 165, 210, 213

rhetoric, xvi, xix, xxi–xxii, 6–8, 12, 16–17, 30, 40, 45–46, 49–50, 58, 67, 72–75, 77–78, 83–86, 88–90, 92, 96–99, 102, 105, 111–112, 115–116, 133, 137, 142–143, 147, 149, 172–173, 190, 192, 196–199, 203, 207–208, 215–218, 223; faculty, 6, 8; rhetorical education, 17, 84, 89; rhetoric of science, 8, 16, 73, 78; rhetoric studies, 78, 80, 92, 149, 223; rhetorical triangle, 97; theory, 89, 147; visual rhetoric, 40, 97, 215–216
rhetorician, 70, 83–87, 89, 92, 96–100, 102, 112, 147, 177, 189
rhetoric and composition, vii–xxiii, 1, 19–20, 32–42, 44–45, 47–50, 64–67, 70–71, 74, 78, 80–81, 83–84, 86, 132–134, 136–137, 141–143, 169, 174, 192, 201, 208–209, 211, 213–215, 217–220, 222–224
Richardson, Mark, 45, 50
Rife, Martin, xxi, 191
Rogoff, Barbara, 34, 50
Romano, Susan, xii–xiii, xxii
Rudd, Mysti, xi–xii, xxiii
Rude, Carolyn, 136, 138–139, 144

Sam, Cecile, 62, 68, 106, 116
Schall, Svenja, 221
Schell, Eileen, 3, 16–17, 36, 50, 56, 68
Schlarb, Damien, 215–216, 226
Schultz, Lucille M., 20, 31
Schuster, Jack, x, xxiii, 103
scientific research, 10–11, 13
Scudder, Vita Dutton, 211
Segall, Mary T., 7, 17
Sen, Amartya, 60–62, 66, 68

service learning, xxi, 85, 177, 179, 180–184, 186, 188, 210–213, 224
Sexton, Megan, 215
sexuality studies, 88
Shakespeare, William, 23, 162, 205
Shaughnessy, Mina, 24, 28, 31
Slevin, James, 43, 50
Smart People, 44, 50
Smart, Robert A., 7, 17, 44, 50
Smit, David, 37, 41, 50
Smith, Lara, xxii, 174, 209
social media, 191
Social Sciences and Humanities Research Council (SSHRC), 78
Society for Technical Communication (STC), 132, 134
Sommers, Nancy, 28, 31
Sosa, Julie Ann, 146, 148, 157
South Atlantic Modern Language Association (SAMLA), xxii, 210, 212–225
South Atlantic Review (*SAR*), 213
Space Shuttle Columbia, 99
Speer, Tom, 46, 50
St. John's University, 57
St. Martin's College Press, 148
Standard American English, 124
stasis theory, 100
storyboarding, 10, 12
students: first-year, 18; graduate, x–xi, xiv–xxi, 8, 10, 21, 29, 33, 36, 38, 42, 54, 62, 71, 78–79, 82, 84, 86–87, 118, 134, 140–142, 147, 158–159, 161, 163–164, 166, 192–195, 197–200, 206–207, 214, 219, 224; MA, xx, 151, 162, 164, 167; nontraditional, 22, 35, 133; PhD, ix, xiv, 162, 202, 209
Stygall, Gail, 35, 50

subject matter experts (SMEs), xx, 134, 139
Sunstein, Bonnie, 182, 190
Swift, Jonathan, 119, 131

Tarutz, Judith, 137, 144
Taylor, Tracy, xxiii, 36, 50, 131, 174, 197, 208
Teachers of English to Speakers of Other Languages (TESOL), 164
teaching assistant, 146, 161, 194
teaching assistant (TA), 148, 151, 161, 163, 169, 171–172, 197, 207–208
Teaching English in the Two-Year College (TETYC), 31, 43, 50
technical communication, xix, 4, 75–76, 105–106, 111–113, 115, 133, 139, 142, 211
Technical Communication, xvii, 76–77, 106, 112, 116, 132, 143–144, 226
Technical Communication Quarterly, 116, 132, 226
technical editing, 132–134, 136–137, 142–143
technical editor, xix, 132, 134–140, 142
technical writing, xiv, 8, 10, 23, 76, 85, 110, 133–134, 153, 155, 168, 213, 216–218, 221
Telecommunications Research Associates (TRA), 135
tenure, xi–xii, xiv, xvi–xvii, xix, xxi–xxii, 3, 12, 14–15, 19–22, 26, 40, 46, 54, 58, 60, 66, 69, 71–73, 82–83, 92, 102, 104–105, 154, 157, 166, 173, 175–176, 189, 202–203, 209; non-tenure track, ix, xvii–xviii, xxi, 29, 33, 38, 67, 70, 175; tenure track, vii, ix–x, xviii, xx, 29, 32, 35, 37–39, 44–45, 48, 51–53, 55–57, 59, 61–65, 67, 70, 75, 77–78, 81, 91, 117, 121, 132–134, 145–146, 148–150, 156, 158–160, 164, 167, 169, 170–172, 180, 186, 193, 204
textbooks, 8, 23, 40, 43, 75, 77–79, 147, 152, 154
Thaiss, Chris, 7, 17
theory: feminist, 89, 91, 95; literary, 85–86, 89; postcolonial, 92, 95; queer, 101; rhetorical, 89; stasis, 100
Thompson, Isabelle, 49, 106, 116, 159, 174, 186
Thrush, Emily A., 138, 144
touchpoint story, 107
tribal colleges, xvi–xvii, 32, 39, 41–42, 45–46
Trice, Andrea, 184, 189
Trimbur, John, vii, xxiii
Twitter, 155
two-year college, xvii, 18–19, 21, 29–30, 33, 40, 81, 133, 165, 193

University of Arizona, 36, 46
University of Massachusetts, Amherst, 146–149
University of Mississippi, 219
University of Missouri, 108, 147
University of Sussex, 88
US News and World Report, 48–49
usability, 114–116, 137, 142, 195
user experience (UX), 105

Varnum, Robin, 20, 26, 31
Villanueva, Victor, 11, 17, 30
Visitor, The, 44, 50
Vygotsky, Lev, 173–174

Walden College, 149
Ware, Kay, 217
Weaver, Constance, 24, 31
Web 2.0, 194, 200

Welch, Nancy, 172, 174
Wellesley College, 211
Wenger, Etienne, 196, 207
Western Michigan University, 57
Wilcox, Linda J., 8, 17
Williams, Joseph, 49, 124; *Style: Ten Lessons in Clarity and Grace*, 124
Winsor, Dorothy, 6–7, 12, 17
Wisdom, Shannon, xix, 132
workplace writing, 110–111, 132, 143
workshops, 8–9, 94, 108, 150–152, 163–166, 202
Worley, Linda, 162–163, 173
writing: business, 222; collaborative, xx, 96, 133, 141, 173, 187; creative writing, xix, 37, 105, 107–108, 113, 162, 164–165, 167, 172, 177, 214–215, 218; digital, 191, 194; freelance, 170; grant, 13, 217; legal, xx, 117, 119–122, 124, 128–129; technical, xiv, 8, 10, 23, 76, 85, 110, 133–134, 153, 155, 168, 213, 216–218, 221; workplace, 110–111, 132, 143
writing across the curriculum (WAC), xvi, 4–5, 7, 9, 13, 15–17, 78, 122, 126, 145, 149, 151–152, 182–183, 187, 189–190
writing center, xx, 4, 24, 110, 117–118, 121–122, 125–126, 145, 149, 151, 164–165, 177, 186, 194, 203; director, xx, 118, 121–122, 126, 145, 149, 151; work, 4, 117, 126
writing consultant, xx, 97, 117
writing curriculum, 74, 117–119, 121, 151, 204
writing fellow, postdoctoral, xi, xxi, 175–178, 185–186
writing in digital environments (WIDE), xxi, 191–208
Writing in Digital Environments Research Center (WIDE), xxi, 193–194, 208
writing in the disciplines (WID), xvii, 4–8, 13, 15, 183
writing program, ix, xxi, 5, 24, 26–27, 37–38, 46, 70, 94, 147, 149, 152, 175, 189, 196, 204, 209, 224
writing program administration, xxi, 24, 37–38, 46, 84, 149, 157, 172, 174, 197, 208
writing program coordinator, 24, 27
writing studies, xix, 74, 78, 80
writing tutor, 24, 109–110, 121, 124, 126, 151, 153, 165, 170, 211, 224

Yancey, Kathleen Blake, 26, 31, 182, 190
Yeats, Dave, xix, 104, 116

Zawicki, Terry Myers, 7
Zorn, Jeffrey, 45, 50

Contributors

Jennifer Ahern-Dodson is an instructor and civic engagement consultant for the Thompson Writing Program at Duke University. Her research interests include community-based research, writing for civic learning, and community-campus partnership development. Currently, she teaches writing-intensive courses about sustainability and civic participation.

Moira Amado-McCoy, PhD, is a teacher of rhetoric and writing with a commitment to engaging ethical civic discourse for community amelioration. She now advises nonprofit agencies committed to educating about gender identity and sexual orientation and is currently spearheading a community collaborative in Taos, New Mexico, which aims to make education relevant, satisfying, and accessible for students of all backgrounds.

Nick Carbone finished his graduate studies at UMass, Amherst, concluding as ABD in 2000. Since 2000 he has been a New Media Editor and Director of New Media (2002) for Bedford/St. Martin's. In 2008 he received Computers and Composition's Charles Moran Award for Distinguished Contributions to the Profession of Computers and Writing. In 2010 he received the Outstanding Technology Innovator Award from the CCCC Committee on Computers in Composition and Communication.

Malkiel A. Choseed is an associate professor at Onondaga Community College, where he serves as the Coordinator of the Writing Program. He received a SUNY Chancellor's Award for Excellence in Scholarship and Creative Activities in 2009.

Sue Doe is an assistant professor of rhetoric and composition at Colorado State University where she coordinates the core curriculum writing integration. Her research interests include WAC, academic labor issues, and the composing processes of Post 9/11 student-veterans.

Lynée Lewis Gaillet is Associate Professor of rhetoric and composition at Georgia State University. She is Past-President of the Coalition of Women Scholars in the History of Rhetoric and Composition and Past-Executive Director of the South Atlantic Modern Language Association. Her recent works include a new edition of *The Present State of Scholarship in the History of Rhetoric* (University of Missouri Press) and *Stories of Mentoring: Theory and Praxis* (Parlor Press).

Amy Goodburn is Professor of English and Associate Vice Chancellor for Academic Affairs at the University of Nebraska-Lincoln. She is the co-author of *Inquiry into the College Classroom: A Journey Toward Scholarly Teaching* and *Making Teaching and Learning Visible* and was inducted into UNL's Academy of Distinguished Teachers in 2002.

Heather Graves is an associate professor at the University of Alberta, where she teaches writing. She has written *Rhetoric in(to) Science* and was the inaugural Scholar in Residence for Arts Research in Nanotechnology in 2011.

Donna LeCourt is an associate professor of English and Director of the Writing Center at the University of Massachusetts-Amherst. Her research focuses on identity difference in composition pedagogy and civic rhetoric on the internet. She is author *of Identity Matters: Schooling the (Student) Subject in Academic Discourse*. Her work has also appeared in *Pedagogy, College English, Computers and Composition,* and other journals and collections.

Kendall Leon is an assistant professor of Rhetoric and Composition at Purdue University. Her research interests include cultural rhetorics, research methodology, new media, and community engagement.

Carrie Leverenz is Associate Professor of English and Director of the Institute for Critical and Creative Expression at Texas Christian University. Her research focuses on writing program administration, ethics, and institutional constraints on difference. She teaches courses on magazine writing, rhetoric and culture, research methods, and writing program administration.

Ildikó Melis earned her first degree in English and Hungarian Studies in Budapest. She has an MA in English as a Second Language and a PhD in Rhetoric and Composition (University of Arizona). She is a full-time writing instructor and publication editor at Bay Mills Tribal Community College on Michigan's Upper Peninsula, and the 2010–2011 recipient of the American Indian College Fund—Mellon Research Fellowship.

Cindy Moore is Associate Professor and Chair of the Writing Department at Loyola University Maryland. Her mentoring scholarship, including *A Guide to Professional Development for Graduate Students in English* (NCTE 2006), is based on her many years of graduate-student mentoring at universities in Indiana, Minnesota, and Kentucky.

Ben Opipari is the founder of Persuasive Matters, delivering writing seminars and coaching to law firms. He also authors the music website Songwriters on Process, which features interviews with songwriters about their writing process. From 2006 to 2011 he was the writing instructor at Howrey LLP, a worldwide litigation firm. Before coming to Howrey, Ben directed the writing center at Colgate University, where he also taught in the department of writing and rhetoric.

Stacey Pigg is an assistant professor of Writing and Rhetoric at the University of Central Florida. She researches the everyday practice and experience of writing with technologies and teaches courses in writing, rhetoric, and civic engagement.

Mya Poe is an assistant professor of English at Penn State University. Previously she was Director of Technical Communication at MIT. She is co-author of *Learning to Communicate in Science and Engineering* (MIT Press, 2010), which provides case studies of MIT students in disciplines ranging from Biomedical Engineering to Aero-Astro Engineering.

Martine Courant Rife, JD, PhD, is a professor of writing in the Communication Department at Lansing Community College, Lansing, Michigan. Her work recently appeared in *Technical Communication* and *Computers and Composition* with pieces forthcoming *in IEEE*

Transactions in Professional Communication and the international journal, *E-Learning*. She is a co-editor of *Copy(write): Intellectual Property in the Writing Classroom* (2012; The WAC Clearinghouse and Parlor Press).

Lara Smith-Sitton is Associate Director of the South Atlantic Modern Language Association and Managing Editor of *South Atlantic Review*. She is also a PhD student in the rhetoric and composition program at Georgia State University. Her areas of study include nineteenth-century women's rhetoric, service-learning, and alternative learning environments.

Shannon Wisdom, PhD, is the managing technical editor for Hill Associates in Colchester, Vermont. Her interests include technical editing, professional writing, and building community in the corporation.

Dave Yeats is a partner at Sentier Strategic Resources, a user-experience consulting firm that provides research services to companies such as AT&T, GE, and JCPenney. His research has appeared in *Technical Communication* and *Technical Communication Quarterly*.

www.ingramcontent.com/pod-product-compliance
Lightning Source LLC
Chambersburg PA
CBHW030133240426
43672CB00005B/119